THE AMERICAN FEDERATION OF TEACHERS, 1916-1961

A HISTORY OF THE MOVEMENT

William Edward Eaton

SOUTHERN ILLINOIS UNIVERSITY PRESS
Carbondale and Edwardsville

Feffer & Simons, Inc.
London and Amsterdam

Library of Congress Cataloging in Publication Data

Eaton, William Edward, 1943–
  The American Federation of Teachers, 1916–1961.

  Bibliography: p.
  Includes index.
  1. American Federation of Teachers—History.
I. Title.
L13.A438E17   331.88'11'371100973   75-14248
ISBN 0-8093-0708-1

For Judy

Contents

Preface

This book is the attempt to answer a series of questions about the teachers' union movement in the United States. Some of the questions considered most important by the author were: 1. How did the movement begin? 2. Who was involved? 3. Are there any organizational patterns that emerge? 4. How does the AFT fit into the more general pattern of American educational history? The failures of this book in not providing a more "inside" view of the organization or in regarding the teachers' union movement from a labor history or political point of view are related to the author's greater interest in the preceding questions.

Most of the time this book focuses on the national organization of the teachers' union and the handful of locals that constituted its bulk. In so doing it omits many of the engaging struggles that took place at the local level. This omission is due to both the recognition of the fragmentary nature of local accounts and to the author's idea of appropriate limitation.

Someday the story of the American Federation of Teachers will be told from a more personalized point of view. This book could not provide such a commentary. The personal papers of early teachers' union leaders are just now being collected, and the personal views of more contemporary leaders are still not open for public scrutiny.

This factual narrative of the AFT ends at 1961. Such a cut-off point will be regarded by some as too arbitrary and incomplete. The decision to end it at 1961 represents a combination of circumstances. The American Federation of Teachers has not released the majority of its correspondence of the

1960s and 1970s and thus, verifiable data since 1961 are difficult to produce. The second circumstance is the blushing embarrassment felt by the historian as he steps across that hazy threshold from the past to the present.

A final word about this book is in order. It was written to present a narrative of the American Federation of Teachers. The intent was that it should be neither a diatribe nor a panegyric about the teacher union movement.

I am deeply indebted to Professors Raymond Callahan, Arthur Wirth, and William Connor for their patience, encouragement, and invaluable suggestions while this book was being developed.

Special recognition must be reserved for Professor Callahan of Washington University's Graduate Institute of Education. He took upon himself the nearly impossible task of transforming an eager but ignorant schoolteacher into a scholar and historian of education. The failures of doing this that are reflected in this book should not be credited to his account however, but rather to the limitations inherent to the raw material with which he was working.

In producing this manuscript the author received support and aid from a variety of sources. It began with the permission of President David Selden of the AFT. It was pushed along by the cooperation of Werner Pflug and his able staff at the Labor Archives at Wayne State University. Financial and tactical aid were provided by the Office of Research and Projects of Southern Illinois University, by the Department of Educational Administration and Foundations of Southern Illinois University's College of Education, and by the Graduate School of SIU. The typing of the manuscript was done by Barbara Anderson and Amy Weaver.

Finally, I must mention the role of my wife Judy to whom this book is dedicated. In many ways she embodies the pluck and determination that has changed the teaching profession around. At one point, during the writing of this manuscript, I dropped her off for her duty on the picket line of Local No. 743 of the American Federation of Teachers while I headed for the research library to try to learn about the teacher union movement. The irony of that scene has left an indelible impression.

WILLIAM EATON

Carbondale, Illinois
Autumn 1974

The American Federation of Teachers, 1916–1961

Education and Unionization
The Background

*Education and the Final Quarter of
the Nineteenth Century*

The final quarter of the nineteenth century overflowed with events and movements that affected the booming republic in a variety of ways. Immigration, industrialization, urbanization, unionization, and other such phenomena changed the evenness of the pastoral tempo of the earlier decades of the nineteenth century into the unevenness of the last quarter.

The American public school was a significant part of this era. The public-school crusade of the 1830s and 1840s had been interrupted by the Civil War but emerged again at the end of the conflict in even larger ways. The reconstruction of the South meant the building of large numbers of public schools. Several of the constitutions of the former confederate states were rewritten to include provisions for public schooling. The high schools, few in numbers before the war, became evident in larger numbers especially in urban areas of the North. The final quarter of the century saw the public-school movement come of age with the development of state teachers colleges, the rise of the professional school administrator, the growth of the National Education Association, and vast curricular changes that were the result of new educational philosophies and reflections of the infant science of psychology.

Central to the story of public education in the late nine-

1

teenth century was the teacher. Whether found in one of the
thousands of one-room school districts in the country or in a
large school of the city, the teacher became the visible link between the child and the school. Such a position of intermediacy
took different thematic proportions. For some of the teachers
the intermediacy was an inescapable fact of life, a part of the
job that required toleration and undue patience. But for many
of the teachers the intermediacy was the quintessence of the
task. For these, teaching was a "calling" no less sacred than the
ministry. Their intermediacy between the child and the school
was the symbolic passing of the cup of knowledge, handed
down carefully from generation to generation. For these
teachers the job was more than school "keeping." It was this
kind of teacher who labored in the schools of the cities with
classes usually numbering fifty or more. It was this teacher who
gave freely of her salary to pay for lunches and clothing. It was
this teacher who spent Saturdays tutoring students or climbing
the endless wooden stairs of the tenement houses to visit the
parents of her children. On the vast prairies of the West and
Midwest, in the rural areas of the South and East, it was these
teachers who accepted thankless labor in the educational vine-
yard. Month upon month of hearing the endless drone of reci-
tations in the small schoolhouse, year upon year of encouraging the hesitant scholars, and decades upon decades of bitter
frugality that led to old age—such was the life of the school-
teacher.

To be a teacher meant isolation. Whether city or rural
teacher, the quality of isolation was pervasive and hung heavy
upon all persons who taught. The isolation was due to more
than the feelings of despair that arose from the physical circumstances of the job, although these were contributing factors. The isolation came more from the separation from other
adults and the separation from both the seediness and beauties
of life that give vitality. The teacher was an adult who was im-
posed upon the lives of children. The day was spent in moni-
toring childish whims and in checking immature behavior. The
teacher further experienced isolation through social limitations. The behavior norms for teachers were essentially that of
the minister. The teachers were to leave the school for the
boardinghouse or church and there to busy themselves in

worthwhile activities. Teachers were not allowed to mingle with people deemed socially unacceptable, participate in political affairs, spend their money as they chose, and in the case of women teachers, not even allowed to fall in love. The isolation from meaningful contact with other adults continued outside of the classroom.

The teachers were further frustrated by the physical operation of the schools. Textbooks were usually too old and too few and were selected by school committees, distant educational bureaucrats, or county superintendents who often considered only their cost. A desk for every child and teacher, a waste can, and a chalkboard represented school equipment. Classrooms were usually poorly lighted, poorly ventilated, poorly heated, and too small. Playground equipment was practically unheard of and toilet facilities varied from crudely adequate to scandalously unsanitary.

Further frustration came from the administrative problems of education. In large cities, boards of education were sometimes appointed by mayors, sometimes elected from wards, sometimes elected at large. In smaller communities they were elected and informally represented various power blocs like the farmers and merchants. In every case the process was clearly political and a board member took his office with a set of political debits and credits. Boards of education were legally empowered to appoint school superintendents, principals, teachers, and to grant contracts for equipment and buildings. It is not surprising, therefore, that the politics of education inevitably had an impact on the classroom teacher. The crumbling school plant, the uncooperative custodian, the inadequate textbooks, the shabby equipment, and the tyrannical building principal that many teachers witnessed daily were a direct result of this politicization of schools.

The incentives to take a position in teaching were very meager. Salaries were extremely low and fringe benefits were nonexistent. Many apparently entered the profession with a belief in "service to humanity" and in the "noble calling of the teacher" only to leave after a few short years, broken in spirit and overwhelmed with the forces that worked against effective instruction.

Sometimes teachers banded together. But when they did, it

was usually at the bequest of a school official with the objective of promoting cultural interests. Reading and discussion groups were common among teachers, especially in the cities. Although pleasing to the individual teacher, these groups did not become forums for talking about solutions to the pressing school problems. The teachers would have to wait for new organizational models that possessed an action orientation.

Paralleling these events in American education was the rise of organized labor. The first national union of note was the Knights of Labor founded in 1878. The concerns of the Knights were broad and included most of the reforms of the era. One of their interests was the public school as a vehicle for educating the working class. In fact, education was conceived as the key element in the whole fabric of reform. This position was stated rather clearly by Robert Layton, grand secretary of the order, in testimony before the Senate Committee on Education and Labor in 1883: "if education were successful, his words suggested, social reform would follow as a matter of course." [1]

But the support for education fostered by the Knights was not complete. While favoring compulsory school attendance laws, free textbooks, and evening schools, they were contemptuous of higher education. This contempt extended to the high school which they saw as a college preparatory institution.[2] By 1886, the Knights had a national membership of 702,924.[3]

In 1893, the Knights welcomed the inclusion of women on the New York City Board of Education and supported equal pay for women teachers. But generally the Knights spoke little to the plight of the teacher.[4]

More important to both the cause of public education and the classroom teacher was the American Federation of Labor, which was formed in 1886. Maintaining a strict political neutrality, focusing its organizational efforts on the stable group of skilled laborers, and in other ways taking advantage of the mistakes of the declining Knights of Labor, the new federation grew and prospered.

The First Local

Education was a local matter. For this reason the first union experience among teachers was at the local level. The beginning was made in Chicago. Here, in the nation's second great city, the teachers were faced with all of the classic problems of education in the late nineteenth century. The teachers of Chicago daily faced the horrors of overcrowded, unsanitary buildings stuffed with too many children and controlled by an impersonal bureaucratic structure. This they did with poor pay, no job security, and no pension system. The teachers' first unified action would be in the area of pensions.

In 1895, the state of Illinois passed enabling legislation for a pension law. Such legislation had been supported by existing teacher groups. But even with enabling legislation the fight for an adequate pension was just beginning. Much of the agitation in favor of the legislation was carried by the grade-school teachers. It was among these teachers that the first union was formed. In March of 1897, the Chicago Teachers Federation was formed with Catherine Goggin as its president and Margaret Haley as its driving force.[5]

The early years of the Chicago Teachers Federation were turbulent. After a successful fight for salary increases the union grew to more than twenty-five hundred by the end of its first year of existence.[6] The issues facing the young organization were many. In 1897, the maximum salary a teacher could receive was $825.00 a year,[7] the pension law was already inadequate, and the administrative structure was on the brink of toppling. The weakness of the administration structure had been recognized in 1893 after Joseph Mayer Rice, the educational muckraker, had exposed the Chicago schools in the national press. After a great deal of local consternation, a Public School Committee was formed with William Rainey Harper, president of the University of Chicago, as chairman.[8] The report of this committee was to suggest that the cure for bureaucratic blundering was the need for more scientific management. To the teachers this cult of efficiency was to be as disheartening as the old structure. Efficiency meant bringing to education the spirit and methods of commercialism. And Margaret Haley speaking eloquently to the issue declared:

> Two ideals are struggling for supremacy in American life today, . . . one is that of commercialism, which subordinates the worker to the product and to the machine; the other, the ideal of democracy— the ideal of education, which places humanity above all machines, and demands that all activity shall be the expression of life. If this ideal of education is not carried over into the industrial field, then the ideal of commercialism will be carried over into the schools. Those two ideals can no more continue to exist in American life together than our nation could have continued half slave and half free.[9]

The teachers resented the commission and resented Harper, especially after he voted against a salary increase for them in 1898 while a member of the board of education.[10] They associated him with the Standard Oil Trust due to his working relationship with John D. Rockefeller, the benefactor of the University of Chicago, and resented the attempts of reform that tended to overlook the teacher. In the name of reform the board of education released School Superintendent Albert G. Lane in 1898 and replaced him with E. Benjamin Andrews, former president of Brown University and Harper's former teacher. The teachers' federation objected to the appointment of an outsider and were fearful that this move would further tie the school district to the tail of the University of Chicago.[11] The reform commission submitted to the Illinois legislature a bill for reform measures in 1899. The Chicago Teachers Federation opposed this and with the help of other unions collected fifty thousand signatures in a petition campaign that helped to defeat the measure.[12]

The strident militancy of the Chicago Teachers Federation attracted many teachers and in less than three years it had organized more than half of the city's teachers.[13] In November of 1901, the Chicago Teachers Federation began publication of the Chicago Teachers Federation *Bulletin* with Margaret Haley serving as editor.[14]

Up to this point the Chicago Teachers Federation was a totally independent labor organization. Early in 1902, however, serious thought was given to formal affiliation with the Chicago

Federation of Labor. In November, social settlement reformer Jane Addams was invited to address the Chicago Teachers Federation on the advantages and disadvantages of such an affiliation. Though objective in her presentation Miss Addams was critically questioned upon its completion. "Pushed by a direct question from the floor, Miss Addams replied that the proposed move would be a 'step in the right direction.' " [15] The affiliation took place and the teachers were under the broad umbrella of the American Federation of Labor.

The decision to formally join organized labor was a momentous one. A good portion of the American middle class resented unions. Teachers as a whole, despite their lower middle-class origins, considered unionization to be a low class activity, beneath their dignity. In explaining affiliation, Margaret Haley told one reporter:

> Not only has the time arrived when public school teachers must take a position on the serious economic and political questions pressing for solution . . . but the public school as an institution must be either democratic or autocratic. A democratic form of government cannot be maintained with autocratic principles controlling the schools either in their administration or methods of teaching. The labor interests lie in popular, democratic government, and in the maintenance of democracy. It is the largest organized force of democracy. The only people you can depend upon to act permanently with you are those whose interests are identical with yours. We expect by affiliation with labor to arouse the workers and the whole people, thru the workers, to the dangers confronting the public schools from the same interests and tendencies that are undermining the foundations of our democratic republic. It is necessary to make labor a constructive force in society, or it will be a destructive force. If the educational question could be understood by the labor men, and the labor question by the educators, both soon would see they are working to the same end, and should work together.[16]

The Chicago Teachers Federation's concern for educational and social issues continued. The CTF, still an organization of the grade school teachers, supported many reform movements including woman suffrage, municipal ownership of public utilities, direct primaries, the popular election of United States's senators, and referendum and recall.[17] The CTF is credited as being a force in the successful passage of the Illinois Child Labor Law of 1903 and in helping to persuade the voters of Chicago on the necessity of an elected school board.[18] The CTF was also active in attempting to alleviate the constant financial plight of the school district.

A serious financial handicap for the school district was the loss of revenue which resulted from the failure of large corporations in the district to pay taxes on their capital stock and franchises. This irregularity was found by Margaret Haley. After seeking legal advice from former Illinois governor, John P. Altgeld, the local union undertook mandamus proceedings against People's Gas, Light and Coke Company, the Chicago Telephone Company, and Edison Electric Light Company.[19] After successful litigation these three companies were ordered to pay $597,303. Of this amount $347,749 went to the city and $249,554 to the board of education.[20] But once again the board was in no mood to give any regard for its teachers and the amount received, although due to the efforts of the teachers, was placed in a fund to pay for coal and building repairs. This forced the teachers back into court, this time with the legal talent of Clarence Darrow at their disposal.[21] But it was 1904 before they received the pay increase.[22]

At the board of education meeting held June 21,1905: "The Board then voted 13–6 to condemn teacher affiliation with the Chicago Federation of Labor as 'absolutely unjustifiable and intolerable in a school system of a democracy.' "[23] Five of those voting with the majority were at their last board meeting.[24] Although the issue was forestalled the intent was clear. The conservative and traditional school leadership recognized the Chicago Teachers Federation as inimical to its conception of school board—employee relationship. In 1909, however, the situation was eased with the appointment of Ella Flagg Young as superintendent of schools. Mrs. Young was a former instructor at John Dewey's laboratory school at the University of Chicago and the former principal of Cook County Normal School. Mrs. Young was an ardent believer in democratic administration. She instituted a system of teachers councils which allowed the teachers to assist in formulating general policy. She was forced to resign in 1915. Her biographer credits her approval of the union movement among teachers as a factor in her dismissal.[25] The next superintendents: John D. Shoop, 1915–18; Charles E. Chadsey, 1918; Peter A. Mortenson, 1918–24; and William McAndrew, 1924–27, were far less tolerant of the union.[26]

Unperturbed by both official and unofficial criticism, the Chicago union prospered and fought the board of education's 1915 campaign to break the union with a "yellow dog" contract, (a contract prohibiting a person from joining a union). During that struggle sixty-eight teachers were fired, forty of them being union members.[27] This situation caused the union to seek legal action against the board but after lengthy litigation the Illinois Supreme Court ruled in 1917 that the board had the power to arbitrarily decide against union membership for its teachers. Reaching the end of its legal course of action the local was forced to temporarily disaffiliate from the American Federation of Labor and retained only its local labor affiliations. The president of the Chicago women's local and several other important union leaders had been among those dismissed.[28] Thus, the promising beginning of a teachers union affiliated with a national labor body was struck a temporary death blow.

The Teachers and a National Union

Although the Chicago Teachers Federation was the first teachers union it was not the first to affiliate with a national union. The first formal affiliation of teachers with national organized labor was that of a teachers' group in San Antonio, Texas, which asked for and was granted a local charter by the AFL on September 20, 1902.[29] "Low salaries for teaching in San Antonio reflected all of Texas; the state ranked thirty-eighth in the nation in its financial support of education. At a time when San Antonio firemen and policemen were earning from $50 to $70 per month, the starting salary for elementary teachers was $35. A high school teacher with 10 years' experience could make only $54 per month." [30]

But the affiliation of one isolated local with the national AFL was hardly a satisfactory arrangement except on the local level. The AFL was an amalgamation of large national unions and the teachers could only be taken seriously after forming a national of their own. The leadership of the Chicago federation recognized this and in 1899 Catherine Goggin and Margaret Haley attempted to form a National Teacher's Federation in Los Angeles. Six of the eight officers were from Chicago. But this attempt ended in failure.[31] Another attempt was made in 1902 with Margaret Haley as president. Permitting only grade teachers to join, the organization did attract about 180 members nationally. Twenty-six of these were from New York City, and there were others from Los Angeles, St. Paul, and a scattered membership in Mississippi, Illinois, Maine, and Minnesota. But with over half of the membership in Chicago the group had no true national representation and eventually withered on the vine.[32]

The Failure of the National Education Association

One common theme that was echoed again and again by Margaret Haley and those teachers of kindred spirit was the failure of the National Education Association. The NEA had no division for classroom teachers. The leadership of the organization was in the hands of a select group of college presidents and school superintendents. The role of the classroom teacher, and more specifically the woman, was limited to listening. When Margaret Haley addressed the NEA in 1904, she became the first classroom teacher to deliver an address before the group in its near fifty-year existence. Taking advantage of the situation she entitled her speech, "Why Teachers Should Organize." [33]

Aaron Gove, the superintendent at Denver, was indicative of the NEA leadership. Speaking before the NEA on "The Limitations of the Superintendent's Authority and of the Teacher's Independence" he stated:

A dangerous tendency exists toward usurpation by teachers, thru organization, of powers which should be retained by the superintendent. An apparently growing feeling seems to exist—in truth does exist, that the public school system should be a democratic institution, and what the body of teachers constitute the democratic government. This is a false conception of democracy. The truth is that boards of education are the representative bodies of the democracy—the people—for whom they are making laws, and to whom they are responsible for their acts.[34]

The NEA did have concern for broad national education questions and it would be difficult to criticize the organization for most of its programs. The sins of the organization were sins of omission. The NEA did not speak to the problems of the classroom teacher. There was no concern for the poor pay and benefits. As one historian of the NEA in the period 1884–1921 concluded:

> The Association had never concerned itself to any degree with problems of teacher welfare, the general feeling of its leaders being that it was not the "professional" thing to do, and the very thought of teacher participation in decision-making was utterly foreign and most threatening to such autocrats as Aaron Gove, who for three decades had personally employed every teacher, selected every textbook, planned every building and set every policy for the Denver Schools.[35]

One victory for the classroom teachers who belonged to the NEA came in 1910. At that summer convention Ella Flagg Young, the democratic-minded Chicago superintendent, upset the wishes of the nominating committee comprised of the "old guard" and was elected president of the NEA. Her election was greatly aided by the efforts of Margaret Haley and by Grace Strachan of New York City. Though not a classroom teacher but a principal, Grace Strachan was the leader of the grade teachers in the city and had organized fourteen thousand teachers into the Interborough Association of Women Teachers, the largest local organization in the world.[36] Haley and Strachan had joined forces for this important election.

The Chicago Teachers Federation was jubilant about the election. That same year Mrs. Young had testified before a committee of the Illinois State Senate and had said:

> The growth of the grade teachers in a general civic sense, and recognition of the rights of the human being, has been remarkable since the organization of the teachers federation. . . . not only the federation but the various clubs are beneficial. Whatever makes teachers appreciate the life of the community, the spirit of the nation to which they

belong, helps the school. The great drawback in education in the past has been that teachers knew their books and didn't know life outside.[37]

The Formation of the American Federation of Teachers

Events similar to those in Chicago had been taking place in the nation's first city. Although New York City did not experience the same degree of financial disaster as did Chicago, the other situations were parallel. Different, however, was the organizational thrust of the teachers. Grace Strachan's Interborough Association of Women Teachers did not choose to associate with organized labor. The agitation for teachers' union began slowly and was centered with the men teachers.

The roots of the teachers' union in New York City had begun with the publication of the *American Teacher* magazine, the first volume of which appeared in January of 1912, under the editorship of Henry R. Linville. Dedicated to "Democracy in Education; Education for Democracy," it began and grew under the simple observation that "The American teacher is expected to teach Democracy, but the relations of this teacher to his fellow worker, his relations to those above him and his relations to those below him are not such as naturally cultivate the spirit and virtues of Democracy." [38] Articles in the early issues of the journal condemned the authoritarian and paternal attitudes of the school administrators and pushed for greater participation by the teachers in administrative decision making. Other articles concerned the need for better salaries, tenure protection, maternity leaves, and the greater politicizing of the teacher. In December of 1912, they offered these beliefs in the following statement:

We believe that the hope of educational regeneration for the schools lies in the possibility of arousing the teachers themselves to realize that their professional and social standing is far too low to enable them to produce effective results in teaching.

We believe that teachers owe it to themselves, as well as to the public, to study the relation of education to social progress, and to understand some of the important social and economic movements going on in the present-day world.

We believe that with an intelligent outlook upon life, teachers will be able to contribute from their experience in teaching the best ideas for the adjustment of education to the needs of human living.

We believe that the work of teaching must be done by men and women of high purpose, without narrowness and without sex-antagonism.

We believe that unless some tangible and important function in educational management and control is granted to teachers, it will be useless to expect much improvement in the professional and social spirit of teachers.

We believe that teachers will never get the right to a "voice and a vote" in the work for which they are especially trained, until a considerable number of them demand it themselves.[39]

The growing circulation and favorable response to the journal's position emboldened the editor and his staff to issue the following manifesto in the February issue of 1913.

A CALL TO ORGANIZE

While the *American Teacher* is in press the subjoined is being prepared for the purpose of bringing together those teachers who think that something constructive can be done by teachers themselves.

TO THE TEACHERS OF NEW YORK CITY

Believing that the time has arrived for founding an organization of teachers on progressive lines, we, the undersigned teachers of the City of New York, issue this call to teachers and other citizens to organize an association which shall have for its objectives improved working conditions for teachers and better educational results for children.

On the ground that teachers do the every-day work of teaching, and understand the conditions necessary for better teaching, we propose the following principles for the new organization:

Teachers should have a voice and a vote in the determination of educational policies.

Teachers may justly claim the right to seats in the Board of Education, for the reason that they only can bring first-hand information to the representatives of the people concerning the actual working of the educational system.

The right to seats in the controlling body should carry with it the right to vote, as an aid in rendering effective the information and the point of view brought by the chosen representatives of the teachers.

The granting of legislative opportunity to the teachers would inevitably contribute to the development of a strong professional spirit, and the intelligent use of their experience in the interest of the public.

We advocate the adoption of a plan that will permit all the teachers to have a share in the administration of the affairs of their own schools. In no more practical way could teachers prepare themselves for training children for citizenship in democracy.

We urge the scientific study of educational experience, to the end that the lessons of past successes and failures in education may be known to all.

There is evidence that the public schools are being freed from the domination of party politics. Let the public and the professional interest in that direction continue until the more insidious form of personal politics be eliminated, wherever it may be manifested in the appointment of officers in the school system.

Those conditions that affect each individual teacher in his position may be, and often are, serious enough to make him dissatisfied and unhappy, and hence unproductive, in his work. It is, therefore, necessary that public notice be taken of this matter. Among the most important of these unfavorable conditions are, the size of classes, the unhygienic conditions of many schools, the excess of clerical labor, the salaries and ratings of teachers, and the lack of opportunity for professional improvement during tenure of office.

A general meeting will be held in Milbank Chapel, Teachers College, New York City, Friday, February 28, 1913, at 8:15 P.M.[40]

The result of the declaration was the formation of a Teachers League which continued to follow the editorial stance of the *American Teacher.*

Men teachers were also active in Chicago. In February of 1912, a Federation of Men Teachers was organized and, on March 1, received charter number 14,221 from the American Federation of Labor.[41]

In other American cities substandard salaries and unsatisfactory working conditions were causing teacher groups to take a more militant posture. Many of these were showing interest in the growing labor movement. On June 1, 1915, President Charles B. Stillman, of the Chicago Federation of Men Teachers sent out a letter that began: "Believing that the trend toward firmer organization among teachers throughout this country and the deepened bonds of sympathy between the

working classes and the teachers indicate an advanced step, the
Chicago teachers submit this proposition for the formation of a
national federation. It is expected that this organization shall
be affiliated with the American Federation of Labor." [42]

On April 15, 1916, the three Chicago teachers' unions and
one from nearby Gary met at 315 Plymouth Court in Chicago.
With instructions from three other locals not in attendance the
American Federation of Teachers was born. The first officers
were:

Charles Stillman, President
Ida Fursman, Vice-President
Margaret Snodgrass, Corresponding Secretary
Mary Dwyer, Recording Secretary
Freeland G. Stecker, Financial Secretary
James A. Meade, Treasurer
Margaret Haley, National Organizer [43]

By May 9, 1916, The Chicago Teachers Federation; the
Chicago Federation of Men Teachers; the Chicago Federation
of Women High School Teachers; the Gary, Indiana, Teachers
Federation; the Teachers Union of the City of New York; the
Oklahoma Teachers Federation; the Scranton, Pennsylvania,
Teachers Association; and the High School Teachers Union of
Washington, D.C., became the first eight locals and were duly
received by President Gompers into the American Federation
of Labor as the American Federation of Teachers.[44]

The decision to affiliate the new national with the AFL was
automatic. If there had been any doubts they were swept aside
the previous February when Hugh Frayne, an organizer for
the AFL, stated the position of the AFL toward education. He
declared that the union stood for:

1. The abolition of all forms of involuntary servitude, except as a
punishment for crime.

2. Unrelenting protest against the issuance and abuse of the in-
junction process in labor disputes.

3. A work day of not more than eight hours in the twenty-four-
hour day.

4. A strict recognition of the eight-hour day on all federal, state or

municipal work and a wage of not less than the prevailing per diem wage rate of the class of employment in the vicinity where the work is performed.

5. Release from employment one day in seven.

6. The abolition of the contract system on public works.

7. The abolition of the sweat-shop system.

8. Sanitary inspection of factory, workship, mine, and home.

9. Liability of employers for loss of life or injury to body.

10. The passage of anti-child labor laws in states where they do not exist, and rigid defense of these laws where they have been enacted.

11. Free schools, free textbooks, and compulsory education.

12. Suitable and plentiful playgrounds for children in all cities.

13. Continued agitation for the public bath system in all cities.

14. Qualifications in permits to build, of all cities and towns that there shall be bathrooms and bathroom attachments in all houses or compartments used for habitation.

15. Woman suffrage coequal with man suffrage.

16. The Nationalization of Telegraph and Telephone.

17. The municipal ownership of other public utilities.

18. The initiative and referendum and the imperative mandate and right of recall.

19. A complete system of United States Government Postal Savings Banks.

20. A system of finance whereby money shall be issued exclusively by the Government, with such regulations and restrictions as will prevent manipulation by the banking interests for their own private gain.[45]

This philosophy encompassed most of the liberal impulses of the times. In this early part of the century when the national optimism stood high, and when the promise of America seemed unlimited, the goals of the American Federation of Labor represented a realistic, tough-minded, and desirable pattern of social reform. The union teachers were pleased to associate themselves with such objectives. They were enthusiastic about joining the AFL and optimistic about their new status as a national union. They gladly accepted the charter offered them by Samuel Gompers.

In the presentation ceremony, President Gompers said,

The American Federation of Labor in the name of all the workers of America welcome the American Federation of Teachers to the fold and the bond of unity and fraternity of the organized labor movement of our Republic. We earnestly hope for a thorough organization of all teachers and progress and success of the new national teachers' federation; that it may bring light and hope in the lives of American educators, and give and receive mutual sympathy and support which can be properly exerted for the betterment of all who toil and give service—Aye, for all humanity.[46]

Chapter 2

The Formative Years
1916 – 1929

The AFT's Relation to the NEA

Initially the American Federation of Teachers saw itself as more of a radical segment of the National Education Association than as a completely independent body. As in the earlier years of the local federations, members were encouraged to attend the annual convention of the NEA. This policy of working within the NEA had been formulated in the early years of the Chicago Teachers Federation. As one writer of the 1905 effort at organizing a national union described it: "The National Teachers' Federation was organized primarily for the purpose of putting into the hands of the grade and classroom teachers a weapon keen enough to cut the N.E.A. loose from the traditions that have bound it to the ideas and ideals of the eastern university people, which the teachers describe as standing for conservatism almost amounting to stagnation." [1]

Said another student speaking of both the Interborough Association and Haley's group: "There is considerable indication that these groups, at the outset, would have welcomed affiliation with the National Education Association either as departments or as adjunct organizations, but the reaction of the Association's management was one of horrified dismay." [2]

This same attitude prevailed after the formation of the AFT. Said one scholar of the era: "Although the leaders of the NEA came to regard the American Federation of Teachers as a rival organization, the union had had no idea of such a role at the time of its formation." [3] James Meade, the president of the Chicago Teachers Federation, recalled that it wasn't until about 1921 that the AFT considered itself a competitor of the NEA.[4] The situation in the National Education Association was similar to many groups, the larger and more diversified it had become, the less it was able to represent the particular interests of any one group. Unfortunately the NEA had overlooked the very faction it should never have overlooked—the classroom teacher.

Operation of the Union, 1916–1929

The operation of the AFT during these early years was about as small and unsophisticated as one could expect. These were schoolteachers and their union experience and managerial skills were only in the developmental stages.

The union was operated from one room of Financial Secretary Stecker's five-room bungalow with a desk, a typewriter, a file case, and a telephone furnished by himself and his wife. The location was good since President Stillman lived next door. Shortly thereafter, Stillman and Stecker hired Miss Lena Hults as stenographer. Miss Hults was to become a nearly permanent fixture in the AFT office. A typewriter table and a mimeograph machine rounded out the national office.[5]

By July of 1918, twenty-eight charters had been issued, and when the union gathered at Pittsburgh for its annual convention, other decisions affecting the operation were made.[6] Most important, perhaps, was the AFL's making Charles Stillman an organizer. This freed Stillman from his teaching duties at Lane Technical High School in Chicago and allowed him to concentrate his energies on building the new union.[7]

The following summer, the secretary-treasurer's position, (they had been combined at the 1918 convention at Pittsburgh) was made a full-time position as well.[8] The AFL continued its cooperation and assigned L. C. Lampson of Washington, D.C., and Isabel Williams of St. Paul as organizers.[9] This kind of support from the AFL was the difference between life and death.

From all over the country letters came into the national office, making inquiries about the union. The situation of many teachers was desperate, and their hope that the AFT could help them prompted their communication. For one brief period the AFT became an international union when a request for membership was granted to a group of teachers in Montreal who were issued a charter, No. 130, on November 7, 1919. Ten months later it was learned that the teachers were teaching sisters of a convent and that the school they taught at was parochial. The constitution limited the AFT to public schools, and so with red faces the charter was withdrawn and the union was not to be international again until 1938.[10]

The existence of the union during these early years was precarious, and the disappointments they faced were many. Several of the locals were being assaulted by their boards of education. In August of 1915, the Chicago Board of Education had passed a rule that barred teacher affiliation with national labor. The result of this ruling was immediately challenged in the courts. But the court upheld the board of education, and in 1917 Margaret Haley's local number one withdrew from the AFT.[11] This loss was almost a mortal wound.

In 1920, the San Francisco Board of Education warned teachers that union membership would cost them their jobs while the same ruling was made in St. Louis.[12] In May of that same year, eighty-two members of the local in Lancaster, Pennsylvania, were dropped by the board of education.[13]

In 1921 the *American Teacher,* finding advertisement difficult to obtain, and the union's treasury incapable of full support, ceased publication. It must have seemed to the organizers of the AFT that nothing else could have gone wrong, but it did.

In 1923 the national economic situation deteriorated to the point where the AFL could no longer retain President Stillman on their payroll, and he had to return to teaching.[14] In 1924 the Gary local, another of the original eight, folded.[15] As if the problems of organization of new locals, an impossible budget, and an overworked staff weren't enough—the problem of infighting emerged.

To run any organization without personal animosities arising would probably be too much to expect. The formation of the national union had caused a jockeying for positions of power. Margaret Haley, the driving force of the Chicago teachers, had been purposefully overlooked for the job of national president by a coalition who feared she was too involved in the Chicago turbulence to provide a truly national perspective.[16] This was the seed of discontent, and it was watered in the first few years of the national. Margaret Haley had a staunch position on every issue, and included in her broad repertoire of issues was the Irish-English conflict. She identified with John Fitzpatrick, president of the Chicago Federation of Labor, and not with Samuel Gompers whom she knew to be an Anglophile. Charles Stillman's early cooperation with Gompers caused her to write him off as anti-Irish.[17]

Yet another source of conflict was the growing animosity between the leadership of the New York local and that of Chicago. The focal points in this controversy were Charles Stillman and Henry Linville. Linville, as editor of the *American Teacher,* which was the official organ of the AFT, was more ideological in his concerns. Stillman, on the other hand, was more of a bread and butter unionist. The more conservative Chicago unionists resented the philosophical stance taken by Linville in the magazine. When the *American Teacher* was begun again in 1926, the editorship was moved to Chicago and added to the duties of the secretary-treasurer.[18]

Politics, the Great War, and Conformity

American education had been involved with politics and politicians in one form or another since its inception. The concern for school tax issues, the election of school boards and superintendents, the granting of school building and maintenance contracts, and the drafting of school laws, were always important activities of the community. But ironically the person most directly concerned with these problems—the teacher—proved to be the most ignorant of the process.

The tradition of political disinterest among teachers was probably related to the historic evolution of schoolkeeping from the ministry. The central thrust of education was stressing moral values which transcended the more mundane considerations of the political sphere. Another factor, perhaps, was the development of the public school idea during a storm of political controversy that led Horace Mann to admonish that: "Principles which might engender strife and controversy were to be excluded in the interest of 'commonness.' " [19] But probably the greatest factor was the use of young ladies and gentlemen as teachers. Limited in experience, educated only in a classical sense, the teaching cadre learned to live under the attitude of political neutrality, and aloofness became a sacred creed with the emerging profession.

This phenomenon continued throughout the nineteenth century and was greatly reinforced during the latter quarter of that century when the organization of strong local political machines and the growing interest in school systems by the entrepreneurial class made political participation by teachers impossible as well as unthinkable. Even as the progressives sought to reform the political machinery of education, they worked *for* the teachers but not *with* them in the process of reform.

With the twentieth century came increased rumblings among the teachers with the realization that they had no control over their working conditions, salaries and benefits, or educational philosophy under which they were supposed to operate. The *American Teacher* picked up this theme early in its publication history. In the third issue of the journal the editors lamented that:

> Education has made rapid strides but teachers still maintain the positions of hirelings and underlings.
>
> Teachers are underpaid and overworked and are treated with scorn and ridicule.
>
> Democracy in Education, a voice and a vote in the government of our schools would help remove the brass collar from the teacher's neck and make him a being independent, self-reliant, self-respecting, fit to initiate and to cope more directly with this transcendently complex problem of education.[20]

But breaking the bounds of traditional silence and timidity required more than will. The established relationship of subservience was vigorously upheld by school boards and administrators. In Boston the school board ruled that teachers could not speak on political issues of that municipality when some of the teachers voiced approval of two candidates for the board who sought to unseat two incumbents.[21] In New York City the school board instructed the superintendent that employees of the board should not participate in an unauthorized conference on school matters.[22] In Winston-Salem, North Carolina, principal James M. Shields was dismissed for writing a book that was critical of the control of local affairs by the R. J. Reynolds Tobacco Company.[23] In Tennessee, teachers were forbidden by law to smoke. Teachers in a village of Westchester County, New York, were required by the board to be in bed by ten o'clock.[24] A small town in North Carolina actually had the following promises written in a teacher's contract:

I promise to take a vital interest in all phases of Sunday School work, donating of my time, service and money without stint, for the benefit and uplift of the community.

I promise to abstain from all dancing, immodest dressing, and other conduct unbecoming a teacher and a lady.

I promise not to go out with any young men except as it may be necessary to stimulate Sunday School work.

I promise not to fall in love, to become engaged or secretly marry.

I promise to remain in the dormitory or on the school grounds when not actively engaged in school or church work elsewhere.

I promise not to encourage or tolerate the least familiarity on the part of any of my boy pupils.

I promise to sleep at least eight hours each night, to eat carefully, to take every precaution to keep in the best of health and spirits in order that I may be better able to render efficient service to my pupils.

I promise to remember that I owe a duty to the townspeople who are paying me my wages, that I owe respect to the school board and to the superintendent who hired me, and that I shall consider myself at all times the willing servant of the school board, and that I shall cooperate with them to the limit of my ability in any movement aimed at the betterment of the town, the pupils or the school.[25]

Such a system of teacher subservience was supported by the growing profession of educational administration. Said Professor William C. Bagley of Teachers College, Columbia, in his 1919 edition of *Classroom Management:* "Unquestioned obedience is the first rule of efficient service. The classroom teacher owes this to his superiors and whenever he cannot yield such obedience, his resignation is the only alternative." [26] Political and economic conservatism was the rule among schoolmen.

In 1927, M. H. Harper published a study entitled: *Social Beliefs and Attitudes of American Educators* based on 1922 data.[27] Using a sample of three thousand teachers and administrators, Harper found the educators to fall definitely to the conservative side of a conservative-to-liberal continuum. Here are a few selected questions with an indication of the percentage of agreement given following the question: [28]

Our educational forces should be directed toward a more thoroughly socialistic order of society (8%).

One should never allow his own experience and reason to lead him in ways that he knows are contrary to the teachings of the Bible (53%).

During the dangers of impending war, our government should prevent any groups of citizens from opposing, through public discussions or through publications, the government's most thorough preparation for the possible conflict (63%).

For the improvement of patriotism, our laws should forbid much of the radical criticism that we often hear and read concerning the injustice of our country and government (30%).

Histories written for elementary or high school use should omit any facts likely to arouse in the minds of the students questions or doubt concerning the justice of our social order and government (35%).

If the teacher was to gain a voice in the destiny of his enterprise, certainly his own self-concept would have to change. The following advice offered by the AFT journal seemed reasonable: "Now, if we look to our schools to turn out courageous, self-reliant, aggressive personalities, we can hardly expect our children to get their inspiration from a class of beings who have been charged with lacking backbones." [29]

The teaching situation in large urban areas like New York City and Chicago was freer than the situation in the more rural settings but still a long way from reasonable. The early fights of Margaret Haley and the teachers' union had made Chicago school authorities at least aware of the teachers as a force. The successful court activities and the willingness to challenge autocratic rulings made the Chicago teachers uncommonly militant among teachers of the entire country. But even in Chicago the superintendent, school board, and political figures held the destiny of the classroom teacher in their hands. After fighting long and hard for a salary schedule, the teacher's federation investigation showed only sixty-two teachers out of twenty-six hundred at the top of the scale.[30] In New York City the educational powers were likewise concerned with combating the teachers and any sign of political liberalism in the schools. When a straw poll for the U.S. presidency was held at New York's Commercial High School in 1920 the district superintendent ordered the results suppressed when he discovered that Eugene V. Debs had received 354 votes from the two thousand students in the school.[31] Samuel Schmalhausen, an admitted Jewish socialist and member of the New York local of the AFT, was fired on the charge of having offensive books on his high school reading list.[32] Benjamin Glassberg, also a union member, was fired from his teaching post at Commercial High School also on the grounds of subversion.[33]

Although political involvement was not the major thrust of the union it recognized from the start the need to understand the political process, especially as it affected public education. What the teachers lacked was resolve. The union hoped that collective strength would create courage and cause the teachers to speak out. Said John Dewey to the AFT in 1916: "We should have a body of self-respecting teachers and educators who will see to it that their ideas and their experience in educational matters shall really count in the community; and who, in order that these may count, will identify themselves with the interests of the community; who will conceive of themselves as citizens and as servants of the public, and not merely as hired employees of a certain body of men. It is because I hope to see the teaching body occupy that position of social leadership which it ought to occupy, and which to our shame it must be said we have not occupied in the past, that I welcome every movement of this sort." [34] World War I had followed on the heels of the founding of the AFT and was to have a significant impact on the AFT and education in general.

Certainly the war served as a potent force in the drive for political orthodoxy. The amount of opposition to the war was relatively small, but even that amount was intolerable to the self-proclaimed patriots. The embers of patriotism were fanned to consuming flames and in the spread of the holocaust many suffered. Even the war's end did not stop the superpatriotic efforts.

Looking back at the decade following the war the American Civil Liberties Union's Committee on Academic Freedom reported that:

1. More laws have been passed interfering with teaching in public schools than in all our previous history.

2. More college professors have been dismissed or disciplined because of their views than in any other decade in our history.

3. Meaningless, formal "patriotic exercises," flag saluting and conventional instruction in the Constitution in public schools are required by law.

4. Special oaths of loyalty to the government, not required of other public officers, are exacted from teachers in some states.

5. History text-books have been revised, to make past history square with today's prejudices.

6. Teachers' unions are generally opposed and in some cases outlawed.

7. More student papers and liberal clubs in colleges have been censored than in any previous decade.[35]

During the course of the war the AFT's small voice supported patriotism but recoiled at the excesses. The union opposed compulsory military training in the high schools; it was suspicious of the fiercely patriotic support of the war by President Gompers of the AFL; and it was defiant toward those patriotic groups and economic organizations that attempted to use the schools for crusades of orthodoxy.

Often these political and economic interest groups combined for a coalition to combat those who questioned capitalism. A Congressional investigation of the National Security League in 1919 uncovered major contributors from New York Edison, Standard Oil, U.S. Steel, DuPont, Carnegie Steel, and the House of Morgan.[36] The National Civic Federation had Elbert H. Gary and August Belmont as major benefactors.[37]

During the crusades for orthodoxy the charges and countercharges often spilled out of the journalistic arena into the political realm. A favorite ploy was to create political committees and commissions for purposes of investigations. Such investigations could invariably find culprits worth condemning. The accompanying publicity that went with such investigations was better than a highly financed campaign for many of the participating politicians.

One of the first of such committees was the Lusk Committee of the New York Assembly created in 1918. The committee was from its inception identified with the "Red Scare" hysteria that infected the highest offices of government. Most of the committee's activities were held in New York City but hearings were also held in Buffalo, Utica, and Rochester.[38] On November 8, 1919, the committee conducted raids upon seventy-three "Red Centers" in New York City. Over one thousand people were arrested and reams of literature were confiscated.[39] The connection of public education with all of this activity was remote, but the discovery that several teachers were involved in communist organizations was enough to convince the committee otherwise. Therefore, part of the final report of the Lusk Committee called for laws which in effect established a required document by teachers promising their intention of living under the constitution.[40] Such a law was eventually passed over Governor Alfred Smith's veto and remained on the books until Smith could repeal it in 1923.

Formulating a Philosophy

Forming an operational philosophy during the period 1916 to 1929 posed no problem. The very birth of the union was a reaction to conditions common in public education. Taking a stand against such conditions became the philosophy of the union. The AFT had adopted as its slogan the ringing phrase "Education for Democracy, Democracy in Education."

More specifically the union came to stand for a set of principles that were presented to the parent AFL at its convention in Baltimore on November 24, 1916. These following principles were endorsed by the AFL:

1. The right of teachers to organize and affiliate with labor must be recognized.

2. If our children during their most impressionable years are to have the benefit of daily contact with examples of upstanding American manhood and womanhood, and not to be exposed to an atmosphere of servility in the schoolroom, teachers must be given warning and a hearing before being separated from the service.

3. The teacher must be guaranteed the opportunity to make his due influence felt in the community, working thru the school chiefly, but free to work thru all the avenues of citizenship.

4. The control of the teaching staff should be removed from the Board of Education, and placed in the hands of the professional expert, the Superintendent of Schools.

5. If our democracy is not to be crippled at its source, democratic school administration must be secured by insuring to the teacher an effective voice in that administration.

6. The schools must be removed from politics by the application of the merit principle of civil service to the employment, advancement, and dismissal of teachers, thus securing tenure during efficiency.

7. The work of the teacher, now notoriously ill-paid, determines the quality of our future citizenship, and should receive financial recognition more clearly commensurate with its importance to the community.

8. Vocational education should be encouraged, but only under a "unit system."

9. The people should directly control educational policies thru the popular election of boards of education.

10. A system of free textbooks is an essential of genuinely free and democratic public schools.

11. Enlightened public policy demands adequate pension provisions for public school teachers.[41]

The following month the American Federation of Teachers held its first annual convention during the Christmas school-break at Chicago. Here they spent most of their time in filling out the educational philosophy outlined before the AFL. The result was a broadly conceived twenty-seven-point platform that concerned itself with questions of national and local school policies, teacher welfare and security, the school plant, and the curriculum.

In the area of policy the AFT called for the creation of a U.S. Department of Education with a secretary of cabinet status. It further favored universal suffrage and the adoption of the initiative, referendum and recall which were gaining popularity as progressive reforms. Locally it advocated a popularly elected board of education that would be paid (to insure representation of the lower socioeconomic classes) and to include at least one teacher on its membership.

To improve teacher welfare and security, the union endorsed a program of tenure, increased salaries, teacher exchange programs, and sabbatical leave plans. It also favored
changing state certification laws to require four years of training beyond high school for all teachers. A special sore point to
teachers was the system of teacher supervisors and ratings that
had been instituted in the name of efficiency but usually
operated on principles of politics and personal favoritism.[42]
The AFT did not oppose supervision but rather called for
more objective rating systems and for the rating of supervisors
by teachers as well!

The federation firmly opposed the overcrowded conditions
of schools that were so common in the era and called for a
decrease in class size. They also recommended increased use of
the school plant by social and civic groups.

One of the charges leveled against the American Federation
of Teachers, especially in later decades, was its failure to speak
to the problem of curriculum. Certainly in comparison to the
Progressive Education Association it was silent on curriculum
matters. But this charge of silence is not completely accurate.
The union stood firm in advocating the inclusion of physical
education and vocational training into the curriculum. It condemned the move toward compulsory military training. It
asked for more programs for the gifted ("supernormal," as the
plank stated it). Strong statements approving experimental
pedagogy were made, and the hopes of a scientific basis for education were expressed.

These planks, then, stood unchanged from 1916 to 1929 as
the educational philosophy of the AFT. As the union moved
into later decades new issues were added and older hopes were
fulfilled. Yet, the basic operating philosophy of the AFT remained relatively unchanged and matters of principle were not
abandoned.

Organizing New Locals

Organizing new locals in the period 1916 to 1929 was extremely difficult. Initial contact with teachers usually found
them too frightened to organize a union. Even in those com-

munities where the teaching conditions had driven the faculty to the point of desperation, no one would assume leadership among the teachers. Even after establishment of a local, its life span was often very short. Pressures from the administration, promotion of union leadership to administrative duties, threats, and payoffs often led to the demise of local unions. Once the disheartened president of the AFT remarked to the writer Upton Sinclair: "The price of a teacher in the United States is fifty dollars—meaning that a teachers' union would agree to disband if the board of education would give them fifty dollars a year increase of wages as the price of their civil rights." [43]

The official records kept by the American Federation of Teachers from the period 1916–29 reveal both the lifespan and causes of the failure at organizing. The Birmingham, Alabama, local founded in 1920 folded after a duration of two years and two months due to lack of leadership. The local at Visalia, California, which had been founded in 1919, folded after seven months—they got their salary increase. At Denver the local that began in 1919 voted to disband when after a ten-month existence the school board got a new superintendent. In Peoria the High School Women had formed Local No. 46 in 1919 which lasted until the board of education drew up a yellow dog contract in 1920. The union teachers of Prince George County, Maryland, responded to public opposition and disbanded after eight months. In Detroit the proposed local never really got off the ground as the newspapers whipped up public opposition. On and on the same story continued. The organizing pattern and problems were only slightly different in the nation's colleges and universities.

During the formative years, the AFT had to decide whether or not to concentrate its efforts solely on the elementary and secondary schools or to also organize the college teachers. Although having no particular plan of action, the union, always desirous of new membership, ventured into college organization.

The same pressures and problems that were facing the public-school teachers of the United States were also facing the American college teacher. Long a bastion of quiet scholarly pursuit, the older colleges and the newer universities were increasingly experiencing disaffection among the academic ranks. No doubt part of this was due to the inclusion of the same business ethic and cult of efficiency that had invaded the public schools. By 1918 Thorstein Veblen, writing in *The Higher Learning in America,* was already sideswiping the corporate image that had superseded the older university traditions and was calling the presidents of the universities "captions of erudition." Paying professors as little as possible, refusing to provide any security through tenure, and constantly violating the tenets of academic freedom were becoming common practices. As could be expected, many of the victims of these injustices would seek recourse. The American Federation of Teachers, realizing the situation, began its long and usually frustrating campaign to organize locals among the college teachers.

The first large university to have an AFT local was the University of Illinois, which was organized in January of 1919 as Local No. 41. Such a venture into the ranks of organized labor by the otherwise staid professors attracted some national attention, and the *Christian Science Monitor* sent a reporter to the Urbana campus to interview Professor A. C. Cole, the local's president. Cole told the *Monitor* reporter that the reasons for organizing included lack of democratic procedures for faculty members and the general dissatisfaction with the salaries.[44]

Another important college local was formed at Yale. Others sprang up in New York City and in various teachers colleges. But the problems involved in organizing the college teacher were many. For one thing academic rank was a stumbling block. Beginning with the instructor and ranging all the way to a full professor was often too broad a range in which to establish consensus. Typically it was the instructors and beginning assistant professors who had the most to complain about. Many of the full professors had relative security and identified themselves more with the university administration than the younger faculty. Another problem was the nature of the college teacher's personality. Wrote the secretary of the Whitewater, Wisconsin, Local No. 80 to AFT headquarters about the faculty: "They are a self-centered lot. If they are satisfied as far as they are concerned, it is impossible to get them to move."[45]

In a letter to President Stillman from the Univeristy of Illinois one organizer complained: "Without a doubt, these men are the most ignorant of the benefits to be derived from organization than any set of educated men I have ever had anything to do with. . . . In this work you shall have all the difficulties to overcome that can be put together in one soul. They are afraid, regard theirselves [*sic*] on a plane above labor, believe in Carnegie pensions, and dream of good pay positions in the future under the present system." [46] The college teachers were even less inclined to identify with organized labor than public-school teachers. Puffed up by doctoral degrees and higher learning they were often critical of organizing for such a mundane thing as better pay. Said John Dewey to such critics in 1933: "Some teachers have the idea that the sole object of a teachers' union is to protect teachers' wages. I have no apologies to make for that phase. I don't see why workers should not have an organization to secure a decent living standard." [47] However, he continued on pointing out that the "foundations of the teachers' unions of the American Federation of Teachers are much wider . . . and I know of no organization except the American Federation of Teachers that stands constantly, openly, and aggressively for the realization of the social function of the profession."

Yet another problem in organizing the college teachers was their feelings of superiority over public-school teachers with the consequent disinterest in mutual association. In fairness to the college teachers though, it should be pointed out that sometimes the animosity was aimed in the other direction. A letter to Charles Stillman written on October 16, 1919, indicates that the Greater Boston Local No. 66 had been originally conceived for all teachers in the area but that the public school teachers were suspicious of the socialistic tendencies of the Harvard and other college personnel and separated to form their own union.[48]

Efforts at organizing colleges prior to 1930 were inevitably doomed to failure. During the AFT's fourteen-year history to 1930, twenty college locals were organized. The nucleus of professors who helped to organize such ventures were usually small. Of the twenty locals formed the average number of members involved was about thirty-one per unit. But usually organized in quick response to a crisis situation and poorly aided by a weak national federation the dawning of the decade of the thirties found but three of the twenty still in existence.[49] In addition to failing for reasons of satisfaction of an immediate need and inability of the national to provide support, other reasons worthy of consideration were given. Pressure from the administration led to the failure of locals at Howard University and Illinois State Normal. Professors at the University of Illinois were given yellow dog contracts after attempting organization. The local at the University of Missouri was opposed by the farmers. The administration at Washburn College of Topeka, Kansas, solved the problem of dissent by firing all the members of the AFT local. Obviously the efforts of the first fourteen years were not encouraging.

Efforts to protect the vulnerability of the college teacher were also undertaken by rivals of the AFT such as the American Association of University Professors, founded in 1915.[50] Yet the conceptual tactics and methods of protecting the teachers were different in the AAUP than with the AFT. The approach to the violations of academic freedom, for example, were shaped by the AAUP's President A. O. Lovejoy who had a negative disposition towards labor affiliation. The AAUP's approach to breaches in academic freedom called for an investigation by a panel or committee of charges and countercharges in a judicial manner. Until such a procedure was completed and conclusions were drawn, no public statements were issued. Even if the panel were to find a complaining professor entirely justified in his or her allegations the only weapon in the arsenal of the AAUP was professional sanctions. Such sanctions, when printed in the official journal of the association, were supposed to dissuade any prospective employee from seeking work at the institution so advertised. Such a procedure, while having an undisputable ethical tone to it, could be as effective as the size of the association membership and the inclination to abide by the sanctions. The economic depression of 1929 and the resulting cutbacks in college expenditures proved the ineffectiveness of such measures. In fact, it could be said that such blacklisting has never been effective.

The Reaction to the Federation

Teachers joining with organized labor was from the beginning irritating to public-school administrators and to boards of education. Superintendents were fearful of losing their authority. In 1929 the magazine *Nation's Schools* carried a feature entitled: "The School Executive Looks at the Teachers' Federation." The conclusion of the symposium was included in the subtitle which read: "Superintendents express views on whether or not the AFT should be supported and the general conclusion of the symposium is that little need exists for such an organization." [51] The following quotations from superintendents who responded are typical:

Teachers naturally belong with the groups interested in professional-social advancement. No organization of teachers should stand before the American people tainted with the suspicion of economic-social aims.

A board of education, working under the laws of a state, must have complete control of the school system that is placed under its charge. Any organization that attempts to nullify or scatter this authority is working towards chaos in American public education.

Strife and contention seem to follow in the wake of many organizations of the American Federation of Teachers. The cause of education does not prosper in such an atmosphere. I prefer to secure the aims of the educational program more slowly and keep the good will of every portion of the community.[52]

Said one reporter about the prospects of a unionized teaching profession: "No professional standards can be raised by affiliation with labor unions. The effect will, in the long run, be found to be directly contrary not because labor unions are not excellent institutions—they are more than that, they are a necessity of the times—but because affiliation with labor unions, the linking of the name 'school teacher' with the name trade unionist' does not sound well upon the ears of the laity." [53] After building up more steam over the following pages of the article the author concluded by saying: "And when every teacher who is charged with the sacred obligation of planting the seeds of good citizenship in the hearts of the men of tomorrow, and with nourishing the instinct of motherhood in the breast of the wife of tomorrow, is branded with the union label and saturated with the stench of ward politics then will the federation have attained its goal." [54]

The incidence of an antiunion position in Chicago has previously been mentioned. Its occurrence was common. In 1914, Cleveland's school board released eleven women teachers for trying to affiliate with the local federation of labor.[55] In 1922 the local in New York City was harassed by an investigating committee of the board of education. Here the charge was lack of patriotism and in the committee's report entitled: "Exploitation of the Public School System of New York City," the recommendation was for union teachers to be dismissed. Two of the strongest arguments used by the committee included the fact that Abraham Lefkowitz, the legislative representative for the local, had supported the pressmen's wildcat strike of 1919 and had sat on the same platform with William Z. Foster of the Communist party at a rally.[56] In 1919, the St. Louis, Missouri, Board of Education ruled against union membership for its teachers and instituted a yellow dog contract that was enforced until 1937.[57]

Among professors of education there was much ambivalence toward the AFT. Due both to the quality of its program and the vast number of students it handled, Teachers College of Columbia University was tremendously influential in American education. At Teachers College the ambivalence was obvious. Dean William Russell thought that teachers should not affiliate with organized labor.[58] David Snedden and William Heard Kilpatrick, of the same faculty, were similarly opposed.[59] On the same faculty, however, were George S. Counts, John L. Childs, and R. Bruce Raup, all of whom were extremely favorable to union affiliation and joined the AFT in the 1930s.

The most successful coup of the AFT among professional educators was gaining the membership of John Dewey. Dewey joined the New York local in 1925 and, with his usual zeal, offered his services as a publicist and philosopher for the AFT. In 1928 he wrote a short document entitled: "Why I am a Member of the Teachers Union." [60] This statement was reprinted in other journals and later issued as an independent publication of the federation. Among various plaudits contained in the paper, two paragraphs emphasize his feelings: "We live in an industrial age and it is academic folly and mere phantasy to suppose that the conduct of public education can be divorced from the prominence which economic, industrial, and financial questions occupy in all other phases of our social life. . . . I say without any fear of contradiction that there is no organization in the United States—I do not care what its nature is—that has such a fine record in the program of liberal progressive public education as will be found in the printed records of the American Federation of Labor." [61]

In 1929 the federation still lived but its existence was precarious. The 1920s were turbulent times for American labor and the AFT was no exception.[62] Beginning with a membership of twenty-eight hundred the federation declined to less than five hundred between 1917 and 1918. The peak had come in 1920 with a membership of around nine thousand but then steadily declined to a low point of three thousand in 1926.[63] In attempting to assess these growth patterns of the 1920s, Mary Barker, a president of the union in this era offered the following explanations:

1. Following the World War, capital made a widespread attack against organized labor. The American Federation of Labor lost millions of members and the American Federation of Teachers, affiliated with it, lost its share.

2. Teachers have long been a conservative and yielding group and have been made a target for criticism because of their status as "employees of the public."

3. There is a strong prejudice against public servants affiliating with labor.

4. Labor, when its own crisis came, was forced to withdraw help which it had been giving to the A.F.T. and therefore all national organizers had to be recalled.

5. Teachers flocked to the Federation for economic and social aid and when help came they forgot the source which it was derived.

6. Teachers entertain an "inferiority complex" concerning their affiliation with labor.

7. The N.E.A. has been waging a fight against the A.F.T.[64]

In addition to problems of membership the AFT had had some difficulties with the leadership in the parent American

Federation of Labor. From the beginning the AFT advocated national reforms beyond the goals of Samuel Gompers. Gompers's brand of pure and simple unionism was not enough to satisfy those persons seeking change in the basic fabric of society. Gompers had become increasingly conservative with his own advancing age and had joined the business community in condemning those opposed to World War I and opposing such leftist labor groups as the International Workers of the World. Gompers failed to place representatives of the AFT on the AFL's Committee on Education. In 1921 the situation deteriorated when two of the three AFT delegates to the AFL convention supported John L. Lewis in an unsuccessful attempt at replacing Gompers as president.[65]

Plagued with questions of philosophy, fighting to build a membership against overwhelming forces, faced with internal squabbles, the AFT was also financially impoverished in these early years. From the start the dues had been set purposefully low to attract a large membership and to compete with the NEA. But if the organization was to prosper it would cost money. As of July 1, 1918, the treasury had held $235.87.[66]

Yet with this shaky beginning and with these several problems the AFT stood in 1929 with thirty-nine locals, 5,255 paid-up members, and eternal optimism.[67]

Chapter 3

The Depression Years
1929 – 1935

The Depression Descends

The crash of the stock market in October of 1929 signaled the beginning of the economic struggle. Despite the inflation of the 1929s the American worker never was as well off as he was before the collapse. Wages had gone steadily up as America had become the supplier of food, munitions, and manufacturers of war-torn Europe. But for the American teacher the slump became even more bitter when he considered that he had never really enjoyed the fruits of prosperity.

Public education in the United States qualifies as one of the more interesting cases of historical irony. That public education was held in high regard in 1929 is probably without question. The Lynds attested to this fact in their 1924 investigation of Middletown and reported that the people placed "large faith in going to school" and that the "public schools of Middletown [were] the city's pride." [1] But that this idealistic concern was seldom translated into public action or paralleled with some of the more "pressing" problems of the times can also be shown. In 1929 an august group of Americans who formed the executive council of the National Economic League met at their Beacon Street address to give consideration to just the question of what the pressing problems of the nation were. On this executive committee were:

John Hayes Hammond, Mining Engineer
William Allen White, Publisher
James Rowland Angell, President of Yale
A. Lawrence Lowell, President of Harvard
Roger W. Babson, Statistician
Frank O. Lowden, Ex-Governor, Illinois
David Starr Jordan, Ex-President, Stanford
George Wickersham, Ex-Attorney General
Nicholas Murray Butler, President of Columbia

It is interesting to note that of this group, four of the nine, were directly involved in education. But when they issued their report in March of 1930 which was entitled: "Paramount Problems of the United States for 1930" the tabulations were as shown in the data below.[2]

Subjects

Administration of justice	2209
Prohibition	2068
Lawlessness, disrespect for law	1699
Crime	1642
Law enforcement	1573
World peace	1235
Agriculture, farm relief	996
Taxation	877
World court	862
Reduction and limitations of arms	811
Conservation	810
Efficient democratic government	735
Foreign relations	672
Education	654

From its position in fourteenth place in 1930, education dropped to twenty-fourth place in the 1931 report and fell to thirty-second position in 1932.[3] Just as the public failed to consider education in general as pressing, they likewise failed to show interest in the more specific problem of low pay for teachers.

Just how badly teachers fared economically in the period 1914 to 1929 can be shown in several ways. Using 1913 as a base year and assigning it the index number of 100.0, the cost of living had increased to 162.0 by December of 1929.[4] By 1930 the average salary had climbed to $1,420.00 representing a 177 percent increase in salary and in actual gain in real dollars.[5] Such an increase probably served to convince the boards of education and general public that teachers were advancing on a sound basis. This misconception was probably further enhanced by noting that from 1910 to 1928 average daily attendance had climbed from 12,827,307 to 20,608,353 and that per pupil expenditure moved from $24.93 to $86.77.[6] The dilemma arises when careful consideration is given to the economic position of the teacher relative to other occupations. The national pay average of teachers of $512.00 in 1913 was abysmally low. In that same year the United States government paid its employees an average of $1,136.00, salaried employees averaged $1,066.00, ministers averaged $899.00, wage earners averaged $594.00 and the factory workers $578.00.[7] Even in comparison with other local government employees the $512.00 figure was only 70 percent of that of policemen and 71 percent that of firemen.[8]

In addition to the problem of starting from an extremely low base, actual changes in the composition of the profession must be considered. The most significant was the increase in the number of men teachers and the dropping of provisions by many school boards that no married woman could teach. The result of this change was an increase in the number of dependents among teachers. In the short period of 1929–33 a study of teachers in Spokane, Washington, showed a 15 percent increase in the number of dependents among the teachers of that city.[9] Another factor was the general tightening of policies that affected certification. The most significant change in this direction was the requirement of college training for the elementary schoolteacher.[10] Both of these factors were important to the salary picture, the first meaning an interesting need among teachers for more money and the second a factor that accounts for the increase in average pay levels. Yet another reason for increased pay levels was the lengthening of the school year. In 1910 the average school year was 158 days. In 1928 it was 172 days.[11]

Still another dilemma was the pay differentials among teachers and supervisors. Most salary averages that were computed were based on data from regular classroom teachers as well as supervisory personnel. When it is considered that the differential between teachers and high school principals was 2.4 in 1927 the position of the teachers becomes even more discouraging.[12] Thus, the economic data indicates that the teachers remained in 1929 in the disadvantageous position they had been in 1913.

The depression descended and blanketed within its midst all segments and groups of the population. Not escaping the economic devastation—the school-age population too became enmeshed. Especially hurt were the young people age fifteen to twenty-five. Layoffs in all sectors of the economy meant an extreme burden on those who were just entering the job market in the early thirties. Estimates as to the number of young people who thus found themselves unemployed and out of school by the period 1933 to 1935 range from three to six million.[13] Those who had entered college found themselves short of funds and unable to finish their studies.[14] Those that did finish college during the period found the job market no less glutted. In 1932 an Unemployed College Alumni group was organized in New York City and their estimates showed that 10,000 graduates were unemployed in that city alone.[15] A survey conducted by Dr. Esther Lloyd-Jones of Teachers College and Clyde R. Miller of the Bureau of Educational Service revealed that in the fifty-four colleges and universities located all over the United States that they had surveyed, 21,974 men and women who held degrees were without positions.[16] Hardest hit of all the professions was teaching. The Lloyd-Jones and Miller survey showed that of the 21,974 unemployed, 12,420 were teachers.[17] The colleges and universities hardest hit were not those of marginal reputation. The chart that follows indicates the ten universities which suffered greatest.[18]

Also suffering were the younger children. In 1932 the New York City Health Department reported that 20.5 percent of the schoolchildren examined in city schools were suffering from malnutrition.[19] Clinics in that city reported a substantial increase in rickets.[20] The year previous an investigation revealed

University	Number of Reported Unemployed Graduates
Ohio State University	2,097
University of Chicago	1,798
University of Illinois	1,445
Teachers College, Columbia	1,255
Carnegie Institute	844
Temple University	687
New York University	575
College of the City of New York	550
University of Minnesota	528
Princeton University	450

that 11,000 hungry children were being fed by the New York City teachers.[21] Charles E. Picket, secretary of the American Friends Service Committee, testified before Congress that his study of counties in Illinois, West Virginia, Kentucky and Western Pennsylvania indicated that 10 percent of the children were underweight.[22] By the end of March 1933, nearly one-third of 1 million schoolchildren were at home as districts closed their schools. Georgia had closed 1,318 of its schools which affected 170,790 children. Alabama had 81 percent of all rural whites on forced vacation. In Ohio the Dayton schools opened their doors three days a week, and by the first week in May 1933 Akron owed its teachers $330,000 in back salaries.[23] In 1934 the National Education Association's research, shown in the chart below, revealed the extent to which school programs were retarded.[24]

Educational Items	Year to Which 1934 Figures Have Declined	Number of Years of Development Lost
Number of teachers, supervisors, and principals	1927	6
Average salary of teachers, principals, and supervisors	1921	12
Total expenditures	1924	9
Capital outlay	1913	20
Cost per child enrolled	1922	11

Retrenchment and Response

What followed on the heels of the depression was retrenchment. As the decline continued state and local governments reacted swiftly to shrinking revenues by cutting down or omitting their services. Public education was not spared the process.[25] The problem was with the political weakness of the educational lobby. The years of calculated ignorance about the political power systems and the usual aloofness maintained by the teacher organizations made them extremely vulnerable to the caprice of the budget cutters. Apparently many saw this situation brewing and hastened to forewarn against this inevitability. Early in the slump Ellwood P. Cubberley, the patriarch of school management warned: "We can wait for streets, parks and many forms of public improvements and service, but we cannot postpone education." [26] To this Al Smith, certainly no stranger to political realities added: "Whatever may be the exigencies, whatever may be the reasons for drastic reductions in appropriations, one thing must not happen. There must be no curtailment of educational facilities." [27] And lastly, Herbert Hoover, now on the outside of the house on Pennsylvania Avenue chided: "However the national economy may vary, or whatever fiscal adjustments may need to be made, the very first obligation upon the national resources is the undiminished financial support of the public schools." [28]

But talk wasn't enough to save the schools. The move to cut back on education came slowly during 1930 and 1931. Some writers have described the school operation during these first two years as usual.[29] But the situation deteriorated and one investigator reported, presumably in a serious vein, that his research of state education journals in the period 1929 to 1931 revealed that finance rose as a topic from tenth place in 1930 to seventh place in 1931 while jokes and anecdotes dropped from 16.2 percent of column space to 5.4 percent.[30]

Possibly part of the problem of retrenchment evolved from various segments of the educational profession which regarded large cutbacks as so inevitable that they offered little resistance. In its twenty-seventh annual report the Carnegie Foundation for the Advancement of Teaching pointed out that "the public school system (from elementary school to university) is in much the position of a hotel that has for long offered a bill of fare of lavish proportions, in which one did not always find a simple and wholesome meal. The time has come when it can no longer offer so extravagant a menu." [31] "The same document went on to suggest that in addition to cutting the curriculum, the children and not the state should purchase their own textbooks since: "The American people [were] being made soft by this sort of coddling." [32] It further offered that secondary schools should institute formal admission standards and charge tuition.[33] Attitudes similar to this were just the kind of soothing balm that legislators desired.

In the 1933 session of the Iowa assembly, thirty-two new laws affecting the schools were passed. All but one were concerned with economy. The appropriation for the Iowa State Department of Public Instruction was cut by 30 percent and the state's minimum income for teachers was set at forty dollars a month.[34]

In Idaho the legislators cut educational expenses 20–30 percent of the 1931 level. In Oregon the minimum salary law for teachers was invalidated.[35]

In Chicago the economic program, as originally adopted, suggested "closing half the kindergartens, eliminating manual training and household arts from elementary schools, disbanding or drastically reducing the staffs devoted to child study, vocational guidance, and the care of adolescent difficulties, abolishing the parental school and the junior college, closing the swimming pools and reducing physical education." [36] In addition to this the junior high school system was to be dismantled, the supervisory staff was to be decreased and every elementary school principal was to supervise at least two schools.[37]

A report issued by John A. Wieland, Illinois Superintendent of Public Instruction, offered the comparisons for a three-year period [38] as shown for the years 1931–34.

Perhaps the depths were reached in a small community in North Dakota which advertised in a newspaper for teachers stating that: "The low bidders, if qualifications are satisfactory, will teach in the four schools of a rural district near here." [39]

	1931	*1934*
Per capita cost of education	$119	$94
School term		Shortened 11 days
Average teacher's salary		Cut $385
Teachers employed	48,976	46,161

As the depression deepened, financial issues and problems served as a wedge to split into even wider differences many political, social, racial, and economic ideologies. This wedge worked on the uneasy alliance that had been made in the nineteenth century between education and commercial interests. This alliance had held together during earlier economic fluctuations. One study showed that the depression of 1929 would be the first to adversely affect school support.[40] Searching for the reasons in the breakdown in this relationship seems to indicate not only the fact that this depression was extremely severe but also that the local school budgets had grown so significantly in the twentieth century as to demand the largest percentage of local revenues of any taxing agency. So perhaps the key factor was the conspicuous nature of school budgets.

In 1920 school budgets were supported by local revenues. In that year the federal government contributed only three-tenths of 1 percent, the state and counties contributed 27.9 percent leaving 71.8 percent support to the community. By 1930 this amount had increased to 72.3 percent.[41] Leading experts in school finance like Paul Mort and George D. Strayer of Teachers College, Columbia University had realized before the slump began that such heavy dependence upon local sources of revenue was not only inequitable, due to economic differences from one community to another, but also hazardous in that local or regional cyclical declines would have significant negative impact on education. But little was done to alleviate this problem before the depression.

The business community, especially those organized into national groups, turned their energies toward cutting school expenditures. C. Weston Bailey, president of the National Board of Fire Underwriters, probably spoke for many businessmen when he complained of "exorbitant taxes and bureaucracy" in the educational system and demanded a "prompt stopping of this riot of waste." [42]

In the spring of 1932 a National Economic League was formed to offer suggestions as to how the tides of the depression might be stemmed. Selected as chairman of this League was Admiral Richard E. Byrd.[43] Serving with Byrd on the advisory council were former President Hoover, Newton Baker, Elihu Root, John J. Pershing, Alfred E. Smith, former President Coolidge, and Admiral Sims.[44] Using this great prestige the League was organized in thirty-five states and began their assault on governmental expenditure. On the national level they reserved their major salvos for the veterans' appropriations, which at the time accounted for approximately one-fourth of the national budget.[45] On the local level much of their attention was on schools. Other national groups included the National Organization to Reduce Public Expenditure organized in June of 1932 at Chicago under the auspices of the Chicago Association of Commerce, the Illinois Manufacturing Association and the 648 other cooperating groups like grain and trade associations and local chambers of commerce. The National Association of Manufacturers formed the National Committee for Economy in Government in the summer of 1932.[46] Without national affiliation were a host of local community tax and business protective groups that wielded their influence to cut the strings of the public purse.

The group with the best formulated plan for attacking school budgets was the United States Chamber of Commerce. Holding conventions every year, this national amalgam of local businessmen had previously supported education and had listed it as one of its "major programs of the year" every year. In 1932 this priority was dropped and the central program was for "drastic cuts in government expenditures." [47]

Adopting this as its new objective a letter entitled: "Possible Fields of Economy in School Retrenchment" was sent to local members. The letter offered twenty areas that might be considered in order to shave expenses:

1. Purchase of supplies.
2. Operation of physical plant.
3. Reduction in cost of collecting school funds and of debt service

by consolidation and refunding of outstanding indebtedness where possible.

4. Postponement of new capital outlay for buildings and replacements.

5. Transfer supervisors to classrooms.

6. Simplify curriculums.

7. Simplify overhead administration and centralize responsibility.

8. Shorten school day one hour.

9. Increase size of classes.

10. Increase teaching hours.

11. Repairs and maintenance of physical plant.

12. Suspend automatic increases of salaries.

13. Reduction in teachers' salaries not to exceed 10 per cent.

14. Shorten school year not to exceed 12 per cent.

15. Discontinue kindergarten.

16. Discontinue evening classes.

17. Reduce elementary curriculums by consolidation from eight to seven years.

18. Reduce high-school curriculums by consolidation from four to three.

19. Transfer one-third of cost of all instruction above high-school level from taxpayers to pupil.

20. Impose fee on high-school students.[48]

Measuring the impact of such recommendations is nearly impossible, but the June 1932 issue of *School Management* showed that of the cities, towns, and villages it surveyed: 62 percent were reducing teachers salaries; 50 percent were reducing administrators salaries; 37 percent were employing fewer teachers; 19 percent were reducing school year; 38 percent were increasing class size; 33 percent were postponing building; 54 percent were postponing equipment and supplies; 8 percent were eliminating subjects; 3 percent were reducing the top age on compulsory attendance; 8 percent were eliminating free texts; 10 percent were cutting budgets by other means.[49] The apparent relationship, between the program of the chamber and the realities of the situation is no doubt attributable, in part, to the high percentage of membership of businessmen on local boards of education.

The response of teacher groups to the great depression was largely on the verbal level. The AFT took the strongest steps to translate some of its words into action. The Progressive Educa-

tion Association was largely silent. The National Education Association's response was essentially bureaucratic.

The major reason that the PEA was silent during the depression on fundamental economic questions was due to its organizational objectives. Characteristically concerned over matters of methodology and curriculum it saw no need to make
economic action its new emphasis. Of the sixteen major committees formed by the PEA from 1930 to 1938 only two were
even related to economics. One was Counts's Committee on
Economics and Sociology and the other was Paul Mort's Committee on Federal Support to Education.[50] The first produced a
report that was unacceptable to the leadership and the second
was not formed until recovery was imminent. The major energies of the Progressive Education Association during the thirties were reserved for its eight year study on the relation of the
secondary school and the college.[51]

The NEA investigated the negative effects of the depression
through its research facilities and did appoint several committees to offer possible solutions to the economic crisis of the
school. The Department of Superintendence appointed a Committee on Education for New Social and Economic Rela-
tionships. This group did turn out a report with some recommendations. Another group was the Joint Commission on the
Emergency in Education. Formed of both superintendents and
educational experts their offering was long-range planning and
recommendations in tax structure.[52] The superintendents also
cooperated with the parent organization in forming the Educational Policies Commission in 1935. Created for a five-year
period, the commission was to consider all aspects of education
but certainly the financial crisis had to capture its central interest in 1935. The objectives of the commission were sufficiently
vague enough to offer the group unlimited horizons. As established, they sought:

1. To stimulate thoughtful, realistic, long-term planning within
the teaching profession, looking toward continued adaptation of education to social needs.

2. To appraise existing conditions in education critically and to
stimulate desirable changes in the purposes, procedures, and organization of education.

3. To consider and act upon recommendations from all sources for the improvement of education.

4. To make the best practices and procedures in education known throughout the country and to encourage their use everywhere.

5. To develop understanding and cooperation among all organized groups interested in education improvement.[53]

In addition to many shorter bulletins the net product of the commission's five year existence was four basic reports issued under the heading of "Education in American Democracy." [54] The objectives of the commission, although worthy, were not aimed at seeking immediate solutions to the pressing problems of education and were therefore lauded and set aside.

The NEA did a better job of responding to the depression in its warnings and condemnations that were offered as resolutions and speeches at the annual conventions. But even here the record is inconsistent. Continually striving to hold the goodwill of the business sector, the NEA courted the men of commercial affairs throughout the depression. The NEA's general session of 1931 passed resolutions condemning budget cuts but reserved a significant segment of its program to hear speeches from Milo H. Stuart, assistant superintendent of Indianapolis on "Educating for Better Business," Paul Codman, executive secretary of the San Francisco Stock Exchange on "The Business Man Surveys the Graduate," and A. M. Jones of the Chase-Manhatten Bank on "The Contribution of Education to Banking and Capital Investment from a Banker's Point of View." [55] Perhaps the NEA's response to the depression could best be described as intellectual and passive. In a speech delivered in the 1932 general session, Joseph Rosier, president of Fairmont State Teachers College, stated: "The problems growing out of this depression must be solved by our intellectual classes. In the laboratory, the library, the classroom, and in mental contacts we must find the plans and the remedies for the curing of our ills." [56]

The research department of the NEA published a document entitled, "The Teacher's Economic Position," in September 1935. While recognizing inadequate salaries the document went on to advocate that teachers still try to save 20 percent of their income and contribute 18 percent more to charities.[57] In a concluding pitch for capitalism the bulletin reminded teachers that "the economic system of the nation must be so ordered as to maintain the safety and productiveness of personal investments, and to prevent major changes in the purchasing power of money." [58]

The response of the American Federation of Teachers was more active. Although using rhetoric and committee to condemn the educational cutbacks the union moved beyond these to the arenas of political and social action. At the Fifteenth Annual Convention held in Chicago in the summer of 1931 the AFT passed resolutions favoring the replacement of the local property tax with a graduated state income tax, called for the establishment of federal unemployment insurance, asked for government planning of public works, and advocated a shorter work week.[59] The publications of the AFT also came directly to grips with the depression. The *American Teacher* gave 12½ percent of its column space in 1930 to economic and social problems.[60] But from the start the editorials and articles in the official journal offered more than palliatives for the pressing matters of school finance. Many articles went beyond these issues and concluded that the depression was but a manifest symptom of a graver social illness. Citing instances of gross inequities in the distribution of wealth, showing the injustices of existing social arrangements, and denouncing the power of industrialists and commercial interests, the magazine became a muckraking forum with an educational slant. In the October 1931 issue, the subscriber could read an article by the British socialist Harold J. Laski on "The Teachers Union in a New Social Order." [61] In the February 1933 issue Charles J. Hendley, an officer of the New York City local, wrote on "The Dictatorships of the Bankers." [62] In April of 1933, John Dewey used an article to blast citizens economy groups as tools of concentrated wealth, cited instances of school curtailment, sideswiped the National Association of Manufacturers and the U.S. Chamber of Commerce, and concluded by stating that: "Organization, union, combined and concerted thought and action, is the answer and the only answer I can see to the adequate solution of the problem of the crisis." [63]

Indicative of both the economic realities of the depression

and the efforts of the union was the situation in Chicago. The financial picture there had been dark even before the crash of 1929. Plagued by an inefficient bureaucracy and a notoriously corrupt tie with politics, the school system was in deep financial trouble. The failure of the tax assessor's office to adequately assess property meant glaring inequities in the tax structure. With the beginning of the slump and the resulting delinquency in tax payments came greater crisis. Although the stock market did not crash until October of 1929 the effects were felt as early as January 1930 in Chicago where teachers' checks were held until March 4. "From then on, the salary situation went gradually from bad to worse until the summer of 1934. During this entire period of four and one-half years, nine salary checks were received on time, and the remaining payments were delayed for periods ranging from one week to ten months, with accumulated arrearages amounting at the end to as much as nine months salary." [64]

As things grew worse a Citizens Committee was formed under the leadership of Fred W. Sargent, a Chicago railroad executive. One teacher in Chicago reacted to the activities of this committee by stating: "It is the Committee that is our enemy—made up of bank presidents, railroad presidents, packers, and directors generally of the wealth of the second city of the United States. There is no possible doubt of their intention; they are attempting to starve the teaching force into submission to their programme and to cripple the city's educational system. They would like to reduce public education in Chicago to the three R's." [65] In July of 1931 the board of education moved to issue script. When legal action by the teachers blocked this, the board issued tax anticipation warrants in small denominations to the teachers in lieu of payment. [66] By 1932 the school term was shortened by two weeks at the beginning and two weeks at the end. Teachers were not paid for holidays and salaries were cut by 23.5 percent. [67]

The teachers' reactions to these machinations came slowly. One of the problems was the division among teachers. George S. Counts had investigated the schools of Chicago in 1928 and found that the most powerful teacher groups were Margaret Haley's Chicago Federation of Teachers, the Chicago Principal's Club, the Chicago Teachers League, the Federation of Women High School Teachers, and the Federation of Men Teachers who were affiliated with the AFT. Groups of lesser power were affiliated with the Illinois Education Association, the Schoolmaster's Club, the Eighth Grade Teachers Association, the Ella Flagg Young Club, the Elementary Manual Training Teachers Club, and the Chicago Household Arts Club. In addition there were some nineteen other groups.[68]

During the crisis of the 1930s there was a strong move among teachers to unify in order to consolidate their power. The vehicle for accomplishing this end was achieved in the formation of a Save Our Schools Committee with representatives from all of the teacher groups. The major force behind this being the AFT leadership in the city.[69]

In the midst of this confusion Chicago was readying itself for the 1933 exposition to be called "Century of Progress." The teachers, hopeful that such a title would not be entirely misleading, had established a relationship with Mayor Anthony Cermak who promised them the influence of his office to correct the adversity. When Cermak was assassinated while on tour with President Franklin Roosevelt this ray of hope was extinguished.[70] Acting Mayor Corr would not sign the schools' tax warrants.[71] Under special state provision the city council appointed Edward J. Kelly mayor.[72] In May the new mayor issued a warning through the press that there were to be no demonstrations on the part of teachers when the fair opened.[73] The month previous to that the teachers showed their first signs of unification when twenty-eight thousand of them with sympathizers marched to the banking district. After tying up Loop traffic for over two hours, they entered former U.S. Vice-President Charles Dawes's bank to protest the refusal of Chicago banks to even honor the tax warrants. Upon determining that the mood of the crowd was not to be mollified with hasty maxims the former vice-president said: "To Hell with trouble makers!" and returned to his private office.[74] In that same month of April a group of teachers interrupted a flag-raising ceremony at the exposition by singing the national anthem and carrying signs of protest. One sign read: "Chicago, the Wonderful City, has 14,000 Unpaid School Teachers." [75]

Earlier that same year Fred Sargent, chairman of the Citizens Committee, traveled to the nation's capital with the advertised intent of getting a loan for government employees and teachers. Sargent was able to get $8 million from the Reconstruction Finance Corporation which had already advanced $32 million to Sargent. But like the first monies this second loan went to the Chicago and Northwestern Railroad of which Sargent was president.[76]

As the opening day of the World's Fair came close, many business leaders in Chicago were growing nervous. It was hoped that the event would attract thousands of money-spending tourists to the city. John Fewkes, the president of the Chicago Men Teachers of the AFT, used both his influence as chief officer of the local and as the leader of the Save Our Schools Executive Council to play on this fear of the men of commerce by threatening to organize a mass march of teachers on the day of the fair's opening. The day before the opening ceremony the following circular was sent from the superintendent's office to all schools: "Information has come to Mr. Bogan's office from high authority that the bankers will refuse to provide the $12,000,000 for salaries for October, November, and December if the proposed demonstration or parade of teachers is held tomorrow." [77] As the parade was about to form the next day, John Fewkes arrived to call off the demonstration with freshly gained gilt-edged promises from the bankers to loan the district money.[78]

But cuts in the school budget continued. Meetings of the board of education were heavily attended by both uniformed and plainclothes police to protect the board.[79] In July the teachers staged a mass meeting to avow their militancy. Throughout the crisis the power and leadership of the locals affiliated with the AFT grew. Their influence was unquestioned. The grave situation continued, however, until the federal government made massive loans to Chicago. Even this was made possible by help from the union. Lillian Herstein, an officer in the Chicago local, used her longtime friendship with Secretary of the Interior Harold Ickes, to solicit federal interest in the educational plight of Chicago.[80]

At the national level the federation also mobilized its

strength to combat the efforts of the budget cutters. In their activities the AFT received support from the AFL. Early in the depression the AFL passed the following educational program:

1. Waste and extravagance must be determined by careful study, the responsibility placed where it belongs and no economies which harm the children permitted.
2. No curtailment or elimination of any school activity necessary to maintain and *improve* educational standards.
3. Raising the top-age of compulsory school attendance.
4. No reduction in teachers' salaries.
5. No increase in size of classes.
6. No shortening of the school year.
7. No lengthening of the school day.
8. No elimination of valuable subject matter.
9. Free text books for all.
10. Widest extension of the program of adult education.
11. Tenure laws for teachers.
12. Maintenance and improvement of teaching standards.
13. Adequate school buildings adapted to the needs of modern education.
14. Increased revenues to maintain and develop public education. More money for public education, not less. Our complex social order, the complications of our economic system, call for our public schools and require larger instead of restricted appropriations.
15. Equal educational opportunities for *all* children.[81]

The AFT and the AFL were in perfect harmony in their programs.

The dire economic situation of the 1930s also had consequences for the internal politics of the AFT. The polarization between the working classes and the capitalists grew. The leftists in all segments of society were finding many of their Cassandric predictions of the 1920s coming true. The situation of the thirties lent itself well to socialist and Marxian theory.

Leftist elements, always present and active in the AFT, were becoming even more vocal. They were quick to publicize the problems of American society. The *Social Frontier* journal was quick to point out that at the low ebb of the depression in 1934 the following Americans made the following incomes: [82]

William Randolph Hearst, $500,000, newspapers
Mae West, $339,166, Movies

B. D. Miller, $337,479, Dime stores
C. W. Guttzeit, $323,250, Electricity
Charles M. Schwab,$250,000, Steel
Bing Crosby, $192,948, Crooner
George Hill, $187,126, Tobacco
R. B. Bohn, $140,860, Aluminum
F. B. Davis, $125,219, Rubber
Arthur C. Dorrance, $112,500, Soups

Many of the members of the AFT were equally intrigued with such paradoxical phenomena of the era. This led such members to draw up ideological battle lines between those who favored a social revolution with an accompanying collectivist democracy and those who still hoped for a recovery of capitalism. Such battle lines were reflected in the conventions held by the AFT in the 1930s. During this period the federation elected four presidents: Harry R. Linville, 1931–33; Raymond R. Lowry, 1934–35; Jerome Davis, 1936–38; George S. Counts, 1939–41. Of these four men, all but Lowry had clearly expressed themselves in favor of social reconstruction and economic collectivism.

Organizing in the 1930s

The strength of any union is the size of its membership. Recognizing this principle the American Federation of Teachers strove to organize new locals throughout the 1930s. This was usually done through a variety of methods such as using the regional vice-presidents, utilizing the state federations, receiving help from organized labor, or by efforts of individual AFT locals.

The executive council of the AFT was formed of the president, secretary-treasurer, and vice-presidents. The vice-presidents represented geographic areas of the country. In 1929 this division was not too well defined, but by 1940 the vice-presidents had specific areas laid out for them and had their efforts supplemented by special organizers in those areas that were especially large or fertile.[83]

The organizational efforts of the vice-presidents and the special organizers were usually made possible by general inquiries, leads, or by campaigns. General inquiries were often made to the national office from a teacher or teacher group who had heard or read about the federation and desired more information. These inquiries were referred to the regional vice-presidents who followed up either with a letter or personal visit and often a stack of the official literature.

Such a system often allowed the union to step into a ready-made situation when a clear grievance was already in existence. Specific leads came from AFT members who knew of such dilemmas in nearby towns or from district councils of organized labor who made the national office or regional vice-presidents aware of particular instances. Said one organizer: "In starting in a new community, I found it very essential to have 'leads'—as many as I could possibly collect. I have secured the best of these from members of existing locals in nearby towns." [84] Special campaigns were used with varying success. These were conducted by the regional vice-president or special organizer who made arrangements to speak to existing teacher groups on a swing through a particular territory.

State Federation of Teachers affiliated with the AFT were very useful in organization operations. Unfortunately these did not emerge as a significant factor until a later era. There were state federations in Wisconsin, Minnesota, Pennsylvania, and Ohio formed in the period 1935–36. Where they existed these state federations could pay for and coordinate organizational work on the state level.

The help rendered the AFT by other unions in forming new locals cannot be overestimated. Even with positive leads, the organizers needed the cooperation of local labor councils or strong individual unions. The councils or unions would often arrange the meeting places and times and even encourage teachers to attend. AFT organizers carried credentials from both the AFT and the AFL and often letters of introduction from specific unions.[85] One regional vice-president reported: "In one county we went directly to the President and Secretary of the Saw Mill and Timber Workers' Union. We found that they had organized every other craft in the towns of that county and were delighted that there should be one more to conquer." [86]

Strong individual locals were also useful in aiding organizational efforts by becoming the locus of activity and discussions. Their very existence generated talk into nearby areas that often paid dividends in organizing new locals. Local officers often visited nearby regions for such discussions and were often besieged by letters requesting information on specific local programs dealing with salary, welfare, and tenure.[87]

Of all the particular methods used to organize new vocals during the 1930s the one that seems to have had the greatest overall success was using an existing strong local as the center of activity. This was useful not only in organizing but in maintaining locals since isolated locals with no moral support from surrounding union teachers had to depend too heavily on the efforts of the always-too-small national office.

During the decade of the thirties the AFT was far more successful in organizing college locals than it had been in the previous decade. No doubt aided by a general federation that was now stronger and better equipped, the organizational efforts were also helped by the negative effects of the depression. From 1930 to 1936, twenty-five teachers were dismissed and fifty-nine compelled to resign at the University of Pittsburgh by an administration who refused any criticism.[88] In 1935 Connecticut College prohibited any discussion on the question of compulsory military training.[89] In the annual meeting of the AAUP in 1936 the statistics of the association revealed that some college teachers had received pay cuts as high as 50 percent. The average decline in salary was 15 percent. Data compiled by the U.S. Bureau of Education for seventy-six private colleges, comparing salary declines in 1934–35 with 1929–30, appear below.[90]

	1929–30	1934–35	Percent Declined
For presidents	$5469	$2708	32.2
For deans	3375	2500	25.9
For professors	3030	2336	22.9
For associates	2646	2156	18.5
For assistants	2235	1864	16.6
For instructors	1775	1559	12.2

Leaving the realm of statistics, President Jerome Davis of the American Federation of Teachers observed that during the 1930s:

A larger number of laws have been enacted interfering with teaching than in all the other decades of American history combined. . . .

Special loyalty oaths are required of the teachers in twenty-two states.

More student papers and liberal clubs in colleges have been censored than in any other period.

More college professors have been dismissed than in any similar period in our history.[91]

During the period 1930 to 1940 the AFT organized thirty-three college locals with memberships running from the 7 members who formed a unit at the University of Chicago to the 610 members of the college teachers local of New York City. Not including the unusually large New York local, these units had an average starting membership of about 20 persons. But more important than average size or range was the fact that of the thirty-three organized in the decade, twenty-eight carried on into the next.

The purposes and objectives of these college locals varied from campus to campus but the aims of the New York local, as expressed in their own publication, indicate the scope of their interests.

"I. To protect and advance the economic interests of college teachers and other educational employees

    A. The college section aims to secure at the public and private colleges:

        1. Uniform rules of appointment, salary and promotion, and uniform enforcement.

        2. Guarantee of minimum salaries and stated increments.

        3. The establishment and preservation of a system of permanent tenure to provide security for component educational employees.

        4. The establishment of an appeals machinery for

all cases of dismissal. Appellants shall have the right to open trial, counsel, cross-examination of witnesses and all other legal safeguards.

II. To improve the character and extend the scope of college education

   A. The college section seeks to accomplish this in the following ways:

      1. By promoting the maintenance of high standards of teaching and research among members of the profession.

      2. By influencing educational policy. Education for democracy means education for peace, for the social welfare, and in the realities of the modern times. We shall oppose domination of the colleges by private, political, religious, or economic interests.

      3. By supporting Academic Freedom actively and vigorously. We believe in the right of staff members and students freely to criticize any social policy.

      4. By stimulating educational employees to exercise the full rights of democratic citizenship. We shall oppose any restrictive regulation on the outside activities of the teacher. Participation in the affairs of the community will benefit the community and inspire teaching by bringing it closer to life.

      5. By opposing restriction of scientific research and its utilization for anti-social purposes.

      6. By fostering cooperation between teaching staff and the student body.

      7. By opposing educational retrenchment. We favor increase of the present facilities and staff so as to provide individual attention for all students and in opening of collegiate opportunity to a much larger sector of the population than now enjoys it.[92]

The AFT followed up its new-found ability for organizing college locals and formed a special Committee on College Teachers. In 1935 this committee of ten was chaired by Harold M. Groves and included both Paul H. Douglas and John Dewey.[93] By 1938 the AFT was naming one of its vice-presidents as vice-president of the college section. George Axtelle served in this capacity from 1938 through 1940. In the era of the thirties the college local had become a major area of concern for the AFT.

CHAPTER 4

Social and Philosophical Concerns 1929–1941

The Growing Question of Minority Rights

The federation's concern for the Negro teacher was one of several involvements undertaken in the name of social justice. The number of black teachers was small in 1916 and largely confined to segregated school districts south of the Mason-Dixon line.[1] But those who did teach in the northern urban areas found an early ally in the union. Part of the concern for the Negro was undoubtedly based on existing reality. The initial stirrings of the teachers' union movement had been in large urban areas like Chicago and New York where the Negro had already established himself and sent his children to the city schools. The earliest union movements among Negro teachers were in the nation's capitol. Here the black population was on the rise and the number of Negro teachers and school-children paralleled this growth. Interest in unionism was strong among both the black and white teachers in Washington, D.C., this phenomena a reflection of the unenvious position of teaching in a system where Congress always operated too slowly, where the population had no recourse to the ballot box, and where the teachers couldn't bypass a reluctant, appointed school board and take issues directly to the public. The high-school teachers of Washington were charter members of the AFT and formed Local No. 8 in 1916. These teachers represented the Caucasian teachers in a school district that was racially segregated. They were shortly followed, however, by the Negro teachers of the Armstrong-Dunbar High School who organized and became Local No. 9 of the AFT on September 14,1916. The elementary teachers soon followed suit and the white teachers formed Local No. 16 early in 1918 and the Negro teachers formed the Elementary Colored Teachers Union in the late spring of 1918. But union activity among the Negro teachers was more than confined to public-school teachers in northern urban areas. In addition to those mentioned, the locals with all-Negro membership, chartered 1916–40, are shown below.

Local Number	Name	Location	Chartered
18	Dunbar Teachers	Garvin Co., Okla.	3/11/18
25	Norfolk Teachers	Norfolk, Va.	5/20/18
33	Howard University	Washington, D.C.	11/18/18
295	Pulaski Co.	Little Rock, Ark.	4/20/34
312	Conway Co. Teachers	Conway Co., Ark.	5/08/34
521	Tuskegee College	Tuskegee, Ala.	7/15/37
536	Jefferson Parish	Jefferson Co., La.	12/10/37
611	Fiske University	Nashville, Tenn.	12/29/38

It should be pointed out that these locals represented total Negro memberships but in no way reflected the total black membership of the AFT. The policy of the federation was to organize locals according to the system of school organization found in the local community. Therefore, the locals that were totally black were found in areas where separate black and white school districts existed. To do otherwise would not have made sense because issues of salary and teacher welfare had to be negotiated with separately ordained boards of education. Where school districts were not so organized, which was essentially north of the Mason-Dixon line, the Negro teachers were invited to join a racially unified teachers federation. The AFT asked for no racial indication on membership applications and for this reason there are no statistics on Negro membership in the American Federation of Teachers, only convincing evidence that the union was greatly concerned for the black teacher.

This concern was shown in several different ways. In November of 1918 the *American Teacher* carried a supportive editorial for the Negro.

Education of the Negro is no longer a Southern problem but an American problem, and as such, should receive the support of all Americans.

The backwardness of the Negro means the backwardness of the nation and that is something that concerns all of us. Teachers, it is your duty to see to it that your colored brothers and sisters get a square deal! That every colored school be as well equipped as every white school! That every colored child shall have the same school year that every white child enjoys. If our colored brothers and sisters can give their all for America and for humanity, the least that America can do for them is to stand by its principles of democracy and give the Negro what he deserves—"a square deal, and not charity." [2]

In April of 1919, Julian S. Hughson, a Negro member of Local No. 25 in Norfolk, Virginia, wrote an article in the *American Teacher* calling for Negroes on school boards, compulsory attendance laws for Negro children, lower grade curricula in black schools, and more pay for the teachers. After these points he concluded: "It redounds as much to the benefit of the Caucasian as to the African that the reforms or modifications in the educational system of the South herein discussed shall be immediately made into law and enforced." [3] In addition to trying to make their members aware of the racial inequities the union attempted to translate its feelings into action. During its convention of 1919 a discussion of the problems of the Negro and his education led the delegates to organize a petition campaign to notify members of Congress of their strong support for a greater appropriation for the operation of Howard University. Howard had been dependent upon federal grants since its inception but the usual grant of $100,000 was woefully inadequate in 1919. The petitions called for an appropriation of $1.5 million.[4]

At the AFT's 1928 convention the assembled delegates passed the following resolution:

WHEREAS, The writers of history in the past have failed to recognize the part played by the Negro in the development of our nation and,

WHEREAS, This failure of recognition tends to rob the Negro of that self-respect without which no group can play its part in the Nation's life therefore be it,

Resolved, That the A.F.T. commend the action of local 27 . . . [Washington, D.C. Elementary Teachers] . . . in its attempt to call attention to the achievements of the Negro in the past in order that our histories may develop a more tolerant attitude between the races that constitute the nation.[5]

Among the locals there was also activity in behalf of the Negro. In New York City the union teachers formed a Harlem Committee in 1935 which undertook to provide teachers with materials about Negro history and culture. The journal of the New York local, the *New York Teacher*, published bibliographies of scholarly works on Negro history, art, literature, and the labor movement.[6] In 1936 the local responded to the shifting population in the Bedford-Stuyvesant area by forming a special regional committee.[7]

The American Federation of Teachers wasn't the only organization a Negro could join, he could also join the National Education Association or the American Teachers Association. The NEA accepted Negroes into membership in local associations organized along racial lines and also segregated at the state and national levels. Negro teacher groups that were affiliated with the NEA had their own state and national conventions. Such a method of organization combined with the failure of the NEA to express itself forcibly against the racial inequalities in either national or local school issues made many Negroes suspicious and skeptical of the NEA leadership and participation was therefore limited.[8]

Many Negroes interested in belonging to national teachers' groups belonged to the National Association of Teachers in Colored Schools. This organization had been formed in 1904 by Dr. J. R. Lee, a mathematics instructor at Tuskegee Institute.[9] Formed with the blessing of Tuskegee's president, Booker T. Washington, the association became an amalgam of several state groups for black teachers and struggled with a limited membership until it changed its name to the American Teachers Association in 1937. Even then its effectiveness was small and it could only boast of twenty-five hundred members

in 1938 with a bank balance of $196.71.[10] The more important
state federations that were affiliated with the National Association of Teachers of Colored Schools appear in the chart
below.[11]

State	Name	Founded	Membership
Arkansas	Association of Teachers of Negro Youth	1886	700
Delaware	State Colored Teachers Association	1918	145
Florida	State Teachers Association	1891	857
Kentucky	Negro Education Association	1877	1410
Maryland	State Colored Teachers Association	1914	1117
Mississippi	Association of Teachers in Colored Schools	1906	801
Missouri	State Association of Negro Teachers	1884	772
Oklahoma	Association of Negro Teachers	?	1250
Tennessee	State Association of Teachers in Colored Schools	1923	1000
Texas	Colored Teacher State Association	1884	2109
West Virginia	State Teachers Association	1890	985

As can be seen from the chart, the enthusiasm for a national
affiliation was less than that for state affiliation.

The thrust of the NATCS was largely discussion-oriented
and the association held little influence or political clout nationally. This was due not only to the relatively small membership, small treasury, and racial realities but also to the conceptual purpose of the leadership. Stamped with the
philosophy of Booker T. Washington it accepted segregation as
a *fait accompli* and sought only amelioration of the Negro's
most pressing problems. In characterizing Negro education in

1937, Ralph Bunche, then professor of political science at Howard University, observed that: "The Negro school, its principal or president and its teachers, are content to seek refuge in the tranquil atmosphere of the academic cloister and to look down upon the problems of the group and its neglected masses, in 'scholarly' detachment." [12] In the 1940s the American Teachers Association chose to include itself under the umbrella of the National Education Association. But it was not until 1952 that the NEA allowed them direct representation at their annual conventions.[13]

Certainly the problems of educating Negro children in the period 1929 to 1941 were awesome and in great need of attention. In 1930, 15 percent of rural southern Negro adults had no formal schooling, 48 percent had not gone beyond the fifth grade, and only 5.5 percent had any high-school training.[14] In the school year 1933–34, the class size average for black elementary schools in the South was forty-three pupils while white classrooms average thirty-four.[15] The average salary for the teacher in a black elementary school in 1935–36 was $510 a year while his white counterpart could expect to average $833.[16] Clearly the plight was significant and was to grow to even greater proportions.

The American Federation of Teachers responded to these situations during the period 1929–41 by creating a greater awareness of the inequities, increasing their efforts at organizing black teachers, and demonstrating to their black members that the federation would hold true to its own pronouncements about democracy and equality. In trying to foster a greater awareness, the union continued to use its journal as a forum for discussion and description of the issues. In the March–April number of 1937, Charles H. Thompson called for a "New Deal" for the Negro and provided a good analysis of the situation in the schools.[17] Thompson pointed out that the American Negro population of approximately 13 million in 1936 had some 3½ million children of school age within its composition.[18] He then moved to document the vast differences in educational provisions and experience between the white and black schoolchild. One of the problems was forced separation of schools: "In 19 states and the District of Columbia Negroes are forced by law to attend schools set apart for them; in three states, separate schools are legally permissive; in 12 states, they are prohibited and in 14 states, the law is silent on the question." [19] Another problem was the differences in physical facilities between the schools of black and white children:

The physical plants of the Negro separate schools are almost invariably inferior to those of the white schools in the same communities. It is estimated that there are 25,000 separate Negro elementary school buildings in the country, and some 600 separate high school buildings. More than three-fourths of the elementary schools are one or two-room structures. And despite the building of more than 5,000 school buildings with the aid of the Rosenwald Fund, the typical Negro elementary school building is still a ramshackle, dilapidated affair sadly in need of replacement. Nor are there enough of these to "house" the Negro pupils enrolled in school. A fairly recent survey (1932) showed that 48 per cent more classrooms than are now provided would have to be built if Negro pupils now enrolled in school were to be "housed" to the extent as white pupils in the same communities are. Moreover, the value of school plants for each pupil enrolled in school was $37 for each Negro pupil and $157 (or more than four times as much) for each white child enrolled in school. It would take $242,000,000 just to bring the physical plants of Negro common schools up to the level of the white school plants in the same communities.[20]

Another complaint was the length of the school term: "In 1910, the average length of the Negro school term was 5½ months; that of the white school term in the same community, 6½ months—one month longer. In 1932, the Negro school term was 6¾ months; the white 8¼ months—1½ months longer." [21] The largest complaint among black elementary teachers was in the pay differences: "The Negro elementary school teacher, although she has 70 per cent as much training and teaches 38 per cent more pupils, nevertheless receives only 47 per cent as much salary." [22]

In regards to high school: "A survey in 1932 found 230 counties in which there was at least one high school for whites in each of these counties, yet in not one of them was there a single high school for Negroes. And this, despite the fact that 158,939 Negro pupils of high school age lived in these counties, and despite the fact that in no county was the Negro population less than one-eighth of the total population." [23] In terms of per-pupil expenditure the differences were even more alarming:

In 1930, the per-capita expenditure for each white child in common schools was $44.31; for each Negro child $12.57. Some 252% more money was spent on each white child enrolled in school—with a range of 28.5% more in Oklahoma to 731.9% more in Mississippi. . . . In 1934–35, Louisiana spent more money ($1,816,266) merely to haul 121,341 white pupils to and from common schools than it spent ($1,749,427) for both current expenses and capital outlay on the entire common school education of all the 172,629 Negro pupils enrolled in school.[24]

The situation was no better in higher education: "In 16 states there is not a single state-supported institution where a Negro may pursue graduate or professional work, yet some 15,000 white students receive such training at state-supported institutions." [25] Thompson went on in this article to attempt to account for some of those differences by talking about the legal restrictions, the social discrimination, and the failure of white society to even allow the Negro to have a say in the administration of his educational program. He concluded by pointing out: "Where Negroes have school opportunities that approximate the whites we find their educational status correspondingly approximates that of the whites. Where the school opportunities of Negroes are lower we find Negroes' educational status correspondingly lower." [26] In January of 1940 the entire issue of the *American Teacher* was devoted to the problem of the Negro and education.

Organizing Negro teachers was yet another way the AFT demonstrated its commitment to equality. During the year 1934 the American Federation of Labor undertook a special campaign in the South. This campaign was under the direction of George L. Googe of the AFL, working with Googe was Allie Mann of the AFT.[27] In New York City, Local No. 5 of the AFT had elected Miss Layle Lane a vice-president in 1935. Miss Lane, a Negro, volunteered at the AFT convention to spend her sabbatical leave doing organizing work among the Negroes in the South and West.[28] At that same convention Doxey Wilkerson, a professor at Howard University, became the first Negro to be elected a national vice-president of the American Federation of Teachers. He was one of fourteen Negro delegates at the convention and was instrumental in aiding the organizational efforts of Negroes during his terms in office.[29]

The liberal racial position held by the AFT was not without its practical problems. At the convention held in 1934 the AFT moved its entire operation to another hotel when it became apparent that Negro delegates would not receive equal facilities.[30] At the 1937 AFT convention held in Madison, Wisconsin, an incident occurred when a hotel bartender ceremoniously smashed the glass of a Negro delegate as he was ready to leave. Profuse apologies from the management were hastily given after the AFT contacted the local president of the bartenders and restaurant workers union who threatened to shut the hotel down.[31] In 1938 the AFT again moved to a different hotel at the last minute when it was discovered that black delegates were being asked to use the freight elevators.[32]

Yet another area of concern for the American Federation of Teachers was in the move to equalize salaries between black and white teachers. In 1934 the Garland Fund contributed ten thousand dollars to the National Association for the Advancement of Colored People "to be used exclusively for a campaign of legal action and public education against unequal apportionment of public funds for education and discrimination in public transportation." [33] The program moved slowly until 1938 when Melvin Alston, a Negro teacher in Norfolk, Virginia, filed suit on grounds of unequal salary. After rejection by the lower courts the U.S. Circuit Court reversed and granted the petition of Alston in 1940. The subsequent refusal of the U.S. Supreme Court to review the ruling of the circuit court established the legal grounds in fighting unequal pay.[34]

In its midwinter session the executive council of the AFT passed the following resolution:

WHEREAS, The American Federation of Teachers has consistently supported the principle of equal salaries for equal work and has opposed salary discrimination based on differences in sex, race, or marital status; and,

WHEREAS, The average salary of Negro teachers in states where separate schools are maintained is $462.00 yearly as contrasted to an annual average of $937.00 for white teachers; and

WHEREAS, The success of Negro organizations in securing equalization of salaries in Virginia is in line with the policy of the American Federation of teachers; and therefore, be it

Resolved, That the Executive Council of the American Federation of Teachers heartily approve the action of the Supreme Court of the United States which upheld the decision of the United States Circuit Court of Appeals equalizing salaries of Negro teachers in Norfolk, Virginia; and be it further

Resolved, That the editor of the American Teacher be required to give publicity to the decision ending salary discrimination in Virginia so that teachers' locals and professional organizations may be stimulated to press for similar action in other states.[35]

Despite a small budget the federation made annual contributions to various Negro organizations such as the National Association for the Advancement of Colored People. Throughout the period of time 1929–41 there were many issues that splintered the AFT into various factions. At no time, however, is there any evidence that the American Federation of Teachers was anything but unified in its strong advocacy for the black American.

The AFT's position on minority rights was even more fundamental than the racial issue. The AFT became a leading champion for women's rights in education.

By the 1916 formation of the federation, public education already presented the paradox of being dominated by women but controlled by men.[36] The control was possible due to the creation of a set of tacit agreements usually accepted by boards of education that men teachers would receive higher pay and be given the first consideration for promotions. Such agreement was easy in a society where women did not have the right to vote in national elections and where societal norms condemned women who attempted to assert their ideas. When women teachers did attempt to make their ideas known they usually received a cool reception. Said one student of the National Education Association about the situation near the turn of the century: "The classroom teacher was not an active participant in NEA affairs. Women went unrecognized in the Association; only a few unimportant offices had gone to them, and they were notably absent on programs." [37] But when an insurgent group became active in the NEA women were a part of the insurgency. Margaret Haley was a leader in this movement. She first spoke out at the 1903 NEA convention about the rights of the classroom teacher. Her actions, along with those of others, led Nicholas Murray Butler to protest: "I joined in 1885 and gave vigorous and enthusiastic service for some twenty years. Then that organization degenerated into a large popular assembly which quickly fell into the hands of a very inferior class of teachers and school officials whose main object seemed to be personal advancement." [38] When the NEA sought to form a National Council on Education in 1905 by reincorporating the organization, Haley fought the plan as undemocratic. "The undaunted schoolmarm went home to Chicago and immediately began a crusade to prevent Congress passing the Act of Incorporation." [39]

That the AFT should champion equal rights for women was due to more than the fact that some of the early locals were among grade-school teachers. Principal efforts to organize the federation came from the New York City Teachers League and the Men Teachers of Chicago, both of which were groups of secondary-school teachers who were dominated by men. Usually secondary-school teachers were jealous of the prerogatives that they enjoyed such as more pay then the grade-school teachers and fought to maintain these differences. The commitment on the part of the federation was seemingly more idealistic in nature.

In the period of 1929 to 1941 the AFT was no less enthusiastic toward promoting equality than it had been in its earlier period. The attitudes had changed in the period 1910–32 in the larger society, however. Generally there was a relaxation against the out-and-out prohibition against married women teaching and more and more talk about equality of pay. In 1926 the *American Educational Digest* surveyed 954 school superintendents with the question: "Are married women with equal training and experience as efficient as unmarried?" Sixty-three percent of the respondents thought "married women equally efficient." [40] One study done with 146 professors of education as the sample indicated that 86 percent were opposed to discrimination against female teachers.[41] But the exigencies of the depression tended to halt this trend and renewed efforts on the part of the union to protect women educators were once again called for.

Leadership roles in the American Federation of Teachers were commonly held by women. Florence Rood had been president of the AFT in 1923–24 and she was followed by Mary C. Barker who was president from 1925 to 1930. Florence Hanson was the secretary-treasurer of the federation from 1926 to 1934. The vice-presidential positions in the AFT were often held by women. Examination of the names of delegates at the convention show that while proportions vary, about one-half were women. The legislative representative position, a key AFT official was held by Selma Borchardt during most of the period of the thirties and the state legislative representatives of some of the larger locals like New York and Philadelphia were held by women. The number of women holding the presidencies of large local federations like Philadelphia, Boston, and Atlanta was common during the thirties.

The AFT was also interested in seeing the colleges and universities drop their discriminatory practices. In 1939, Willystine Goodsell published a report entitled: "The Economic Status of University Women" for the American Association of University Women. Her investigation showed that at the large state universities only 4 percent of the full professorships were held by women while they held 23.5 percent of the instructorships. The investigation disclosed that 79 percent of the women interviewed reported discrimination against them because of sex and marital status.[42] Such disclosures caused the AFT to realize that extending the union movement to colleges would aid the struggle of women as well as increase the material benefits and security of the college teacher.

Social Reconstructionism

The twentieth century in American education witnessed reaction to the movement that could be described as "education as a laboratory science," and the subsequent growth of a new swing toward interest in the interaction of man, society, and the school. This new concern for the child as a social organism and the school as an instrument of society brought to education the talents of John Dewey and a group of less publicly known scholars and teachers that formed the backbone of the progressive movement in education. The new emphasis attracted men and women of broad vision and concern for sweeping reform akin to the spirit of the earlier progressive movement in American politics. Like their predecessors they held to an eternal optimism that hinged on such basic assumptions as the perfectibility of man and his institutions, but unlike their spiritual forerunners they envisioned the school as the new intermediary of reform. At first, content with attacking the formalism that encrusted both the schools and the doctrines of education, they moved to expand their interests to a more cosmic concern with greater mind for contemporary issues and problems. This new orientation brought them closer to political progressivism and also signaled the beginning of sharp doctrinal disputations and factionalism. As Lawrence Cremin suggested, this new world view caused the movement to lose not only its innocence but cast it into "a paralyzing partisanship from which it never fully recovered." [43]

In the late twenties and early thirties, Teachers College of Columbia University found itself in the position of being the single most important center of educational progressivism. Its importance was largely due to a core of the faculty that was strongly committed to progressivism and who were aided by having the strong mind and voice of Dewey close at hand. Led by William Heard Kilpatrick, the progressive elements were able to disseminate their ideas due to the large size of the student body at Teachers College as well as the clarity and appeal inherent to their position. It has been estimated that Kilpatrick alone taught thirty-five thousand students during his career.[44]

This particular group of progressive educators gave birth to a program of ideas that was labeled social reconstructionism. The philosophic rationale for social reconstructionism was clearly within the progressive educational tradition but worthy of special delineation within the tradition because of its own special singularity. To Dewey belongs the distinction of making the first significant pronouncement of the concept of the school as an agent of social change. Dewey's 1916 publication of *Democracy and Education* was a manifesto calling for the schools to become the agent for a democratic society. It was this general plea that became the nucleus of social reconstructionism.

The beginnings of social reconstructionism as an identifiable stream began in 1927 with the formation of a discussion group at Teachers College. "Regularly from 1927 to 1934, intermittently from 1934 to 1938, and then regularly again for several years, this group—joined by Dewey and others for varying periods of time—carried on bimonthly discussions under the chairmanship of Kilpatrick." [45] In the group were Harold Rugg, George Counts, John L. Childs, R. Bruce Raup, Goodwin Watson, Edmund de S. Brunner, Jesse Newlon, Harold F. Clark, and F. Ernest Johnson. [46]

Like any set of complex beliefs shared by complex men the basic credo of the social reconstructionists is difficult to simplify. Perhaps the summary provided by John L. Tildsley, a critic of the group, is adequate. Tildsley characterized the group as sharing six commonalities. [47]

1. That the ultimate objective of the Frontier Thinkers (as of socially-minded thinkers generally) is to bring into being a social order which will secure for the common man a much larger measure of well-being and a greater share in determining the economic, social and political institutions and practices which condition his well-being.

2. That to this end, the group in the main favors a society not dominated by the profit motive, a society labelled as a *democratic collectivist society.*

3. That the group is not united as to the method of creating such a society; that one faction headed by George S. Counts maintains that it is the first obligation of the schools of this country to do all in their power to establish this democratic collectivist society; that this desirable goal is to be attained by first winning the teachers to this aim; that the teachers then by immediate and direct propaganda are to convert the boys and girls they teach into active workers for this democratic collectivist society.

4. That the philosophy of education of the Counts faction, as necessarily implied in their program, is that *in the school the child is to be dealt with as a means to an end, not as the end itself.*

5. That the Frontier Thinkers generally hold that the world is

changing so rapidly that very little is to be gained from the study of the experience of the race, and that children should be educated for the changing world of the New Social Order primarily by direct exposure to present economic, social, and political activities.

6. That the Frontier Thinkers are primarily Social Reformers, New World-Makers rather than School Masters, and are therefore seemingly indifferent to the quality of the education actually in operation in our schools today. To them Freedom of the Teacher and a Democratic Collectivist Society loom larger than the fullest growth of the children.

Obviously such characterizations are overly critical and the reconstructionists would have been quick to rebut that the child would never get lost in their system.

The institutional involvement of the group began with the Progressive Education Association. This interest in the PEA was spurred not only because of common sharing of Dewey as intellectual progenitor, but also to the natural desire to become identified with any group that shared the similar conviction about the importance of the school. Although the social reconstructionists never achieved high office or administrative control of the PEA their involvement helped to shape the organization. The reconstructionists may well have stayed comfortably within the camp of the PEA if they had been willing to soft-peddle their ideologies. But the nature of the group was contrary to such a consideration and the reconstructionists became a faction within the PEA. The starting point for this split probably came with the speech of George S. Counts before the PEA's 1932 convention entitled: "Dare the Schools Build a New Social Order?" Calling for the reshaping of most of the country's basic institutions with the school as the major instrument, the assembled educators found themselves confronted with propositions far beyond their usual considerations of how to improve school curricula. The immediate response was the formation of a Committee on Social and Economic Problems, chaired by Counts and membered by several liberals among them being Newlon and Watson.[48]

The report of the committee brought the issue of differing opinions to the forefront. Fearing that the ideas of the committee were too political the report was never given official sanction from the PEA.[49] Subsequent failures of the PEA to either debate or act on matters of national concern led the reconstructionists to the position of only halfhearted participation in the PEA for the remainder of the decade.

The speech of Counts had challenged the PEA but the gauntlet had been ignored. In his speech he had equated the PEA with a society that "like a baby shaking a rattle, we seem to be utterly content with action, provided it is sufficiently vigorous and noisy. In the last analysis a very large part of American educational thought, inquiry, and experimentation is much ado about nothing." [50] With a strong thirst for action he concluded: "That the teachers should deliberately reach for power and then make the most of their conquest is my firm conviction." [51] It was such sentiment that led Counts and reconstructionists of like mind to the American Federation of Teachers. By the mid-thirties the AFT had already proven itself capable of exertive action in championing the rights of children and their teachers; it had already shown tireless interest in national affairs; and it had already lived up to the spirit of its motto: "Democracy in Education; Education for Democracy."

In 1934 reconstructionists began publication of the *Social Frontier,* a journal devoted to education and national issues. Edited by Counts, it became an important vehicle for expressing the ideas of such diverse thinkers as Dewey, Carleton Washburne, Broadus Mitchell, Charles A. Beard, Norman Thomas, Earl Browder, Harold J. Laski, Sidney Hook, Roger Baldwin, Louis Hacker, and Harry Gideonse. Dropping the speculative approach in favor of frank discussions and open proposals the journal developed its own program for educational change. In a 1936 contribution written by Harold Rugg, the call was for a vast program of federal aid and involvement with the schools, a major school building program to alleviate unemployment, a mammoth program of adult education, further protections for academic freedom, and an entire reconstruction of the curriculum.[52] The journal also became a forum of debate over the question of whether teachers should affiliate with organized labor. This understandably became an issue at Teachers College where the debate naturally spilled over.

Although the bulk of the staff at Teachers College was

amenable to the basic tenets of progressive education there were both specific objections to the reconstructionists and to the participation of teachers in the labor movement. Professor I. L. Kandel ridiculed the reconstructionists for oversimplification and further quipped: "if the implication is that the school can anticipate change or can build a new social order, then the new program of social reconstruction through education is mere nonsense." [53] Dean William F. Russell of Teachers College, bemoaning the increasing militancy of both faculty and the students, added that: "Revolution is so much easier than evolution." [54]

On the more specific issue of labor affiliation the gulf was even wider. For here even the reconstructionists were split. Those active in the teachers union movement included Counts and John L. Childs. But Kilpatrick and Newlon, although sympathetic, were skeptical of union affiliation. Both of these issues served to create a whirlwind of controversy at Columbia. These debates became pubic knowledge when James Wechsler wrote an article for the popular magazine *Nation* in 1938 which hinted of the firings of Kilpatrick, Counts, Childs, Watson and Roma Gans from the faculty.[55] The article further related the growing problems of Dean Russell in attracting financial contributions to a college that was already identified with ultraliberal leanings. In the later 1930s a doctoral dissertation by Zalmen Slesinger took a Communmist point of view on education and, when published in 1937 under the title of *Education and the Class Struggle,* condemned the liberalism in progressive education as ineffectual.[56] When Counts directed a doctoral paper by William Gellerman that attacked the educational programs of the American Legion Dean Russell anxiously addressed the New York State Legion convention on "How to Tell a Communist and How to Beat Him" and had copies of the speech distributed to potential benefactors including the entire membership list of the American Bankers Association.[57] The body of the address was fairly liberal but undoubtedly the title had been designed to soothe fears.

In addition to the division over unionism within the ranks of the reconstructionists, there was opposition to unionism from without. These differences caused a direct confrontation between Childs and Dean Russell in the summer of 1936. In noting this meeting the historians of Teachers College observed: "While the Dean made it clear that he was appreciative of the contributions of unions to American life, he did not see a role for them in the conduct of education. The tactics of labor, he noted, did not befit a profession, and the teacher is a member of a profession, not a worker. The whole effort of the union to introduce policy management by faculties into American schools was pictured as abortive and conductive to the worst possible autocracy." [58]

Despite such opposition George Counts, John Childs, and Goodwin Watson were active in the AFT. The participation and interest of Counts continued throughout the decade. The interest of Childs and Watson remained until they felt that events had caused the New York College local from fulfilling its promise of democracy through democratic procedures.

The membership of these prestigious figures in the American Federation of Teachers was significant in the 1930s. Their very presence attracted national attention and added membership to the ranks of the union.

Chapter 5

The Critical Period
1935—1941

The AFT and the WPA

Franklin Roosevelt's New Deal, being a shotgun approach to welfare was bound to scatter some of its pellets in the field of education. Early in 1934 the United States Congress passed the Civil Works Emergency Relief Act which emerged in 1935 into the Works Progress Administration. One of the many programs of this operation was to train the unemployed as adult education teachers. One such program was conducted in Chicago where those that qualified for the program were trained at the University of Chicago. Involved in the training program were several members of the AFT such as Martin Krueger, and Lillian Herstein. It was largely due to their influence that on September 10, 1934, these trainees organized the Adult Education Teachers of Chicago, elected Harold J. Gibbons their first president, and became Local No. 346 of the American Federation of Teachers.

At this point in time the national office had no particular policy in regards to such specialized locals and there were no violations of their current constitution. At their 1936 convention in Philadelphia the AFT officially decided in favor of not only accepting WPA teachers but in devoting some of their energies toward their organization.[1] To instrument this new policy the federation made Harold J. Gibbons, who had led Local No. 346 to prosperity in Chicago, a national vice-president in charge of WPA locals.[2]

From the beginning the WPA locals proved to be problematic for the AFT. Typically the WPA local that affiliated with the federation was too small to be effective, was split with political factions, short-lived due to the nature of their founding and to the natural decline of the Works Progress Administration, and had different interests than the public-school teacher. Harold Gibbons reported that the Chicago WPA local had quickly organized itself into Socialist, Communist, Trotskyite, and Lovestoneite caucuses within Local No. 346.[3] This was undoubtedly a reflection of the typical member who was young, cynical, ultraliberal, and without devotion to the established order. Such factionalism was dangerous to a national federation already overburdened with internal differences. In locals that accepted WPA teachers along with regular classroom teachers the WPA faction often became a separate force. In Seattle, Washington, Local No. 200 had this occur when President Lila Hunter, a classroom teacher, was replaced by Hugh DeLacey of the WPA group. Such situations led to distrust among the leadership of the regular teachers.[4]

But despite such problems, the organization of WPA locals constituted one of the major efforts of the American Federation of Teachers in the 1930s. Beginning in 1934 through 1939 the AFT organized some forty-seven such locals.

AFL-CIO Controversy

Nineteen thirty-seven was the year for the real rise of the CIO. Ostensibly created to fill the need of organizing unskilled and semiskilled workers, it also caught the eye of the liberal community in America. The American Federation of Labor had worked to disassociate itself from politics and controversy so successfully that most liberal thinkers thought them stodgy and irrelevant. The AFL's record on public education was meritorious. But its position on organizing the less skilled, its relation to the Negro worker, and its stand with the economic establishment made it suspect in many people's minds. With a large body of liberal membership it is not surprising that the AFT showed great interest in the development of the CIO.

John L. Lewis, president of the United Mine Workers and the first President of the CIO, wrote an article for the March

–April issue of the *American Teacher* in 1937. In it he reviewed the historic relationship of labor and education, equated the economic struggles of the teacher and the worker, and closed by assuring that "it should be also emphasized that the labor movement needs the help of the teachers. Because of their professional background they have something to contribute to the labor movement which the movement has often lacked— namely, scholarly attainments, a training in clear thinking and an appreciation of the cultural values of life." [5] Such flattery was bound to be attractive after considering that much of the communication received from William Green and the AFL was threatening.

In May of 1937, the AFL-CIO clash had its first real impact on the A.F.T. In that month John Fitzpatrick, President of the Chicago Federation of Labor and the most influential labor leader in the Midwest, expelled the AFT's WPA Local No. 346 from its council. The action was taken when Fitzpatrick found out that Harold J. Gibbons, president of No. 346 and an AFT vice-president, had become interested in the CIO and was organizing for the Textile Workers.[6] Since the question of the CIO and its relationship to the AFL had not been completely settled many took the action as high-handed.

The question of AFL or CIO affiliation captured the interest of many AFT members. From September of 1937 to June of 1938 the question was the central theme in the *American Teacher*. At the 1937 convention of the AFT a resolution was offered calling for affiliation with the CIO but instead of leaving the resolution to delegate vote it was decided to pose the resolution in a referendum. The entire resolution serves to both indicate the scope of interest as well as the attitude shown the AFL.

RESOLUTION FOR REFERENDUM

WHEREAS, The American Federation of Teachers stands for unity in the American labor movement; and

WHEREAS, A united labor movement is necessary for the continued success, both economically and politically, of the trade union movement in the United States; and

WHEREAS, At the 1936 convention the American Federation of

Teachers went on record as being sympathetic to the aims and purposes of the Committee for Industrial Unionism; and

WHEREAS, The CIO has achieved great success in its organization campaigns in the steel, auto, rubber, and other mass production industries; and

WHEREAS, The Committee for Industrial Organization has influenced and aided both the unionization of teachers and the securing of progressive teacher legislation; and

WHEREAS, This convention of the American Federation of Teachers now has before it the question of the next step in its relation to the Committee for Industrial Organization, therefore,

Be it Resolved, That the American Federation of Teachers reaffirm its endorsement of the principles of industrial unionism, and

Be it Further Resolved, That the American Federation of Teachers at this twenty-first convention direct the Executive Council to undertake a referendum of the membership on the question of affiliation of the American Federation of Teachers to the Committee for Industrial Organization; such referendum to be conducted in accordance with existing constitutional provisions at a time and under conditions to be set by the Executive Council; such referendum to be conducted no sooner than February first, 1938; and

Be it Finally Resolved, That for the purpose of uniting the American labor movement this Twenty-first convention go on record as favoring the holding of a national convention of all bonafide trade unions, A.F. of L., C.I.O., and accordingly instruct our delegates to the 1937 convention to the American Federation of Labor to introduce a resolution into that convention.[7]

This resolution not only indicates the growing interest in the CIO and declining favor toward the AFL but also a third position—that of trying to make the AFT a conciliatory agency. This last tact was pursued especially by President Jerome Davis. But the AFL was in no mood for conciliation. Within the AFT the arguments both pro and con CIO affiliation were being vigorously asserted, and the pages of the *American Teacher* were filled with letters expressing the beliefs of the membership. Most of the letters expressing favor for CIO affiliation came from New York City or from the WPA locals. The arguments given in favor of CIO affiliation tended to be based on two major premises: 1. the CIO had the more progressive program and 2. the activities of the AFL were detrimental to American labor.

In arguing that the CIO was more progressive, the letters pointed out that industrial unionism was the pattern of the future while craft unionism was outmoded. The CIO's attempt at staying within the AFL camp was lauded, and the structure of the CIO was characterized as exemplary democratic. The tremendous organizational success of the CIO in its short existence led some of the writers to infer that with CIO affiliation the AFT could likewise expect an organizing boom. Two writers from the Chicago WPA local pointed out that the CIO had taken a position in favor of organizing unemployed professionals while the AFL had not.[8]

The bulk of affirmative opinion in regards to CIO affiliation seemed to come from a negative view of the philosophy and practices of the AFL. Celia Lewis of Local No. 5 in New York City said that the actions of the executive council of the AFL in removing certain unions were blatantly undemocratic and that after early CIO successes the AFL moved to recognize rival unions even if they were company organized. She further accused William Green of telling General Motors not to deal with the CIO.[9] Selden Menefee of Seattle pointed out that in his area the CIO had been bitterly opposed by Dave Beck of the Teamsters and a thug element within that union that controlled the Seattle Labor Council had actively worked against the CIO.[10] Another part of the argument which never appeared in print in the *American Teacher* was the position of the two rivals in organizing the Negro worker. The AFL activities on behalf of the Negro were less than laudatory. Doxey Wilkerson, the Negro vice-president of the AFT, became a strong supporter and advocate for the CIO for this reason.[11]

Those who argued against the proposal for CIO affiliation used arguments generally based on (1) history and (2) practicality. The historical relationship that the AFL and AFT had had in the past was positive. These arguments had a great deal of validity in Chicago where the AFL's local trade council had worked closely with the teachers ever since the organizational efforts of Margaret Haley in 1902. Daryl Belat of Portland, Oregon wrote to remind the readers of the *American Teacher* the role the Portland council had played in getting the tenure law and in having restrictions against married women teachers removed.[12]

The practical argument against dropping AFL affiliation was offered by several writers but most lucidly by Lillian Herstein of Chicago. She pointed out that the most important aspect of belonging to the AFL was the existence of a large network of both state and local trade councils. These, she argued, were most valuable to public-school teachers since education was organized along state and local lines. If, she contended, the AFT were to go with the CIO about 50 percent of the existing AFT locals would be without such city trade councils.[13]

The executive council of the American Federation of Teachers, as directed by the convention resolution, established machinery for an investigation of advantages in belonging to the AFL or the CIO. Chairing the committee was Doxey Wilkerson, also on the committee were Vice-Presidents Michael J. Eck and Stanton E. Smith. The last two members balanced the favorable CIO attitude of the chairman.

The committee worked diligently on the project and utilized questionnaires, interviewed CIO officials, and gathered pertinent statistics on both the CIO and the AFL. In January–February the issue of the *American Teacher* printed the assembled information. It showed exactly what the various disputants had been saying:

(1) The CIO was growing fast. "Out of 374 elections held by the National Labor Relations Board to determine the collective bargaining agent preferred by workers in various industrial plants, some 291, or 78% were won by C.I.O. unions."[14]

(2) The AFL was better prepared to give state and local support. As of December 15, 1937, the CIO had 124 Industrial Union Councils and 6 State Industrial Union Councils.[15] The AFL as of January 1, 1938, had 49 state councils and 738 city central labor unions.[16]

The referendum concerning the CIO affiliation never came to a vote. Perhaps the executive council realized the wounds that would have resulted. It seemed clear that the AFT locals in Chicago, Atlanta, St. Paul, and Detroit wanted no part of the CIO. The stream of events was moving on for the AFT and new issues would capture their attention. Doxey Wilkerson, perhaps the leading advocate of the CIO, remained on the executive council of the AFT for a couple of more terms and then quit the union in June of 1943 to become an active officer of the American Communist party.[17] Politics now became the center of controversy. But the AFT-CIO issue had further helped to determine the sides in the upcoming struggle.

Teaching and Communism

The American educator's interest in communism and the Communist's interest in American education is a difficult episode to relate. Perhaps the greatest difficulty lies in interpreting a historical movement from a later perspective when events and people have caused changes in both basic definitions and political attitudes. In 1930 a Communist was a person who advocated any one of several different ideological positions. The person could be a theoretical Marxist, a Trotskyite, a Lovestoneite, or a Stalinist. Each position shared a general belief in state ownership of the means of production but, beyond that, varied considerably in their relation with Moscow and in the matter of revolutionary ways and means. Because of their agreement about public ownership those of the Socialist persuasion were often categorized, usually despite loud protest, as Communists. By the 1920s, the Communists in the United States were attempting to organize themselves into formal groups most of which earnestly attempted to copy the European model of organizing the working class toward social and economic reforms. In 1920, William Z. Foster had formed the Trade Union Educational League which was aimed at informing and moving its members toward a Communist philosophy.[18] When such small efforts as these failed, the Communist International declared in July of 1921 that such efforts at dual unionism were fruitless and that Communists should attempt to "bore-from-within" already established unions.[19] The American Federation of Labor recognized such a strategy and as early as its 1923 convention refused to seat a Communist delegate from Butte, Montana.[20]

In addition to both overt and covert union activities the American Communists formed a formal Communist party structure which concerned itself with political activities. Much of the early membership in this latter group was formed from members of various foreign language federations that were initially formed through ethnic and social concerns.[21] There was thus a division of efforts in American communism as well as innumerable factions within each group. But the labor and political groups did cooperate during times of national election such as in 1924 when the Communists appeared on the national ballot for the first time with Foster as the candidate for president and Benjamin Gitlow of the political organization as vice-presidential candidate. The 33,361 votes that they received was far short of the 500,000 to 1 million that Foster had bragged to Moscow that he thought he would receive.[22] This vote was indicative of the relative ineffectiveness of American communism during the early years.

The involvement of the Communists with teachers began as a small and not too highly planned affair. The Communists were in the advantageous position of having a large segment of the college academic community greatly interested in the Russian experiment and highly anxious to know more of its theoretical and practical basis. In 1926, the party arranged for an American delegation to visit Moscow and in addition to inviting three American Communist party functionaries and three labor union leaders, Professors Arthur Fisher, Rexford Guy Tugwell, and George S. Counts were invited.[23]

Other professors went further than just a simple interest and participated in the party's political activities. Bertram Wolfe, Jay Lovestone, and William Weinstone were three such intellectuals interested in the party and earned from William Z. Foster the sneering nickname of the "City College Boys." [24] But at these early stages the involvement of academics with communism was a personal commitment and no formal strategy existed for either the infiltration of teachers' groups or the control of American youth by Communist teachers.

Of all the events in American history, the one that aided the Communists the most was the depression. The tragic realities of the depression seemed to dictate the need for radical reappraisals and commitments. To those who had been in the middle of the road, collectivism now seemed more acceptable. To those who had been collectivists before the slump an even more radical stance seemed necessary. "Becoming a Socialist right now," John Dos Passos wrote in the summer of 1932, "would have just about the same effect on anybody as drinking a bottle of near-beer." [25]

As interest in theoretical Marxism and Soviet policies gained a larger following, its respectability among the American left grew. Since a significant proportion of the left was involved in literary pursuits or teaching, the possibilities of influencing public opinion through the school system and its books became an interesting source of speculation. In the October 1935 issue of the *Social Frontier* magazine the editors pointed out that teachers were essentially workers. "In consequence, it was held right and proper for teachers to align themselves with labor and to utilize the school in an attempt to bring about a decision which is favorable to the working population.[26] The article went on to advocate that: "Most Americans still believe that they live in a classless society. The school could contribute to the dissipation of that illusion. When that is achieved, America will have made considerable headway toward the goal of democratic collectivism." [27] The position of the editors was more idealistic and theoretical but other contributors were less so. In an article by Theodore Brameld entitled "Karl Marx and the American Teacher," the author affirmed Marx's tough-minded principles that "the opposition of the class in control of capitalist society is so tremendous that nothing short of counter-opposition frequently bordering upon, indeed crystallizing into illegality will suffice to defeat it. When the ruling class is once replaced a period of oppression will continue to be necessary until gradually the citizenry honestly comes to agree that collectivism is a better solution of our troubles than capitalism." [28] Brameld continued in a more specific nature by asking teachers to recognize that they "must then influence their students, subtly if necessary, frankly if possible," [29] toward a position of involvement with society. This could be done by enumerating the problems facing the country and leading the students toward a realization "of the forces aligned against the attempt to bring into being a collectivist society." [30]

Yet despite such overtones of indoctrination a specific plan for the Communist infiltration of teacher groups and the schools was largely undeveloped and vague. William Z. Foster spoke only in the broadest terms about American schools and communism in his published books. But strategies that were formulated often saw the AFT as a natural way of gaining influence among teachers. This was due not only to the liberal nature of the AFT but also to the organizational structure and to the relationship that the AFT had to the more familiar pattern of union organization. In his Marxian interpretation of American society in 1936, Howard D. Langford suggested that: "Where a teachers' union already exists it should be built up and brought under rank and file control. All such unions should become locals of the A.F.T., to which the educational workers should give special attention as a strategic nationwide instrument for furthering their purposes." [31] In a publication called the *Communist,* Richard Frank wrote:

> The task of the Communist Party must be, first and foremost, to arouse the teachers to class consciousness and to organize them into the American Federation of Teachers, which is the main current of the American labor movement.
>
> In the effort to organize the teachers, every care must be taken to bring together in united front actions all existing teacher organizations. Especial attention must be paid to secure such action with the A.A.U.P., N.E.A., and the Guild. Our party members in these organizations must work actively toward this end.[32]

Those educators that did have interest in communism in the early 1930s were often attracted not only due to the Bolshevik program but also as a more reasonable alternative than Fascism. This implies that many saw only these two possibilities, and the literature of the 1930s seems to confirm that many did see the world in such narrow dichotomous terms. The Fascists had already established their regimes in Italy and Germany and their educational programs were a source of great trepidation among American schoolmen. The *Social Frontier* and other magazines of liberal persuasion fed such fears in nearly every issue. In quoting from a letter from a German schoolboy the *Social Frontier* included this paragraph: "Germany is the most powerful state of the world with the best army, the best leader, the best government, the best idea. No country will be able to defeat us. The will of Adolf Hitler is stronger than the will of the sum of all other statesmen. He is sent by God to free our country, and the world from the despotism of the Jews and the capitalists." [33]

Of all the liberal intellectuals in the United States, John Dewey was one of the few that saw communism and its educational consequences as dangerous as fascism. Dewey's objections to communism were both philosophic and practical. On the philosophic plane he objected to dialectic materialism as an adequate theory of history, to the adequacy of class conflict as an initiator of social progress, and to the necessity of an armed revolution. Practically, the concept of insurrection and violence as a means to peace ran completely contrary to his fundamental belief in the relationship of means and ends. He particularly found the Communist strategies of gaining influence in American Society abhorent. Said Dewey:

It is not irrelevant to add that one of the reasons I am not a Communist is that the emotional tone and methods of discussion and dispute which seem to accompany Communism at present are extremely repugnant to me. Fairplay, elementary honesty in the representation of facts and especially of the opinions of others, are something more than "bourgeois virtues." They are traits that have been won only after long struggle. They are not deepseated in human nature even now— witness the methods that brought Hitlerism to power. The systematic, persistent and seemingly intentional disregard of these things by Communist spokesmen in speech and press, the hysteria of their denunciations, their attempts at character assassination of their opponents, their misrepresentation of the views of the "liberals" to whom they also appeal for aid in their defense campaigns, their policy of "rule or ruin" in their so-called united front activities, their apparent conviction that what they take to be the end justifies the use of *any* means if only these means promise to be successful—all these in my judgment are fatal to the very end which official Communists profess to have at heart.[34]

The specific involvement of Communists with the American Federation of Teachers, like the pattern established in the larger society, began in a very small and innocuous manner. The union was essentially an urban phenomenon and as such had among its membership a significant number of persons of recent foreign extraction who saw collectivist schemes as less objectionable than the nativists. In 1937, 61 percent of the total population in New York State was foreign born.[35] The vast majority of these lived in New York City. The New York State Teachers Association, the NEA affiliate, was an upstate organization with only 400 of its 46,000 members in New York City.[36] This left the local teachers union to represent the city teachers whose political and economic philosophies ranged from fundamental conservatism to radical communism but leaned more heavily toward the left than the right. As such an organization, the union presented itself as a ready target for any highly organized minority to take advantage of such diversity and to gain control through legal means.

In 1923 several members of Local No. 5 formed a Research Study Group. The group all shared a warm sympathy for communism. This group was headed by Benjamin Mandel, who was also the membership chairman of the local.[37] The group pushed for affiliation with the Educational Workers International, an organization created by the Comintern in 1923. This move was resisted by the larger membership of the local and the infighting that resulted led to the recall of Mandel as the local's convention delegate. Shortly thereafter he left the union and teaching to become a full time Communist party worker.[38] After this, the interest in communism among many of the local's members continued, but particular incidents or confrontations were avoided. In fact, Mandel returned to the union as a staunch ally of the President Linville in 1932 after Mandel had broken with the Communist splinter group known as the Lovestoneites.[39] In 1928, William Z. Foster formed a Trade Union Unity League which had within its membership several teachers who were also members of New York Local No. 5.[40] But relative harmony prevailed until the early 1930s. The historian, Robert Iverson, commented: "Although Stalin had ordered the American Communists to Bolshevize their party and prepare to convert the economic crisis into a revolutionary crisis, the coming of the Depression found the communists virtually powerless within one of America's largest institutions—the schools." [41]

Communist activity began afresh in the New York City local after 1930. Much of the sentiment was direct response to the precarious position the teachers found themselves in and to the need to express themselves against the growing retrenchment programs. Thousands of underpaid substitutes were brought into the school system.[42] By 1933, salary cuts among the system's regular staff were at the ten percent level.[43]

Despite the protests of Linville and the more traditional local leadership the substitutes were invited to join Local No. 5. This caused the regular leadership to lose control and in 1932 Linville's leadership was challenged when a large dissident group within the local, calling themselves the Rank and File Caucus, ran Donald Henderson for President. Linville won the election easily, 558 votes to 63, but the Caucus did place Isidore Begun, one of its members, on the board of directors.[44] More important than the small victory, however, was the effective inroad made into the leadership of the local. Hoping to stave off this erosion of the traditional leadership's power, Abraham Lefkowitz, the local's legislative representative, moved in executive board session to expel from the union all members of the Rank and File Caucus. After passing the executive council, the issue was taken directly before a trial committee. Here the trial committee was asked to determine the justification of expelling Isidore Begun, Alice Citron, Clara Rieber, Abrah Zitron, Joseph Leboit, and Bertram Wolfe on grounds of: 1. attempting to discredit union officers; 2. engaging in calculated and continuous misrepresentation of the executive board and its acts; 3. exercising minority control at meetings; 4. pursuing disruptive tactics aimed at objectives alien to purposes of the union and the will of its membership.[45]

The trial committee that was selected was chaired by John Dewey and consisted of Esther Gross, Max Kline, Raphael Philipson, and Charles J. Hendley. Each case was heard separately with the accused being allowed counsel. After twenty-four meetings with the hearing of sixty-three witnesses for the plaintiffs and forty-six for the defendants, the last session came to a close February 22, 1933, with the committee recommending six months suspension of the accused. But in order to satisfy the constituted procedures this recommendation required a two-thirds approval by the general membership. Taken before the local, the recommendation fell short of the two-thirds requirement by fifty-nine votes.[46] Said an irritated Dewey: "One may conclude that the Left Wing caucuses have some end in view which they did not hold as expedient to avow publicly, and moreover that they regarded that end as so important as to justify any means of misrepresentation and abuse that could be employed to further that end." [47] Said a perplexed Lefkowitz: "Between the bankers and the Communists, we're having a hell of a time." [48]

As the situation became more tense within the local, the parent AFL became more jittery. William Green, the president, was no radical in either economics or politics. But more important than Green's philosophy was the thought and action of Matthew Woll. A longtime unionist, Woll was the AFL vice-president and chairman of its Education Committee. In this capacity he was more than just passively interested in the activities and tribulations of the American Federation of Teachers. To complicate matters Woll was a leading member and president of the National Civic Federation, a group held in suspect by liberals as being only slightly to the left of fascism. In 1935, Woll sent a letter to Representative McCormack, who was then chairman of a congressional committee investigating un-American activities, encouraging him to give serious consideration to William Randolph Hearst's allegations that many professors were engaged in teaching subversive propaganda.[49] This letter was stoutly condemned even by Henry Linville who wrote to William Green protesting:

For several years teachers' unions have been trying to further the organization of the college teachers who are friendly to organized labor. We are obligated to state frankly at this time that the most serious obstacle we have met in this endeavor is the current belief among educators that Mr. Woll represents a reactionary and fascist spirit; and because of his frequent public utterances of that character, such spirit tends to be charged against all labor leadership, no matter how progressive it may actually be.[50]

All these combined currents meant by 1933 the leadership of Local No. 5 in New York was faced by both a hard-core group of Communists aimed at controlling the union and heavy pressure from the AFL to squelch all unorthodoxy. Either alternative would have meant the demise of the local.

As the situation among the membership of Local No. 5 continued to boil over, the federation found itself in a nearly impossible position. From the national office in Chicago it was impossible to tell if the turmoil in New York City was more the fault of the Communists or of the Linville group who was resorting to charging dissidents with being communists in order to preserve its tottering regime. Of practical consideration was the fact that the New York local was the largest single union in the AFT and the national could not afford to antagonize any faction for fear of breaking the union in half. Realizing this, the national sat tight and waited.

Pressure Groups and Supporting Agencies

The 1930s were times of deep social and economic unrest. Radicalism and reactionism vied with each other to pull the middle-of-the-road American to its own extreme. Just as there were those groups that debated the economic questions of rugged capitalism versus social collectivism there were groups who used the political system as the topic of debate. Of special concern to the AFT were those groups that saw the schools as an important agent in the process of political and economic training.

The National Association of Manufacturers showed great concern for the schools. In 1934 the NAM began a publicity campaign on the advantages of capitalism. They had forty-five thousand billboards which read: "What is Good for Industry is Good for You!" The NAM published a weekly newspaper, *Young America,* for schoolchildren. When hearing that the textbooks might be harboring ideas contrary to the spirit of capitalism they appointed a committee and went over 563 of them.[51]

More active than the NAM was the American Legion. The relationship of the Legion to education in the period of the thirties was very important. By 1931 the Legion had an organization of over one million members and a treasury of about one-half million dollars.[52] More important than just size and wealth was the commitment made by the Legion to the schools. The Legion's particular concern was the promotion of Americanism. At the first national convention ever held by the American Legion they recommended that all schools devote at least ten minutes daily to patriotic exercises.[53] In 1921 they began their long cosponsorship of American Education Week with the National Education Association. In 1926 they sponsored their own American history textbook entitled: *The Story of Our American People,* edited by Charles F. Hornes.[54] In 1925 they had endowed a chair of Americanism at the University of Florida.[55]

During the 1930s, the legion maintained a very strange relationship with educators. Educators, eager for allies in the battle against retrenchment, found the legion an ally. But the price of this relationship was high. Often anti-intellectual in its pronouncements, usually opposed to basic tenets of academic freedom, and determined to use the schools for their Americanism programs, the legion became a source of unending worry for educators.

By the mid-thirties the legion was very strong, with 16 of its members in the U.S. Senate and 130 in the House.[56] By 1936 the legion had 11,129 posts.[57] Using this strength it carried on campaigns against pacifism and radicalism. In trying to promote orthodoxy the legion fought for loyalty oaths for teachers. This, more than any other issue, brought them into conflict with the American Federation of Teachers.

In writing an editorial for the Hearst newspaper chain in November of 1935, Commander Joseph V. McCabe warned teachers to concentrate on subject matter and suggested that teaching ideas of social change was an invitation to chaos.[58] The drive for state loyalty oaths was one way the legion believed that such subversives that might have advocated social change could be kept out of the schools. At the legion's sixteenth annual convention held in 1934, the delegates passed a resolution that put the machinery of the state and local posts into motion for loyalty oaths.[59] Joined by other patriotic societies the loyalty oath movement picked up steam. From the period of 1929 to 1935 thirteen states added a loyalty oath provision for teachers to their school codes. This brought the total number of states having such oaths to twenty-two.[60] After swearing allegiance to such an oath a teacher could be readily dismissed for any infraction that might be interpreted as contrary to the established form of government and economic system.

But the legion was not alone in its crusade for political orthodoxy. At various junctures it was eagerly joined by a host of both large and small patriotic societies. One of the largest was the American Coalition of Patriotic Societies, which was another prime force in the teacher oath movement. The coalition was formed of eighty-five groups such as the Betsy Ross Corps, the Anglo-Saxon Federation, the Immigration Restriction Association of Chicago, and the Junior American Vigilante Intelligence Federation.[61] The activities of similar groups often brought them into the schools. The American Defense Society distributed ninety thousand annotated copies of the U.S. Constitution to schoolchildren, distributed one hundred thousand pictures of Theodore Roosevelt with the caption "Keep Up the Fight for Americanism," and sponsored a speaking tour for former army general J. J. Pershing.[62] Other patriotic groups published journals. One of the ones with the largest following was the *National Republic:* "A Magazine of Fundamental Americanism," which featured covers that generally had General George Washington on them and carried regular features such as "The Enemy Within Our Gates," and "With the Patriotic Societies." The articles of the *National Republic* were opposed to immigration, pacifism, the Tennessee Valley Authority, international alliances, the radicalization of religion and Soviet recognition. They favored military preparedness, high protective tariffs, fundamental Christianity, and the protection of property rights. The articles often concerned education. When the editors found out, for example, that seventy out of ninety-two faculty members at Grinnel College in Iowa were opposed to the type of capitalism personified by former President Hoover, the editor contended: "Perhaps if these professors were thrown directly into the business world where they would meet individual and corporation competition, they might judge things differently." [63] In reporting the AFT convention of 1936, the *National Republic* noted that the American flag was not in the assembly hall; that the most popular exhibits were those of the

American League for Industrial Democracy, the American Birth Control League, the War Resisters League and the *Social Frontier* magazine. The writer further claimed that the unofficial floor leader of the convention was Frank Palmer, director of the communistic Federated Press.[64] Said the *National Republic* of George S. Counts: "The doctor's interest in sovietism is far from being merely academic, a perusal of the products of his pen and tongue conclusively reveals. Dr. Counts has been and is one of the most aggressive disseminators of Communist doctrines, and one of the most active champions of the red deal, to be found in the United States." [65] Said the *National Republic* in its February 1937 issue: "Be Loyal to America or Leave It!"

Other patriotic efforts were run on a small scale with only infrequent publications. One small pamphlet, issued by John E. Wright of Worthington, Ohio, and entitled: "The A.B.C.'s of the Fifth Column" said to its readers: "The American Federation of Teachers is Communist and radical controlled. Eighty percent of its members are duped into belonging for Special Benefits and for the cause of Labor. (Ask Your Teachers If They Belong.)" [66] One individual effort of important consequence was the publication of a book entitled: *The Red Network* by Elizabeth Dilling. The author compiled in a dictionary form hundreds of names of both individuals and organizations she thought to be subversive. The contribution to the world of literature became a handbook for every patriotic society and investigative agency. Said the author about the AFT: "Radical; stands for abolition of R.O.T.C.; recognition of Russia; full academic freedom to teach anything, including Socialism, Communism, or Atheism; closely allied to A.C.L.U.; received financial aid from Garland Fund, which gives only to radical agencies; monthly organ the *American Teacher*." [67] In the second part of her book Elizabeth Dilling had a "Who's Who in Radicalism." Just about every literary figure in America made it, also included were the following members of the AFT: Selma Borchardt, George Coe, George Counts, Jerome Davis, Solon DeLeon, John Dewey, Paul H. Douglas, Albert Einstein, Florence Curtis Hanson, Lillian Herstein, Granville Hicks, William H. Holley, Abraham Lefkowitz, Henry R. Linville, A. J.

Muste, Scott Nearing, Reinhold Niebuhr, David J. Saposs, Charles Stillman, Goodwin Watson, and Bertram Wolfe.[68]

Perhaps the only ally that the American Federation of Teachers could rely upon for support was the American Civil Liberties Union. Organized in 1920, the ACLU devoted itself to free speech, free press, the right of strike, the right of fair trial, racial justice, and an end to censorship.[69] Another interest was freedom in education. In establishing guidelines on education the ACLU offered the following nine:

1. No interference with freedom of teaching in adult or higher education except upon judgment of juries of educators; nor in lower schools except upon judgments of composite juries of administrators, community, and teachers.

2. No limitation on classroom discussion relevant to the subjects taught.

3. Outside of schools, the same freedom for teachers as other citizens, with encouragement of participation in public affairs.

4. No interference with the right of teachers to organize for their own protection and freedom of teachers to affiliate with labor.

5. Strong tenure laws in all states to protect teachers against unfair dismissals.

6. Opposition to all special oaths of loyalty for teachers as unfair discrimination and as harmful to free and open critical inquiry.

7. No unreasonable interference by legislatures with the school curriculum, the control of which should be vested in educational authorities and the teaching profession.

8. No compulsory religious practices in the schools, such as Bible-readings.

9. Protection of the rights of students to organize for discussion of public issues, without faculty control. No disciplinary action against students because of religious, political, or other views or activities.[70]

These views were shared by the American Federation of Teachers, and, in fact, the original National Committee of the American Civil Liberties Union included AFT leaders Henry R. Linville and A. J. Muste.[71] The Academic Freedom Committee of the ACLU included on its membership George S. Counts, John L. Childs, Sidney Hook, John A. Lapp, Alonzo F. Myers, and Reinhold Niebuhr— all members of the AFT.[72]

As the pace of events and political splintering increased in velocity the social reconstructionists group found itself confronted with growing internal differences. These differences were based both on philosophy and organizational questions.

On the philosophical plane the always tenuous consensus broke apart. The central issue concerned the nature of the school and the economic system. While both sides accepted the primary reconstructionist assumption of the importance of the school in the remaking of American society, variance appeared over the question of attitude toward the existing order. The positions were outlined in the November issue of 1938 in the *Social Frontier*. Here Professor Boyd Bode of Ohio State University stated his belief that society could be reformed without a full-scale attack on the free enterprise economic system. The opposite view was expressed by Professor John Childs of Teachers College, Columbia University, who equated the economic system with antidemocratic forces and therefore concluded that to accept the structure of free enterprise was undemocratic and antireformist. The arguments and counterarguments were offered with the serious quality of academic disputation and without any realization that there was not much basic difference in the two points of view. John Dewey pointed this out and tried to hold the differing viewpoints together.[73] But it is just such small chinks in the mortar that cause strong walls to collapse.

What Bode was seemingly reacting to was the growing severity of the attack on capitalism made by both elements within the reconstructionist group and the American Federation of Teachers. The activities of the New York local often amounted to a declaration of war on capitalism and the rhetoric was becoming hotter. But in becoming more vociferous the local managed to alienate several important allies—among them John L. Childs. Childs was more sensitive to language and events than many of his colleagues at Teachers College due both to his natural inclinations and his philosophical disposition. During the growing years of the College Section of the New York local he had angered some of the ultraliberals and Communist party followers by his continual questioning and hesitation. By 1935 the meetings of the college section were characterized by repeated parliamentary maneuvers. The result of such machina-

tions were usually to coerce a reluctant majority into supporting resolutions and procedures purposefully conceived by the
radical minorities of the local. The net result was to endorse
and support programs regardless of the means necessary to
their implementation. At various times the New York locals
marched with a red flag, circulated Soviet literature, and
sought wide endorsements for the Spanish Popular Front.[74]
Tiring of these tactics and no longer willing to be associated
with the local, Childs resigned. The radicals of the local immediately rushed to brand Childs a reactionary, antiunion, and
antiliberal.[75] H. Gordon Hullfish, also associated with the reconstructionists and a professor of education at Ohio State, was
a member of a local with a far less blatant brand of activism.
His withdrawal from the AFT came when be believed that the
socialism and economic position of the union had rendered the
organization useless in leading school reform due to the unac-
ceptability of their philosophy to the larger society.[76] Other
reconstructionists such as R. Bruce Raup and Ernest Johnson
also withdrew and left George S. Counts as one of the few to
remain.[77]

The involvement of the social reconstructionists was important to the AFT. While members of the federation they defined
the central issues facing American education and gave to the
federation a respectability among professional educators not as
likely to have existed without their presence. Their departure
was likewise significant. For in leaving the federation they
helped to convince the reluctant liberals of the AFT that new
thought would have to be given to the widening gulfs of ideol-
ogy within the union. In leaving, they provided the very critical
rhetoric that would be used at a later date against the radical
fringe.

First Efforts at a Purge

The pressure exerted by the American Federation of Labor
on the AFT to clean its house of radicalism mounted in the late
1930s. President William Green was becoming increasingly agi-
tated with the AFT and the publicity it was receiving. Green
was influenced on this matter by Matthew Woll.

Like many immigrant Americans, Woll embraced his new country with fervent zeal. Born in Luxembourg in 1880, he had come to the states at the age of eleven. He no doubt looked back on his own earlier life as a chapter out of the American dream. Educated in the public schools of Chicago until apprenticed at age fifteen, he worked his way up in his craft taking three years of law study along the way before becoming president of the International Photo Engravers Union in 1906.[78] By the 1930s he was a vice-president of the AFL, chairman of the AFL's Education Committee, and president of the National Civic Federation. This latter group had been formed in the early part of the century as a cooperative effort between labor and management. By the mid-1920s "the Federation was now only useful to the A.F.L. as a weapon against the communists." [79] The activities of the AFT and its general regard for civil liberties and liberal causes would have probably been enough to gain the enmity of Woll. But there were other more specific instances that had root in the 1920s. The leading instance was the involvement of the AFT with Brookwood Labor College.

Brookwood was founded by A. J. Muste, himself an immigrant having arrived from the Netherlands in 1891 at the age of six. Raised in a strict Dutch Calvinist tradition he kept the religious fervor and strength of conviction even after receiving his divinity degree from Union Theological Seminary in 1913. The ideas gleaned at Union and his early ministry among the working classes made him a committed advocate of trade unionism.[80] Muste's contribution to the movement was his acceptance of the labor college idea and his work toward the establishment of Brookwood.

The labor college idea was based on the premise that many working-class children were denied higher education due to their lack of funds or to the social restrictions placed upon them in traditional educational settings. The idea of the labor college was to develop classes for adults of such backgrounds where they could receive free instruction in both the regular college fare and in labor theory and practice. Such a plan was advanced in order to allow these people to return to their crafts as more intelligent and practical leaders of their own unions. The idea spread rapidly in the 1920s, and most cities with es-

tablished labor movements opened such colleges. Brookwood
was just such a college. The college was very small with a faculty of only five or six. It was financially supported by contributions from the more liberal of the unions such as the AFT, the
United Textile Workers, the Hosiery Workers, the International Association of Machinists, the Brewery Workers, Coo-
pers, Maintenance-of-Way Employees, Railroad Clerks, Railway
Carmen, Painters, Hat and Cap Makers, the International Ladies' Garment Workers Union, and the Amalgamated Clothing
Workers.[81] Abraham Lefkowitz, an important member of the
AFT's Local No. 5 was a member of Brookwood's board of
directors.

The year 1928 seems to be the year that Brookwood first
ran afoul of the expectancies of the AFL. By 1928 Brookwood
had graduated 111 students, many of whom had moved on to
establish other labor colleges.[82] The faculty at Brookwood was
leftist and their conception of the labor movement in the
United States was generally that of the Marxian class-conflict
theorists. Throughout the 1920s students and faculty alike cele-
brated May Day and probably would have continued to do so,
ignored by the AFL, except that in 1928 several students objected to the celebration directly to President Green, and
Matthew Woll was sent to investigate.[83] Woll's resulting condemnation of the operation was predictable. The AFL asked all
of its unions to withdraw financial support. Although several
unions refused to do so, the declining contributions, the financial realities of the depression, and the withdrawal of Muste
from the college in 1933 led to its death.

The Brookwood episode was important in the AFT-AFL
conflict. For not only did the board of the college have important AFT participation, the teachers—including Muste—had
joined the AFT. Muste had become a vice-president of the
AFT in the early 1930s. When the AFL recommended withdrawal of both students and funds, the editors of the *American
Teacher* complained bitterly, and the convention of the AFT
refused compliance. These actions convinced the AFL that the
AFT was becoming a real thorn in its side.[84]

Combined with these activities were the investigations of the
House Un-American Activities Committee, chaired by Martin

Dies. These investigations included the radical activities of teachers and so involved the AFT. In February of 1939, the AFL executive council met in Miami, Florida. Following the meeting, Woll told the press that the AFT should not permit itself to remain "a breeding ground for Communists," or it should withdraw from the AFL.[85] Later, despite denials from Green, the rumor was circulated that the AFT had been given three months to clean itself up.[86]

The central point of radical political activity continued to be New York City. Henry R. Linville, the president of Local No. 5 since its founding, was becoming unable to control the union. Radical elements, many of whom were avowed Communists, had challenged the Linville-Lefkowitz leadership, and when they found themselves unable to vote them out, resorted to parliamentary maneuvering and obstruction. According to one group of investigators—"These Communists continued to use tactics of obstruction, browbeating and namecalling [sic] to such an extent that by 1933 Local 5 in New York had found it practically impossible to function." [87]

In the spring of 1935, Linville asked the executive council of the AFT to withdraw its charter. "The constitution of Local 5 made expulsion of members practically impossible. The local appealed to the Federation to revoke its charter so that a new local could be formed with a new constitution." [88] The matter came before the general convention in the summer of 1935 at Cleveland, Ohio. Here the recommendation that the charter of Local No. 5 be withdrawn was voted down by the delegates 100 to 79.

Following the decision, Henry R. Linville and the officers of Local No. 5 offered their resignations on September 12. In announcing his own resignation, Dr. Linville "placed blame for the final breach squarely upon the American Federation of Teachers for condoning disruptive practices in our local to defeat our professional objectives." [89] Resigning officers other than Linville and Lefkowitz were Vice-Presidents Albert L. Smallheiser and Truda Weil; Clara Naftolowitz, the secretary; and Max Rosenhaus, treasurer.[90]

The controversy received national attention. The October 9 edition of the *Nation* carried two articles on the situation. The first was by Lefkowitz, which leveled charges against the factions as a cause of the breakup. A following article was a joint effort of the United Committee to Save the Union, which blamed the Linville-Lefkowitz leadership for a "rule or ruin" policy.[91] In the October issue of the *Social Frontier,* both sides were invited to present their sides with Linville writing one opinion and Joseph Gallant for the United Committee to Save the Union, the other.[92] Interestingly enough, the same issue also contained a short statement by George Davis, the secretary-treasurer of the AFT. Davis blasted Linville and Lefkowitz and blamed the breakup of the union on their unwillingness to compromise. Said Davis: "The whole truth of the matter is that Dr. Lefkowitz, failing to dominate Local Five, asked us to wreck it and give him a union which he could control. Failing in that, he asks the American Federation of Labor to wreck the national and give him a satellite national. If that fails you may expect to see a dual organization with Lefkowitz the center of activities. The past officers of the local do not seem to care what is done so long as the action revolves about them." [93]

The issue did go to the AFL, when upon the recommendation of Selma Borchardt the AFL executive committee appointed G. M. Bugiazet, John P. Frey, and Thomas E. Burke to investigate charges of irregular procedures in the seating and voting of delegates to the 1935 AFT convention and to the problem of factionalism in Local No. 5. These investigations were made on April 27 and 28, 1936.[94]

George Davis, the secretary-treasurer, was outspokenly critical of Selma Borchardt as well as Linville and Lefkowitz. His feelings were that the charges of communism and countercharges were extremely jeopardous to the growth of the union. In a letter to Borchardt in 1936, he blamed her for an inflamatory speech which she had offered before the AFL, which he said had been used by an attorney for the board of education in Wisconsin Rapids, Wisconsin, as the basis for not renewing the contracts of thirteen union teachers. "I would not question your motives but the effect is a rather serious indictment of your tactics in that more than forty new locals have been chartered and the defensive campaigns have to be carried on in the face of activities on your part which are definitely obstructive in effect if not intent." [95]

The forces in the AFT's executive council and general

membership that were determined to purge the union of the radical fringe regrouped after the resignation of Linville and his following from Local No. 5 and found themselves in a difficult position. The executive council members such as Davis, Wilkerson, and Hendley were not willing to consider further action. The AFL was not empowered to vote out locals of a national, only the national itself. This led to the consideration of the voting procedures of the national AFT convention. Thus, a local of 7 members (the minimum demanded for organizing a local) was entitled to 2 votes and a local with a membership of 249 received only 3.[96] Due to the wide differences in the size of AFT locals, this meant that 15 percent of the membership could outvote 85 percent. Thus, the 1935 convention vote of 100 to 79 against expulsion of Local No. 5 found the 100-delegate votes representing 3,700 general members while the 79 represented 5,900.[97] This feature was to be the new tact of those who sought a purge. This voting information along with an explanation of other difficulties was published by AFT Vice-President Stanton Smith of Chattanooga, Tennessee, in the March–April issue of the *American Teacher*.[98] In the article, Smith characterized the major split in the AFT as between "radical policy versus functioning liberal policy." In summarizing, Smith pronounced "radical policy" as unworkable. "To adopt the Radical Policy, then, in our judgment, is to relegate the A.F. of T. to the position of a helplessly small minority, perhaps without labor affiliation, and certainly without strength to make real any improvements or reforms in the school world." [99]

In terming his own program as "Functioning Liberal Policy," Smith offered that "this very program has been considered radical in the past, and perhaps it was so at that stage of development in the social thinking of teachers. It seems ridiculous that we desert this position just as general conditions are driving an increasing number of teachers to this position and make possible, for the first time in our history, the organization of a considerable number of teachers under the banner of the A.F.T." [100] But the most important part of the Smith article was the proposal that the constitution be changed to give each local 1 vote for each 10 members or fraction thereof up to 500, and then 1 vote per 20 over 500.[101] The effect would have been to greatly enlarge the convention and to give more voting power to smaller locals and to take away delegate strength from the New York locals. But this proposal failed and those who sought expulsion of Local No. 5 had to wait for new strategy.

Meanwhile Local No. 5 prospered. A large organizational drive from 1935 to 1939 was highly productive and the local grew to sixty-five hundred members. In 1936 the independent Union of Private School Teachers was absorbed by Local No. 5.[102] In 1938 an individual college section was organized with over one thousand members and became Local No. 453.[103] Yet despite internal prosperity Local No. 5 was being more and more regarded as troublesome. They were active in showing support for the loyalists in Spain; they protested the sale of scrap iron to Japan; they picketed the German consulate; and they led the battle to have the AFT join the CIO.[104] In 1938 the New York Central Trade Council, tiring of their CIO talk, suspended them from the council.[105]

In 1941 the AFT College local in New York City and the regular public-school locals in New York City and Philadelphia were ousted from the federation. The ouster was the result of three major factors: the reorganization of the Chicago local; (2.) the dispute over AFL or CIO affiliation; and (3.) the election of an AFT executive council determined to act on the New York situation.

Expulsion

Primary to the question of expulsion of Communists was reorganizational efforts in Chicago. The story of the 1937 reorganization of the Chicago local is a brief one. The economic tribulations of the Chicago teachers in the early 1930s had convinced many of them that only unity would prevent reoccurrence. The first signs of unity had come in 1933 with the AFT locals providing leadership in the Save Our Schools Committee. By the end of the crisis the assessment among union teachers in Chicago was that even more unity would be necessary.

After Margaret Haley's Local No. 1 had become inactive in

1917, further AFT organization had been done among other grade and occupational levels. In Chicago there was Men Teachers Local No. 2, Women High School Teachers Local No. 3, Elementary Teachers Local No. 199, Playground and Supervisors Local No. 209. There was also WPA Local No. 346, University of Chicago Local No. 259, the Education Secretaries Local No. 244, and the Truant Officers Local No. 237. In 1937 the public-school teachers of Chicago (Locals Nos. 2, 3, 199, and 209) joined together, found a new common ground of agreement, and shook the dust off of the old Haley charter and became Local No. 1.

The result of this unity was twofold: it consolidated the teachers under the presidency of John M. Fewkes, a bread and butter AFL advocate and staunch anti-Communist; and it changed the convention patterns in the AFT since local No. 1 now had ninety-five delegate votes to seventy-seven for New York local No. 5.

Before any active campaign could be waged against radicalism in the American Federation of Teachers, the composition of the executive council had to be changed. The constitution of the AFT empowered the council to not only carry out general policy and the resolutions of the convention but allowed them complete control of the daily operation, the editing of the publications, and the formulations of new programs.

When the political issues and discussions of radicalism had first emerged in the mid-thirties the executive council had been balanced between three forces: those who opposed radicalism; those who didn't; and those who didn't want to confront the issue. In the summer of 1937, for example, the executive council consisted of:

President, Jerome Davis
Secretary-Treasurer, Irvin Kuenzli
Vice-President, George Axtelle, Chicago
Vice-President, John Conners, New Bedford, Maine
Vice-President, Hugh DeLacy, Seattle
Vice-President, Michael Eck, Ohio
Vice-President, Arthur Elder, Detroit
Vice-President, Mary Grossman, Philadelphia

Vice-President, Charles Hendley, New York City
Vice-President, Mary Herrick, Chicago
Vice-President, Allie Mann, Atlanta
Vice-President, Mercedes Nelson, Minneapolis
Vice-President, Paul Preisler, St. Louis
Vice-President, Stanton Smith, Chattanooga
Vice-President, Joel Seidman, Chicago
Vice-President, Harry Steinmetz, San Diego
Vice-President, Doxey Wilkerson, Washington, D.C.

This council could be characterized as fitting the pattern of a
three group division. It needs to be immediately pointed out
that by 1937 standards all were leftists. The distinctions that
can be made between groups, although admittedly somewhat
arbitrary, are useful in analyzing the events that led up to the
expulsion of the two New York and one Philadelphia local in
1941. The major issues that divided the council were: AFL-
CIO affiliation, and whether action was needed to be taken
against the radical stand of Local No. 5 in New York City.
These issues must be viewed in such simplistic terms in order to
show any pattern. Obviously the dangers of oversimplification
must be recognized. To say that the concern for the activities of
Local No. 5 was an anti-Communist crusade would be inaccu-
rate. For the term Communist was too general of a concept.
Specifically the concern was for individuals who had joined the
Communist party, who espoused the Moscow line via Joseph
Stalin, and who were interested in subverting the teachers'
union toward realizations of their own personal power to the
detriment of the general membership.

Taking the simplistic view, the council of 1937 could be
said to provide three groups: 1. those who favored CIO affiliation and opposed action against New York; 2. those who
favored remaining with the AFL and favored action against
New York; and 3. those who were essentially neutral and
favored forestalling action.

In the first group were George Axtelle, Hugh DeLacy,
Mary Grossman, Charles J. Hendley, Allie Mann, and Doxey
Wilkerson. Axtelle's position in this group was the least secure.
Later he would shift sides. But in 1937 he was relatively uncriti-

cal of Local No. 5 and argued for many of their interests and ideas. DeLacy was the president of the Seattle local and a member of the WPA teachers. He later became a member of the United States Congress and was thought by many to be very sympathetic toward the American Communist party. Mary Grossman was president of the Philadelphia local and thought to be a member of the Communist party. Charles J. Hendley, President of Local No. 5 in New York City was a Socialist and as such favored CIO affiliation and obviously was opposed to any action against his own union. Allie Mann, of Atlanta, was very pro-CIO. Doxey Wilkerson, of Howard University was also in favor of CIO affiliation and would later become a member of the Communist party.

Group two was formed of John Connors, Michael Eck, Arthur Elder, Mary Herrick, Paul Preisler, Stanton Smith, and Joel Seidman. Biographical data is scanty on Connors, but he emerges in 1940 clearly on the side of those who favored action against the New York local. Arthur Elder of Detroit was a leader of this second group and as well as being the state secretary of the Michigan Federation of Teachers had organized for the AFL. Michael Eck was in a similar position being the secretary in Ohio. Mary Herrick, long a member of the Chicago local, was clearly in camp two. Seidman was a professor at the University of Chicago and Preisler a professor at Washington University, St. Louis. Both were identified with the Chicago group. Stanton Smith, of Chattanooga, Tennessee, favored action against New York. He could be described as being a bread and butter AFL unionist.

Group three, the neutrals, consisted of Jerome Davis, Irvin Kuenzli, Mercedes Nelson, and Harry Steinmetz. The position that Davis took in trying to promote AFL-CIO harmony has already been mentioned. Kuenzli, made secretary-treasurer in 1936, had been awarded his full-time position on the very fact of his neutrality. His predecessors, Florence Hanson and George Davis, has been in deep trouble because of their partisanship. Kuenzli was apolitical. Mercedes Nelson, a classroom teacher and president of the Minneapolis local, had come from a background of socialism. Her mother had been a leader in the Socialist movement of the nineteenth century, and she had inherited a large tolerance for radicalism. Steinmetz of San Diego served but two terms and did not figure in the controversy.[106] This made the council split 6–7–4.

By 1939 the situation had not changed, with Axtelle, Grossman, Hendley, Mann, and Wilkerson still on the council from group one. Connors, Eck, Elder, Herrick, Preisler, Seidman, and Smith were still on from group two, and Davis, Kuenzli, and Nelson were still on the board from group three.

The position of President Jerome Davis needs further exploration. It can be assumed that the president of any organization has certain power to persuade and act unilaterally due to the very nature of his office. These assumptions seem to be true for the president of the AFT. The question remains as to why Davis maintained neutrality throughout the rather long tenure of his office, 1936 through 1939.

Part of the answer to this question lies with the personality and experience of Jerome Davis. Trained in theology he undoubtedly accepted the role of conciliator with ease. And yet his own bitter experience caused him to be slow to condemn radicalism of any brand. Davis's particular experience concerned Yale University where he became an assistant professor of theology in the Divinity School. After what he thought to be a successful career in teaching he was removed from his position by a vote of the Yale Corporation at the beginning of the term in 1936. At that point he had a contract that was good until June of the following year. The charges against him concerned incompetency. At the time of his dismissal he held the Stark Chair of Practical Philanthropy, was on the executive committee of the American Sociological Society, was the general editor of a social relations series published by D. C. Heath, and was well thought of by the divinity school faculty who had voted him a three year appointment in January of 1936.[107] Fortunately Davis had been a member of the Yale local of the American Federation of Teachers, for despite letters of condemnation from the National Education Association, Progressive Education Association, and the American Association of University Professors, only the AFT took action. Besides letters, resolutions, and systematic publicity, the AFT held mass meetings for Davis's case in New York and New Haven, organized a protest rally held on the steps of the divinity school chapel at Yale, and assembled 250 teachers who dressed in academic gowns and picketed a meeting of the Yale Corporation.[108] The corporation did decide to continue Davis's salary for at least one year but the teaching slot had been filled by another.[109] Most of these actions had been organized by the New York College section of Local No. 5. Shortly after, Jerome Davis was elected the president of the AFT and was looked upon as a symbol of the need for academic freedom.

If action against the New York locals and radicalism was to be undertaken by a president of the AFT, it could not be taken by Jerome Davis. Those members of the executive council who favored action against the New York local worked through the later years of the decade of the 1930s to consolidate their forces. The re-formation of Local No. 1 in Chicago had worked in their favor. The natural decline of the WPA with the improving economy had led to the decline of the WPA teaching locals, which was another factor in their favor. There were also general forces in the society that were working on their behalf.

One of these forces was the growing concern in the nation over the internal threat of communism. The Stalin purges of the later 1930s had caused many American Communists to disaffiliate from the party, and their testimony before investigatory committees and their public pronouncements were causing many liberals to have second thoughts about the legitimacy of the Russian regime. Many liberals could have lived comfortably with the idea of an independent American Communist party. But what they could not stomach was a party so tied to the Moscow line that they were continually caught in a chain of contradictions. It was said in those days that you could figure out how high a party functionary was by how many days he could anticipate the new Moscow line. Most members of the American Communist party were forced to read the new declarations in the *Daily Worker*. Especially alarming to unionists were the revelations concerning communist takeovers or attempts at takeover in organized labor.

To those members who favored action against radicalism it seemed important that they elect a president of like conviction at the AFT's 1939 convention. At the annual AFT convention of 1938, they had tried to unseat Jerome Davis by running Lillian Herstein of Chicago for president. But she had been defeated by a vote of 336 to 274.[110] It seemed clear that it would take a more prominent figure to unseat Davis. Their choice of George S. Counts proved to be a good one. Like Dewey, Counts rejected communism as antidemocratic. Counts had a national reputation as an educator and was certainly familiar with the situation in New York.

The warm-up for Counts came in 1939 before the summer convention when he ran for president of the New York College local. His platform was understood to be anti-Communist. He was defeated by a five to one margin.[111] If anything, the defeat strengthened his resolve and he prepared for the convention at Buffalo.

The AFT convention of 1939 was held at Buffalo, New York, on August 21 through 25. Going to Buffalo, Counts anticipated stiff opposition. The site was favorable to the New York locals who could take advantage of the geographic proximity by having not only their full compliment of delegates but also other supporters. Jerome Davis was to seek reelection, and this would mean having to beat an established incumbent. Counts realized that at the convention the tactics of parliamentary stalling and sidetracking would be used. He was aware, however, of the success that David Dubinsky had achieved in a similar showdown in the International Ladies Garment Workers Union.[112] Dubinsky had been born in Russia and was very much aware of the events of that country as well as the persons in America who had allied themselves with international communism. He had become the president of the ILGWU in 1932 and soon became convinced that American communism was detrimental to labor. After twenty-five years as a member of the Socialist party in America, Dubinsky resigned in 1936 to support Franklin Roosevelt saying: "As to my resignation from the Socialist Party at this hour, I would like to state that by tying up this year with the Communists for a joint May Day parade it was divorcing itself from the labor movement. . . . I hold that there is no 'united front' possible with these eternal enemies of the American Labor movement. . . . Experience has shown that cooperation with the Communists spells disaster for unions everywhere." [113]

Dubinsky was a friend of George Counts, and in 1943 they would cooperate together to form the American Liberal party in New York State. Another tie between Counts and Dubinsky was Mark Starr. Starr had been on the faculty of Brookwood Labor College and as such had first joined the AFT. In 1936 Starr was made the educational director for the International Ladies Garment Workers Union and was running in 1939 on the Counts's slate for vice-president of the AFT.[114]

The convention opened on August 21 and proceded to undertake the agenda. Unknowingly, the Moscow Communists were just about to help George Counts. For on August 23, 1939, the German-Russian Non-Aggression Pact was signed in Moscow. The news hit the American Communist party like a bombshell. All through the 1930s the Communists had been the leaders in the anti-Fascist movement. The *Daily Worker* didn't lose a day, including August 22, 1939, in condemning Germany and Hitler. And now they were allies. Up until the time of the pact, the Communists in America were pleading for military preparedness against the Germans. Now they counseled peace.

George Counts beat Jerome Davis by a vote of 344 to 320.[115] But the struggle was far from over. The executive council was still split with Grossman, Hendley, and Wilkerson winning reelection.

The first term of Counts was spent in preparation for the AFT's 1940 convention, which Counts liked to recall as the "second battle of Buffalo." During that year, Counts took out time from his heavy work load at Teachers College, Columbia, to travel extensively and to talk to many of the federation's locals. On October 11, 1939, he addressed the convention of the American Federation of Labor at Cincinnati. His speech: "Education and Democracy," said of the AFT:

We shall permit no political faction or partisan body, whatever its authority or connection, to obstruct our work, divert our energies to sectarian quarrels, and make of the Federation a tool for the promotion of its special purposes. In particular we are unalterably and unequivocally opposed to totalitarianism in every form, however pleasing and alluring its guise. We are opposed to any movement or tendency that repudiates the civil liberties, nurtures the idea of violence and dictatorship, and looks with favor on a regime sustained by machine guns, secret police, bureaus of propaganda, concentration camps, and firing squads. We are opposed to any part or order that takes its political directives in the least detail from any foreign government or power. In still greater particular, we are opposed without exception to the current world movements known as Communism, Fascism, and Naziism.[116]

Pursuing the favorable impression that he had made on the parent AFL, Counts wrote to William Green the following April. In the letter he asked the AFL to: 1. give $1000 for the publication of the April issue of the *American Teacher;* 2. publicize a statement on Green's position that there ought to be federal aid to education; 3. assist the AFT with a new organizing campaign; 4. give $5000 for the salary of two representatives of the AFT who would address summer school sessions on teachers' unions; and 5. address the next AFT convention.[117] The items demanded must have struck Green as a reasonable price to pay for the campaign against the communists in the teachers' union.

A key to the success of Counts was in convincing the honest liberals of the AFT that communism was a real threat to the union and the issue was not simply an exercise in Red-baiting or conservatism. He may have been aided in this task when in February of 1940 the American Civil Liberties Union, recognized as a genuinely liberal organization, made a move against communism. In that month the ACLU's national committee declared it "inappropriate" for supporters of totalitarian forms of government to be members of the staff or directing bodies of the ACLU. The result of this action led the committee to ask for the resignation of Elizabeth Gurley Flynn from the national committee. When she refused, a series of hearings led to her dismissal.[118]

As the 1940 convention approached, Frederick W. Ringdahl of Local No. 263 in New Bedford, Massachusetts, organized the Joint Progressive Caucus for the purpose of offering a slate of candidates to the convention. The breakdown that follows gives their names, positions, and areas.[119]

Candidate	Position	Area
George S. Counts	President	
Lila Hunter	Vice-President	Northwest
Ruth Dodds	Vice-President	Southwest
S. Amelia Yeager	Vice-President	Minn., Wis.
Arthur Elder	Vice-President	Mich.
Mildred Berleman	Vice-President	Ill., Ind.
Paul Preisler	Vice-President	Ark., Tex., La., Kans., Mo., Ok.
Michael Eck	Vice-President	Ohio, Ky., W. Va.
Stanton Smith	Vice-President	Tenn., Ala., Miss.
Charles Etheridge	Vice-President	Fla., Ga., Va., Carolinas
Ruth Wanger	Vice-President	Pa., N.J., Md. Del.
Jane Souba	Vice-President	N.Y.
John Connors	Vice-President	New England
George Axtelle	College Section VP	
Mark Starr	WPA VP	
Ralph Bunche	At Large VP	

The brochure which advocated this slate was distributed to AFT members. In addition to the slate, it offered a set of principles which the slate was pledged to advocate. Point three was the critical one:

Third, in relation to our own union, we stand unequivocally for the right of any citizen, including members of the American Federation of Teachers, to hold any view on political and social questions and to membership in any legal political party, but we strongly condemn and oppose any attempt at manipulation of the American Federation of Teachers, or its program and policies, by a Communist group or any other group whose activities in the Union are directed primarily toward furthering the ends of agencies, foreign or domestic, external to the Union and its policies.

We stand for election of an Executive Council whose loyalty to American democratic principles and to the American Federation of Teachers comes before every other consideration.[120]

When the Joint Progressive Caucus arrived in Buffalo for the opening of the convention on August 19, 1940, they found that an "Education Defense Committee" had been established by the opposition. Heading this committee slate was John J. DeBoer of the Chicago college local.[121]

The opening of the convention was characterized by hot debate over resolutions and over the address offered by William Green. The reporters of the convention in the *Daily Worker* responded to Green's charges against Local No. 5 and turned on the principles of the Joint Progressive Caucus and referred to the members of its slate as "an intellectual goon squad." [122]

A twist of historical fate once again came to the AFT convention. At the 1939 convention the Nazi-Soviet Pact took the delegates by surprise. On August 20, 1940 (the second day of the convention), Trotsky was brutally murdered in his suburban home near Mexico City. The consequence of this act probably had little direct effect but it must have charged the atmosphere of the conflict with even more electricity. The voting for the executive council resulted in a clean sweep for the Joint Progressive Caucus.[123] On December 29, 1940, the executive council met in Chicago and by unanimous vote moved to investigate Local No. 5 in New York City.[124]

The executive council meeting held in Chicago moved with unaccustomed ease in acting against Local No. 5. On December 31, 1940, the council declared itself a committee of the whole and began the investigation of the local. Appearing before the council to plead their case was President Charles J. Hendley of Local No. 5 accompanied by Dale Zysman, a vice-president of that local, and their legal counsel. Also present was Robert K. Speer, president of the New York City College Local No. 537.[125]

After presenting its case and hearing arguments, the council moved to revoke the charter of Local No. 5 on the grounds that: 1. it had promoted dual unionism by helping to organize school custodians into a CIO union when an AFL union existed; 2. it had violated its jurisdiction when it accepted vocational teachers into membership when Local No. 24 of the AFT was also in the city and existed for that purpose; 3. it had conducted its internal affairs in a manner that created factionalism; 4. it had discredited the AFT's executive council following the 1940 convention; 5. it had gained bad publicity which was detrimental to national organization; 6. it had been expelled from New York City's Joint Committee of Teacher Organizations which tended to bring disrepute to the AFT; 7. that the AFL had been recommending the charter revocation of Local No. 5 since 1935; 8. that it had been expelled from the Central Trades and Labor Council of Greater New York; and 9. "that the leadership of said Local No. 5 has engaged in certain organized tactics and practices inimical to democracy." [126]

Local No. 5 was given the right to submit counterbriefs and to appear before the next session of the executive council which was to be held in Chicago in February, 1941.[127] On January 16, 1941, representatives from New York Locals Nos. 5 and 537 with members from Philadelphia's No. 192 who were opposed to the council's action met in New York City and organized a "Committee to Save the American Federation of Teachers." They mailed letters that protested the council's action and among other things proposed: "To defend locals from attacks—whether from within or without the American Federation of Teachers." [128]

The specific response of Local No. 5 to the nine charges made by the executive council were printed in the February issue of the *American Teacher*. Here the local: 1. denied it had promoted dual unionism; 2. admitted the jurisdictional dispute but pointed out that it had been going on for two decades; 3. claimed that its internal affairs were democratic and that the union had grown greatly from 1935 to 1939; 4. charged that bad publicity was generated by Counts and the executive council and not the activities of the local; 5. overlooked the bad publicity rap; 6. countercharged that since the Joint Committee of Teacher Organizations was antiunion that expulsion was predictable; 7. recalled that the conventions of 1935 and 1936 had already rejected the pleas of the AFL to condemn Local No. 5 so that the issue was not relevant; 8. blamed the dismissal from the Central Trades Council on grounds that the AFL had brought pressure to bear upon the council; and that 9. the charge that Local No. 5 leadership was inimical to democracy was without foundation.[129]

As the charges and countercharges were being prepared,

the newspapers of the country picked up the story. Most pre-
dicted the expulsion of Local No. 5. One of the only newspapers in support of Local No. 5 was the *Daily Worker*, which
sounded this note in its March 11, 1941, edition: "The
teachers, however, will recognize Green's role as one on a par
with that of the Rapp-Coudert Committee, and Dr. George
Counts, head of the Lovestoneite-controlled A.F. of T. executive council. They will realize that all three are bent upon the
destruction of their union, and will, as one man, rally to the
support to the teachers' union in ever larger numbers." [130]

In February the executive council met with the representatives of Local No. 5 in Chicago. The council heard 244 pages
of oral testimony in addition to 43 pages of formal briefs submitted by the local. [131] At the conclusion of the hearing the
council moved to revoke the charter of Local No. 5. It was
decided to carry the issue of expulsion directly to the general
membership by use of a referendum. This was done due to the
momentous nature of the decision and also was based on the
realization that it could be done easier this way than in a convention vote. The entire April, 1941, issue of the *American
Teacher* was devoted to the charges and replies.

In its statement of charges the executive council directly
confronted the issue of communism:

> The Executive Council is convinced that our continued growth and
> influence is strongly conditioned by the reputation of the American
> Federation of Teachers and its locals. We cannot hope to organize any
> considerable portion of American teachers, nor can we hope to have
> the confidence and support of organized labor or the general public so
> long as important locals are in general disrepute.
> The council is in no way critical of any member for his personal
> beliefs. The entire case of the council against these locals rests upon
> the character of their conduct, their strategy and tactics. . . .
> So long as the Communist Party is a significant force in the Ameri-
> can Federation of Teachers we can be united only under their pro-
> gram. It is, therefore, necessary to eliminate this influence. [132]

The council published five charges against Local No. 5. The
first was "that the internal affairs of said Local 5 have been so
conducted as to bring disharmony to the membership and that
factionalism within the Local has resulted in loss of mem-

bership through nonpayment of dues and by resignations which have stopped the growth of Local 5 and make it unlikely that said Local can effect a satisfactory organization of the Teachers of New York City." [133] In documenting this charge, evidence was provided which showed the historic nature of factionalism in the local; traced the relationship of the Communist party line as it appeared in the *Daily Worker* with the editorial stance of Local No. 5's publication, the *New York Teacher;* pointed to the hundreds of resignations which had taken place during 1940 and 1941; and provided membership statistics which indicated that as many as one-third of the local's membership were not in good standing.[134] Charge two read:

> That said Local 5 has disrupted the work of the National Organization and of the several locals thereof in the period following the 1940 convention of the American Federation of Teachers up to the present meeting of the Executive Council (December, 1940), by sending out a large number of general communications to the officers of the several locals and to the Executive Council, which communications have attacked the Executive Council and a sub-committee thereof on the basis of rumors and suspicions not grounded in fact and which have tended to create an atmosphere of hysteria throughout the membership of the American Federation of Teachers.[135]

After developing a case for this charge, the council offered the third, fourth, and fifth charges:

> That publicity coming from the political and other activities of said Local 5 has resulted in loss of members throughout the national organization and tends to bring the American Federation of Teachers into disrepute.[136]
>
> That delegates of said Local 5 have been suspended from the Central Trades and Labor Council of Greater New York and Vicinity, said suspension having occurred in March of 1938; and that efforts of said Local 5 and of the American Federation of Teachers to secure reinstatement in said body have been unavailing; and further the President of the American Federation of Labor has stated that in his opinion the action taken by the Central Trades Council of Greater New York and Vicinity in suspending the delegates of Local 5 was fully justified because of the conduct of this Local, and that it is his opinion that Local 5 cannot as now constituted become affiliated with the said Central Trades and Labor Council.[137]

That the leadership of said Local 5 has engaged in certain organized tactics and practices inimical to democracy.[138]

Also included was the general resolution for revocation of their charter along with that of Local No. 537, the College Teachers Federation of New York City. The case against No. 537 was largely an outgrowth of the one against Local No. 5, since they had only been independent of Local No. 5 since 1938. But some additional evidence, pertinent only to No. 537 was offered too. It was pointed out that internal disaffection had led to the resignation of John L. Childs, John Dewey, Reinhold Niebuhr, Sidney Hook, George W. Hartmann, Louis Hacker, and Wesley Clair Mitchell.[139] It was claimed that the local was Communist controlled and as such was recognized by members of the college faculties at Hunter and Queens as not being an important college teachers organization.[140]

The biggest surprise came when the executive council included Philadelphia's Local No. 192 in its indictment. Earlier published materials had not mentioned Philadelphia, only Nos. 5 and 537 and the possibility of including New York's WPA Local No. 453.[141] The move to include No. 192 apparently came when the investigations made by the council early in 1941 led to uncovering of materials suitable to construct a case against Philadelphia. Another factor that forced the council to act was an investigation made of the Philadelphia local by the Central Labor Union in Philadelphia. Learning of this investigation, a city newspaper, the *Philadelphia Record,* had one of its reporters make an analysis of Local No. 192's *Philadelphia Teacher* in relation to the Communist party line, and the published results in the January 22, 1941, edition corroborated the charge of Communist influence.[142] As far as the executive council of the AFT was concerned the most damaging evidence against Local No. 192 was the role it took in helping to organize the Committee to Save the American Federation of Teachers. This the council characterized as "dual-unionism." [143]

In the same issue of the *American Teacher* the presidents of Locals Nos. 5, 537, and 192 offered their refutations of the charges. They used fifteen pages to bolster the position they maintained in these ten points:

1. The American Federation of Teachers, according to official records, was in excellent condition in August, 1940, and needed no such drastic measures as investigations and charter revocation.

2. Between 1936 and 1940, the years in which Locals 5, 192, and 537 participated actively in the national work of the American Federation of Teachers along with other locals, were the years of greatest growth and achievement for the American Federation of Teachers.

3. The activities and achievement of these locals individually are proof that they are not "detrimental to democracy in education."

4. The democratic functioning of the locals belies the charge of "practices inimical to democracy."

5. These locals are not dominated by communist groups or any other groups.

6. Healthy relations with the American Federation of Labor will not be established by expulsions of locals and surrender of autonomy.

7. The charge of dual unionism made against these locals is completely unfounded.

8. The Executive Council, having co-operated with and encouraged small, discredited factional groups in these locals, brings the spurious charge of factionalism against the responsible officers of the locals, who have the support of the overwhelming majority of the membership.

9. To substantiate its charges the Executive Council has reposed complete and unquestioning confidence in the testimony of a small number of members or ex-members of the locals and has rejected the documented statements of accredited representatives presenting the almost unanimous opinion of the membership.

10. The Executive Council has resorted to undemocratic and unconstitutional practices against these locals.[144]

These positions were presented to the membership who now held the future of these three locals in their hands. Ballots were mailed out by the national office on March 31, 1941, and were to be returned by May 31.[145] According to the *New York Times* of May 29 the voting in Local No. 5 resulted in 28 votes for revocation and 4,635 against. The vote in Local No. 537 was 45 for and 626 against.[146] The final national vote, however, was as follows: [147]

For revocation of Local No. 5, 11,256
Opposed to revocation, 8,499
For revocation of Local No. 537, 11,104

Opposed to revocation, 8,520
For revocation of Local No. 192, 11,054
Opposed to revocation, 8,529

Locals Nos. 5, 192, and 537 were no longer within the American Federation of Teachers. This act reduced the total national membership by about one-third.

Chapter 6

The Hot and Cold War Era
1941—1954

Preeminence of the War

We are at war. We are at war for the second time during the lives of most of us assembled here. We are at war for the second time since the founding of our federation.

The hour of decision in this war approaches. It is the hour of a decision so momentous, so freighted with the possibilities of good and evil, that we scarcely dare to view it with the eyes of candor. Other ages, perhaps, have made decisions equally conclusive, but never so universal in their reach and consequences. In this hour, the fate of the entire world and of all mankind is being decided. . . .

We are teachers. We are gathered here in Gary to clarify our special responsibilities in the winning of both the war and the peace. We are not in the armed forces; we are not working in the defense industries; we are not producing any of the material things for sustaining our people in this struggle. Yet I am convinced that our task is no less important than that of the soldier, the defense worker, or the farmer. . . .

There are at least five responsibilities which, in my opinion, rest uniquely on our shoulders. First, we must lead in the struggle to maintain and even extend our great system of public education during these days; second, we must adjust our program wherever necessary and desirable to the furthering of the war effort; third, we must introduce into the program of our schools and colleges a systematic and realistic study of the background, the issues, the stakes, the problems of the war and the peace; fourth, we must prepare ourselves to shape educational programs to meet the needs of social readjustment and reconstruction following the war; and fifth, we must strive to develop a more adequate and challenging conception of education for our American democracy in the twentieth century. . . .

Our American Federation of Teachers, because of its philosophy of democracy and its organic connection with the working people of our country, is peculiarly qualified to assume a position of undisputed leadership in directing the schools to these great tasks involved in winning both the war and the peace. The burden is heavy and the way will doubtless be long, but to shirk responsibility or to refuse to choose the larger good would be wholly out of harmony with our past. We welcome the opportunity to live in an age of great decision and to help shape the future, not only of our own America, but also of all mankind throughout the world.—Excerpts from the speech of George S. Counts, before the 1942 convention of the American Federation of Teachers

From the beginning of Pearl Harbor in 1941 to the signing of the peace with the Germans and Japanese in 1945, the full attention of the nation was on the war. Certainly the membership of the AFT reflected this national concern and it became a dominant issue in the conventions and in the pages of its publications. Like other educational agencies, the AFT sought to mobilize the resources of the schools, the students, and the teachers toward the successful completion of the war.

Meeting in January of 1942 the executive council of the AFT pledged its support toward the war effort and began the process of translating the pronouncement into positive action. The issues of the *American Teacher* were filled with descriptions of various locals who worked hard in war bond drives, clothing collections, and civil defense activities. Supportive feature stories often concerned teachers who had enlisted into the ranks. Several of the AFT leaders were called to Washington for wartime service in the mushrooming agencies of the federal government. John Fewkes, the president in 1941 and 1942, became director of the War Production Board's Department of Health and Recreation.[1] Lillian Herstein, an important member of Chicago's Local No. 1, became a consultant to the War Production Board on problems affecting women workers.[2] George Axtelle, former AFT vice-president, joined the Price Stabilization Board.[3] Paul Douglas, a professor of economics at the University of Chicago and important member of the AFT, was looked upon as a popular hero after his enlistment and subsequent heroics as a marine.[4]

The convention in 1942 was dedicated to the war activities of the AFT. The federation was joined in this concern for the conduct of the war by the other educational agencies. In February of 1942, the NEA's Educational Policies Commission published "A War Policy for Teachers."[5] This was a first of several statements concerning education and the war. The United States Office of Education was also active and established a fifty-eight member Wartime Commission chaired by Commissioner Studebaker.[6] The USOE changed the name of its biweekly magazine *School Life* to *Education for Victory* in March of 1942.[7] The teachers, like the entire nation, were mobilizing.

From the beginning the AFT also showed concern for both the problems resulting from the war mobilization and in the large questions of postwar reconstruction. One of the questions of concern was the constant bugaboo of military training in the high schools. The war effort quite naturally spurred on those elements who had long advocated compulsory military training and the union once again resisted such measures. They were further concerned about the actions taken against the Japanese-Americans. At the convention held in the summer of 1942 resolutions were passed that urged "all governmental agencies both state and national, which have any responsibility for the welfare of children of Japanese ancestry, provide adequate educational facilities and competent teachers for all such children of school age."[8] A major article in the November issue of the *American Teacher* described the detainment camps of the Nissei with their problems of overcrowding and condemned the actions of superpatriotic groups like the Sons of the Golden West.[9]

The union also showed concern for the anticipated problems of the postwar world. The AFT appointed a Commission on Education and the Postwar World. The commission's first report came in 1943 and it stated:

Our choice is not any longer a choice between national peaceful, self-sufficiency (national isolation) versus participation in some kind of world organization or system of collective security; the real choice is a choice between some form of American imperialism and militarism, versus a program of international economic cooperation and mutual political security.

If the people of this nation want to create conditions for economic progress and political security, they must build bridges across two great gulfs:

a. One is the gulf that divides the capitalist-democracies from Communist Russia.

b. The second is the gulf that divides the white world from the colored world. Postwar conditions must satisfy deep-moving aspirations of the people of China, India, and the so-called Colonial peoples.

c. As tragic events in California, Detroit, and Harlem have shown recently, we shall not have peace within our own country unless we can bridge this gulf of color and get rid of long standing discriminations and prejudices.[10]

So the mobilization efforts of the federation were aimed at more than winning the war. They were aimed at waging the inevitable peace and facing the challenging social questions of the nation.

Organization and Administration

With the critical decade of the thirties behind it, the American Federation of Teachers moved into a new decade that witnessed its coming of age. The 1940s were a period of growth and consolidation. The AFT had been built from the bottom up and the large locals were still the heart of the organization. The need was to centralize and strengthen the position of the national office. This became a central thrust in the period 1941–54.

The problems of administration and organization were crucial. Membership, finance, and union activities in a range of fields became issues to solve in the forties. If the union teacher was to have a national voice he must have a national organization. The principal task was to build membership.

At the beginning of the forties, President George S. Counts issued a challenge to AFT members to organize 10 percent of the nation's teachers. Said Counts: "It seems to me that at least ten percent of the teachers in our schools are sufficiently liberal and labor-minded to make good union members. With such a membership, if at the same time we could hold the support of organized labor and the confidence of the American community, we would be able to assume a wholly unprecedented position of leadership in shaping the course of public education in the United States." [11]

Whether or not Counts really believed that the union could achieve such a growth rate and position of influence is hard to determine, but certainly the growth rate of the early forties was impressive. By 1942 Chicago, Cleveland, New York City, Atlanta, and Minneapolis had AFT locals with more than one thousand in each.[12] During the fiscal year 1941–42, the AFT chartered forty new locals and the following year sixty-one more. Secretary-Treasurer Kuenzli could happily report that two-thirds of the American Federation of Labor's national unions were smaller than the AFT.[13] By October of 1944 Kuenzli could boast that the AFT had added seven thousand new members since Pearl Harbor.[14] Three years later a jubilant AFT President Joseph Landis was reporting ten thousand new members in a period of one year and a total national membership of over fifty thousand.[15]

But looking at total membership numbers doesn't tell all the story. Patterns are better traced by looking at the organization of new locals. An analysis of the organizational endeavors of the AFT from 1945 through 1952 reveals a pattern that was similar to the 1930s with the exception that more locals were chartered in the latter era. The figures for the number of charters and the corresponding year are shown below.

Year	Number of Charters Issued [16]
1945	26
1946	100
1947	52
1948	28
1949	22
1950	45
1951	50
1952	25
Total	348

But the problem of keeping the new locals active remained a serious matter. Of the 348 chartered only 196 of them remained active by October of 1953. This was a retention rate of 56 percent. Further analysis shows that of the 152 that failed to make it, 3 (or about 1 percent) were actually merged with other locals due to school district reorganization and shouldn't be considered as losses. But 37 locals (about 11 percent), were issued charters and never got off the ground. Organizing new locals was becoming easier for a more centralized national office. Retaining them in active membership continued to be a critical problem.

Money was also a problem. Expenditures for 1945–46 were $101,960.01. Below is a chart showing the items of expenditure and the approximate percentages spent.

Items	Percent of Total Expenditures
National office	28.0
American Teacher	18.0
Reserve fund	8.0
Special items	7.5
AFL affiliation dues	5.5
President's expenses	5.5
Organization	5.0
Executive council December meeting	3.75
AFT committees	3.75
AFT literature	3.5
Defense fund	3.5
Secretary-treasurer's expense	2.0
Safety factor	1.75
Washington expense	1.75
Supplies to locals	1.0
Miscellaneous	0.75
Membership fees	0.5
Convention expense	0.5
Special meetings	0.5
Printing and office forms	0.5
	101.25

(Further refinement would require dropping below 0.25 percent.) Actual receipts of income for 1945–46 amounted $104,463.86 for a surplus of $2,503.85. The revenue of the national was in large part solely dependent upon per-capita dues collections. This accounted for approximately 90 percent of all income with lesser amounts coming from advertisements in the *American Teacher*, the sale of AFT literature, and contributions.

The surplus was important to the organization. Surplus funds meant strength and stability for the national organization and the possibility of entertaining new directions. Money was always a central issue, but with the forties came breathing space for the first time in the history of the federation.

Even with numbers and money on the upswing there was still the issue on internal politics. Factions within the AFT had become a way of life ever since the organization of the federation in 1916. This situation continued through the thirties into the forties.

In August of 1943, Joseph F. Landis replaced John M. Fewkes as president of the AFT. Landis was a high-school English teacher who had taught at Cleveland's Collinwood High School for twenty years. Landis had been president of his local and a national vice-president two years previous to his election as president. He ran for president in 1944 without opposition, retained his office in absence of a 1945 convention, and was reelected again in 1946. Landis was identified with the more moderate forces within the union. The more liberal elements, or self-styled "progressives," formed a caucus during Landis's term and moved to seat their own presidential candidate in 1948. At the convention of 1948 two groups emerged, the National Caucus which suported the reelection of Landis, and the Progressive Caucus which sought the election of John M. Eklund of Denver as president.

It would be difficult to ascribe exact roles for these caucuses since the personalities involved were more important, in the last analysis, than the issues. But the participants felt that the National Caucus represented the conservative elements of the midwestern region, and the Progressives the more liberal elements from out of the Midwest. This characterization is hardly adequate since all were certainly left of center in national political terms, and the handle "Midwest" is not clear either. Of the stated leadership of the National Caucus two were from Chicago and Gary which had been an old alliance, another was from Alabama, and another from Rhode Island. Of the Progressive Caucus two of the leaders were from New York and Boston, but there were important members from Illinois, Minnesota, and Kentucky. An analysis based upon regional differences is impossible to construct. It was more a case of the haves and the have-nots. In this instance the haves were the National Caucus members who controlled the national office and planned to keep it that way. The Progressive Caucus wanted the seats of power and quite naturally complained about the policies of the haves. In 1948 the Progressives carried the day, and John Eklund became the tenth president of the American Federation of Teachers.

This was far from the end of caucus activity however. In 1952 the National Caucus returned undaunted to elect Carl J. Megel, former officer of the Chicago local, president of the AFT.

One important change that came with the election of Carl J. Megel in 1952 was the utilization of a professional public relations firm. Public relations heretofore, were handled directly by Secretary-Treasurer Kuenzli. In November of 1952, the Harry E. Caylor Organization of Chicago contacted Megel and convinced him that a professional firm could best do the job.[17] This was, after all, the decade of the organization man and of public relations. The national really couldn't afford an agency, but the project was dear to the heart of Carl Megel and there was a need. But the hiring of the agency proved to be just one of several bones of contention that arose between President Megel and Secretary-Treasurer Kuenzli. The end result of this growing conflict was the release of Kuenzli as secretary-treasurer in 1953.

From 1936 Irvin R. Kuenzli had been the secretary-treasurer of the AFT. He had assumed the office at a critical point in the history of the federation and proved his ability to both manage the affairs of the national office and keep out of the partisan struggles within the union, a very dfifficult thing to do. But by the 1940s he was already being criticized for his efforts. Said one detractor: "Kuenzli may have been an ideal man for the period through which we have just passed, but I feel that he is really not big enough for the job of director of the national office." [18] The truth or falsity of this charge is impossible to determine. Kuenzli did manage to convince enough people of his merits that he lasted until 1953. At this time his services were terminated by the executive council. The termination stirred up a hornet's nest.

The vote of the executive council was close, eleven to five. The charge was that Kuenzli was not "carrying out the responsibilities of his position in the best interests of the American Federation of Teachers." [19] The issue had been building for a while and was hastened by the election of Megel as President. Megel became the first "full-time" president of the national office. The affairs were now to be run in tandem. Unfortunately Irvin Kuenzli had been working in single harness since 1936 and found the new relationship difficult. Said Megel:

> Unfortunately, from the very beginning, on the numerous occasions when I came into the office of the Secretary-Treasurer, he was either indifferent or indisposed to give serious consideration to any item regarding which I sought his advice, suggestion, or opinion. Furthermore, even though we were together in the National Office for a period of 18 months, Mr. Kuenzli during this entire period never at any one time came to my office, or called me into his office to ask for an opinion or offer a suggestion, or give advice, or consult with me upon a single item concerning or regarding any policy or program or matter pertaining to the welfare of the American Federation of Teachers.[20]

In addition to his failure to cooperate with Megel, Kuenzli was also charged with being too secretive and loose about the affairs of the AFT. There was also concern about his accepting the presidency of the International Federation of Free Teachers Unions on the belief that this placed limitations upon his duties as secretary-treasurer.[21]

There was an immediate reaction to the termination. Vice-Presidents Joseph F. Landis and John Fewkes (both past presidents), as well as Geroge Beacom and William Swan were opposed to the move.[22] They expressed this opposition in a statement mailed to the membership and led the fight for the reinstatement of Kuenzli to the convention the following summer. They formed a defense committee designed to organize such an effort.

The mail into the national office regarding the affair was decidedly in favor of Kuenzli. Many locals that he had visited reported favorably as to his abilities and personality. But at the convention of 1954 the move to overturn the termination of the executive council failed.

The organization of the AFT changed drastically with the departure of Irvin Kuenzli. No one was appointed to fill the vacancy. Instead, the duties were absorbed under the office of the president and were undertaken by a single person and later a more complete staff designated as administrative assistant, secretary, or aid to the president. The focal point of the AFT was now the president.

The initial move to dump Kuenzli was related to the larger question of internal politics. Kuenzli, a bread-and-butter unionist, could never please the political leftists nor the grand visionaries. He was criticized by the Progressive Caucus as being too conservative and small-minded. It was charged that he failed to grasp the potential of the state organizations. Predictably, opposition rose from the leaders of state organizations, especially from Herrick Roth, leader of the Colorado Federation of Teachers and the Progressive Caucus. It seems clear that the dismissal of Kuenzli was just another episode in the constant pattern of internal quibbling.

The West Coast Affair

For the second time in two decades, the AFT confronted the specter of Communist infiltration into its locals. This time it was the West rather than the East.

The trouble centered in Los Angeles, San Francisco, and Seattle and reportedly began in 1945, although it was not brought to the attention of the executive council until August of 1947 when it was charged that the Los Angeles local was Communist influenced.[23] President John Eklund made a preliminary investigation, and what he discovered caused him to feel that further action was required. In July a full investigation was decided upon with Eklund, Selma Borchardt, and Arthur Elder undertaking the task which began in September of 1948.[24] Their investigation centered around the Los Angeles local's unofficial affiliation with the CIO. But more important than this unofficial relationship was the formal affiliation the local had with the United Public Workers of the CIO which had been condemned by CIO President Phillip Murray as having a national leadership which promoted communism.[25] The feeling of the three investigators was that too much time was being spent on politics by the local and too little on educational issues. As a consequence of hearing the report of the committee, the executive council approved the following statement: "After a thorough review of the facts, the members of the investigating committee were unanimously of the opinion that the good name and prestige of the American Federation of Teachers in Los Angeles and the Pacific Coast area, as well as nationally, would best be served by revoking the charter of Local 430. After examination of the summation of evidence, the Executive Council voted unanimously to revoke the charter of Local 430 immediately." [26] After their three-day look at Los Angeles, the investigators had moved northward into San Francisco, arriving there September 5, 1948.[27] Here the issue was the involvement of key officials of the local with the California Labor School—the latter branded as a Communist front activity. Upon threat of revocation of their charter the local ordered disaffiliation with the labor school and salvaged their relationship with the AFT.[28]

By September 7, the three investigators had moved into Seattle to look at Local No. 401, the University of Washington's Teacher Union. The issue here was Communist activity and a prima facie case was readily gathered. The strong political activities of the local found them in staunch opposition to America's Lend-Lease program before June of 1941 and also to the war in general. After Germany's invasion of the Soviet Union, the local became suspiciously vociferous in their demands for Lend-Lease, a second front, and U.S. preparedness. The Seattle Central Labor Union had already expelled the local and upon recommendation of the investigators the AFT executive council did likewise making provisions for the college teachers who chose to reaffiliate with the AFT to join the Local No. 200, the Seattle public-school local.[29]

In the spring of 1949 the former Los Angeles local chal-

lenged the executive council on its revocation decision and submitted a rebuttal statement to be printed in the *American
Teacher*. This was disallowed by the council, but the council did
invite the former local to present its case at the summer convention.[30]

At the Milwaukee convention of 1949, spirited debate was
held over the issue of revocation but the final vote of 792 to
108 upheld the revocation.[31]

The expulsions of the locals at Seattle and Los Angeles
demonstrate rather well the determination of the AFT to keep
its house in order. The national feeling against the threat of
communism was so crystallized that the executive council felt
no need for the kind of thoroughness that had characterized
the expulsion of the New York and Philadelphia locals. No
public statement was ever issued by the council that named
names and offered a complete list of particulars. What was un-
deniably true in the matter, however, was the issue of CIO
affiliation. This alone would have probably been justifiable
grounds. But there were less tangible problems as well. The entire state of California was on a Communist hunting rampage.
Jack B. Tenney and Sam Yorty cochaired a California Senate
investigatory commission often referred to as the "little Dies
Committee." [32] The commission reported conspiracy throughout the state that ranged from the Student Union at Berkeley
to the teaching of sex education at Chico.[33] Of interest to the
union was the commission's investigation of the Los Angeles
public schools, where they gathered testimony that charged
Mrs. Frances R. Eisenberg and Mrs. Blanche Bettington with
injecting Communist propaganda into their teaching at a Los
Angeles County High School.[34] Both were members of AFT
Local No. 430.

The charges were undoubtedly blown out of proportion,
and the commission's investigations typically had all the dignity
of a circus. But public opinion was ready to be formed from
such accusations and all the pleas for rationality would go unheard. In any case, the AFT, still sensitive to the fear that the
public wanted to believe their entire operation subversive, had
moved to expel Local No. 430. Said the California senate commission at one point in their report: "The case of Mrs. Eisen-

berg is crystal clear. She is a member of Local 430 of the A.F.T., a thoroughly communist dominated trade union." [35]

Commission on Educational Reconstruction

At the convention of the AFT held in Chicago during the summer of 1944, the assembled delegates voted to create a Commission on Educational Reconstruction. The commission was to serve as a blue-ribbon committee to formulate objectives for American education in the postwar era. Serving as chairman was Floyd Reeves, a noted professor of educational administration at the University of Chicago. Serving with Reeves on the commission were:

John L. Childs, Professor of Education, Teachers College, Columbia University

Joseph Landis, President, AFT

Irvin Kuenzli, Secretary-Treasurer, AFT

Selma Borchardt, Legislative Representative, AFT

George S. Counts, Professor of Education, Teachers College, Columbia University

Milton S. Eisenhower, President, Kansas State College

Roma Gans, Professor of Education, Teachers College, Columbia University

Florence Thorne, Research Director, AFL

Robert C. Weaver, Chairman, Mayor's Committee on Race Relations, Chicago [36]

During its first year of existence the commission concentrated on two issues: military conscription and federal aid. The commission was opposed to the extension of the draft into peacetime which was being advocated by several quarters on Capitol Hill. More effort, however, was expended by the commission in their concern for federal aid. The streets of Washington were littered with unsuccessful attempts at obtaining federal support for the schools. The GI Bill was important but not to the public-school children of the nation. At the first conference of the commission, Chairman Reeves asked the question that was to become central for the following twenty years:

"Is there any hope of getting a program of Federal Aid to Education without having it center largely around National Defense?" [37]

Federal aid to education was one item that many could support in theory. The problem was one of writing a bill that was acceptable to these same people. One immediate problem was that the professional education community tended to oppose federal aid for nonpublic schools on philosophical grounds. Certainly Professors Reeves, Childs, and Counts understood these arguments. But the official AFL statement on federal aid said: "public funds must be administered by public education authorities in each state without prejudice to any child within the confines of the state." [38] Further disagreement centered around the proposal to aid all states. Ohio Senator Robert Taft favored aiding those states whose incomes were the lowest. Dr. Weaver, of the AFT's commission, objected to this scheme and pointed out the needs of urban children in relatively wealthy states like the children in ghetto areas of New York City and Chicago. The commission managed to iron out compromise measures losing only one of its members in the process. Dr. Milton Eisenhower, who could not reconcile his position with the others, resigned from the commission.

The commission was to pursue other problem areas too. Chairman Reeves had high hopes for the commission as a major investigatory and research agency in American education. Unfortunately, his hopes were too high for the AFT treasury. Support was sought for aid from the locals and a special drive did net $5,051.65 for the commission's work. Of this $3,200.00 came from from Chicago's Local No. 1 and the remainder from other locals.[39] The commission was off to a good start only to lose a little momentum as time passed.

By 1950 the commission had a slightly different membership. Reeves had resigned, John Childs had become the new chairman, and Professors Robert Ulich of Harvard and George Axtelle of New York University had been added to the group. The grandiose plans of Reeves had never been accomplished but the commission had been productive. They had expended a lot of energy in exploring such topics as democratic education, teacher evaluation, textbook evaluation, democratic school administration, vocational education, teacher training, teacher rights, and the activities of AFT locals.[40] Their activities, publications, and personnel had given a new degree of respectability to the AFT in the wider educational circles. They had been limited only by a thin budget and a feeling among a minority of AFT members that their efforts were not first priority. Said Kuenzli in a 1945 letter to Reeves: "In travelling among the locals I have heard some criticism in relation to the fear that the A.F. of T. may become another 'research and nothing else' organization like the N.E.A. The failure of the great majority of our locals to make any contribution at all to the work of the commission should probably make us think seriously before devoting too large a proportion of the regular budget to pure research which is unrelated to action." [41]

Intercultural Concerns

During the decade of the 1940s, the federation projected its longtime interest in international and cultural minority concerns into a synthetic position of promoting intercultural understanding. The issues of the union's magazine abounded with such articles as: "Teachers and Children in France," [42] "Discipline in Russian Secondary Education," [43] "Mexican Youth in the United States," [44] and "Postwar Education in India." [45] Such an interest in intercultural understanding represented an amalgam of several concerns. One of these was the plight of minorities in the United States, another was the interest in divergent cultures, and another was an interest in promoting international agencies of cooperation.

During the forties, Layle Lane was made chairman of an AFT Committee on Cultural Minorities. Her reports became a regular feature of the union's magazine. The concern of the AFT was broader than simply the problems of the American Negro. Interest was also shown toward problems of religious bigotry, especially the treatment of American Jews and Catholics. Other American cultural minorities like the Spanish-speaking and Oriental-Americans were also emphasized. But certainly the issue of the Negro remained central. There was a special endeavor at identifying the contributions of the American Negro to American society. In just such an article entitled:

"Why Not Introduce High School Students to Some Negro Publications?" the author offered: "Will a child reared in an atmosphere of anti-Negro prejudice become cured of it because he has heard about Carver or Randolph or Roland Hayes? Hardly! But he will at least realize how little he knows about his colored brother, who isn't merely a problem, but that highly complex, interesting thing—a human being. He will realize how much he has to learn about him. Perhaps he will want to become acquainted. It is only a first step—in the right direction." [46]

The federation took some specific action when at its 1946 convention it passed the following resolution: "*Resolved,* That the AFT: (1) Condemn racial segregation in school systems as a violation of the democratic pattern; (2) urge upon all locals in cooperation with local central trades that they request their school officials to set up committees on intercultural education and provide all types of materials to be systematically integrated into every level and phase of the curriculum." [47]

In terms of international cooperation there was much interest shown toward the new United Nations organization. Members of the AFT were encouraged to support the United Nations Recovery and Relief Agency and feature stories in the *American Teacher* told of the plight of school-age children around the world. When the United Nations Educational, Scientific, and Cultural Organization was established the AFT's executive council immediately supported it. [48] Hundreds of column inches in the magazine were devoted to the work of UNESCO and several AFT members attended international conferences sponsored by UNESCO.

Educational Issues in the Forties

During the 1940s the union continued to formulate and confront issues both of a philosophical and operational nature. In December 1944, the Education Committee of the American Federation of Labor presented for adoption to the AFL convention its program. The program called for: federal aid to education; maximum class size of twenty-five; a $1500 minimum salary for teachers; opposition to undemocratic school administration; more training programs for youth; promotion of junior colleges; the upgrading of current vocational education programs; expansion of adult education; an International Office of Education; opposition to yellow-dog contracts; opposition to child labor; a training and retraining program for veterans.[49] Federal aid to education was especially thought to be important by the AFT and during this era the union worked vigorously to get a measure that they approved through the Congress. Getting federal aid was a significant problem within itself but the issue was further complicated by the fact that the National Education Association was also supporting federal aid legislation of a different type. The NEA-supported bills called for federal aid to school districts for use in program areas. The AFT favored only legislation that would go for supplementing teacher salaries. This issue of salaries was still paramount to the union. In one small study printed in their magazine, the union tried to relate low salaries with student achievement by showing how the army literacy tests indicated that the twelve states paying the lowest salaries had 110 illiterates per 1,000, while states paying the highest salary had only 23 per 1,000.[50]

Federal aid seemed to be the key to meeting the AFT's demands for quality education. The lessons of the retrenchment period of the 1930s had been learned well. The local communities just could not be counted on to vote themselves higher taxes to pay for needed educational improvements.

On Capitol Hill the mood of the legislators toward federal aid was as favorable as it had been for years. This reflected the mood of the general public. A survey taken by the National Opinion Research Center at the University of Denver in 1944 showed that only 23 percent of the American public was opposed to federal aid for education.[51] Proponents of federal aid ranged from liberal to conservative in political persuasion, and the activists for federal aid included such diverse elements as the South's Lister Hill and William Fulbright to the North's Robert Taft and Wayne Morse. The problem in passing a federal aid to education bill in the 1940s was not in generating support for the concept but in establishing agreement over the approach.

One extremely tough question concerned federal aid to nonpublic schools. Most education leaders opposed aid to non-public schools, and this was the official policy of the NEA. The AFT was never as clear on this issue. There continued to be a Catholic Caucus within the federation that actively worked to see the AFT support a policy of federal aid to all schoolchildren. The issue was difficult to resolve. In the winter of 1947–48 the unions' Commission on Educational Reconstruction issued its policy on federal aid which discussed the issue and formulated a program that those who favored aid to nonpublic schools could live with. In January 1947, the national Catholic magazine, *America,* lauded this position and condemned the NEA for their position. But at the AFT convention of 1947, the statement of the Commission on Educational Reconstruction was challenged and a floor fight ensued. The consequences of this fight were a modification of the earlier statement to more of an exclusion sentiment in regard to aid for nonpublic schools.[52] Throughout the 1940s, the position taken by the Catholic educators was one of federal aid for all school children or federal aid for none.

In Congress the issue of public and nonpublic was more or less resolved in favor of excluding the nonpublic sector. The problem here was finding agreement over the administrative aspects of such a measure. Selma Borchardt, the AFT's Washington representative, reported in April of 1947 that there were about a dozen different bills concerning aid to education at various stages in the legislative process.[53] None would pass the Congress.

By 1948 it was clear that no compromise could be hammered out on federal aid. Other bills would be introduced, but all shared the same fate. In the 1950s the issue of school integration clouded the question of federal aid even more. The schools would have to wait for aid until 1958.

Teacher Salaries and Welfare

The AFT had special concern for the level of teacher salaries in the forties. Teacher pay was in more dire straits than it had been during the peak of the depression. By 1947–48, the

average teacher pay in the continental United States was
$2,639. Average teacher pay in 1933–34 had been $1227.
Thus, the raise in salary had more than doubled. Unfortunately the cost of living had tripled, and the statisticians in the
U.S. Bureau of Education had to report that: "Due to the
greatly increased cost of living . . . the 1947–48 average salary
had less purchasing power than the lower average salary in
1929–30." [54] The range of average teacher salaries went from a
low in the state of Mississippi of $1,256 to a high in California
of $3,690.[55]

Low pay in the 1930s has been tolerated by the teachers
since depression was spread among all sectors of the economy,
since prices had dropped, and since there were no alternatives
to quiet suffering. But with the recovery in 1936 the situation
changed. Teachers now had the opportunity of leaving the
profession for better paying jobs in industry. And leave they
did. Despite increased enrollments, there were fifty thousand
fewer teachers in 1943–44 than there had been in 1939–40.
The U.S. Commissioner of Education's Office estimated that by
1947–48 there were over seventy thousand teachers teaching
on emergency certificates to stem the growing shortage.[56] This
large number teaching under emergency provisions had actually been larger two years previous. In assessing the impact of
the war on education, I. L. Kandel, professor of education at
Teachers College, Columbia University, said: "At the end of
the war it was estimated that more than a third (350,000) of the
competent teachers employed in 1940–41 had left teaching, the
majority to accept higher paying positions in business, industry,
and government services. According to estimates of the U.S.
Office of Education, 109,000 teachers were employed on
emergency certificates in 1945–46." [57]

One might assume that in times of such a critical teacher
shortage that pay benefits and welfare programs for teachers
would have been improved in order to attract new teachers.
This seemed to occur only in remote instances. Almost every
other technique was utilized. The states established machinery
for either formally lowering their certification requirements or
simply winked at the loose procedures employed by county superintendents or other certification agencies. Teacher colleges

retooled their training programs to turn out their products faster. Often, student teaching, which even the most vocal critics of teacher preparation consider essential, was waved. Programs were designed to attract new prospective teachers and at the same time win back those who had left the profession. Tuition waivers, short workshops for credit, and other types of special considerations were given to those who indicated they would teach.

The AFT was concerned over these trends since they favored both increased teacher preparation and increased salaries. In 1945 the executive council of the AFT called for establishing a minimum pay of $2,000 nationally.[58] The union was likewise interested in a single salary schedule and fought for its widespread adoption. This was a difficult item to obtain since in the forties there was a campaign at instituting merit pay schemes. The U.S. Chamber of Commerce supported merit pay and promoted it in its publications. If there was one complete point of unanimity between the NEA and the AFT it was in their mutual condemnation of merit pay and in their mutual realization that there was no way of objectively measuring effective instruction.

In addition to its position on salaries and single salary schedules, the AFT supported the following items that concerned teacher welfare in the forties: maximum class size no larger than 25 (resolution passed in 1947); establishment of credit unions for teachers (resolution passed in 1949); establishment of a home for retired union teachers (resolution passed in 1949); health insurance for teachers (resolution passed in 1950); load allowances or additional compensation for teachers with assigned extra-curricular activities (resolution passed in 1951); board paid liability insurance carried on teachers (resolution passed in 1952).[59] By the 1960s most of these policies would represent ordinary school practice.

Collective Bargaining

In the November issue, 1944, of the *American Teacher* was a short and disarmingly simple statement that the American Federation of Teachers local of Cicero, Illinois, had signed a collective bargaining contract with the board of education.[60] This represented a first for the teachers' union and when the announcement of the agreement was made by the local's president to the convention delegates a couple of months earlier, she was besieged with questions concerning its details. The form of the contract was similar to the standard labor union contract which began with recognition of sole bargaining agency, promoted a seniority basis, listed the pay schedules, established a grievance procedure, and ended with revision and renewal procedures.[61] Much of the contract, however, did realize the nature of the occupation and included specific educational items as tenure, recognition of additional college credits, and transferring of personnel to other schools within the district. For the time, the document represented quite an advance. It not only served as the realization of successful bargaining but included provisions in it which were liberal for their day. Teacher pay was determined by a single salary schedule that started at a low of $1300 for beginning nondegree teachers and climbed to a high of $3400 for persons holding a master's degree and having twelve years of teaching experience. The agreement established a sabbatical leave program, pay for extraclass duties, and provisions for renegotiation at the end of one year.[62]

The agreement generated so much discussion that the delegates returned two years later to the convention with the resolution that

the A.F.T. assign one of its committees the task of studying collective bargaining and its application to school management, as well as its application to the setting of wage scales, and be it further

Resolved, That the A.F.T. thru the national office and thru the designated committees collect and keep on file: 1. wage contracts; 2. steward's manuals; 3. other types of education literature prepared by trade unions to train their shop stewards and members in trade union practices.[63]

The possibilities of collective bargaining and the future of American education were not lost on the other educational groups. In 1947 the NEA issued a policy statement that Executive-Secretary Willard Givens termed, "among the most important in our 90 year history," [64] which called for "group action" to gain salary increases. The NEA proposed the following program: 1. election of a teachers' salary committee by the membership of the local education association with authority to represent and act for it; 2. study by the committee of the local salary schedule and financial conditions; 3. submission of a plan of action to the local association for approval; 4. "any understanding reached by the teachers group with the board of education should be approved by the board and then entered in its entirety in the minutes of the board"; 5. "during salary discussions teacher organizations should exert their influence to prevent unprofessional acceptance of appointment replacing teachers involved." [65] Givens stated that "this program was more appropriately described as 'democratic persuasion' than collective bargaining." [66]

Teacher Strikes

The issue of collective bargaining quite naturally led to the question of what weapons did teachers have to enforce a working agreement. There was no such problem for the boards of education. For the boards in states with no tenure provisions, teachers could simply be fired without explanation. This was also true of probationary teachers even in states that had tenure laws. But the situation was almost as insecure for tenured teachers. The problem was essentially a legal one.

Congress had passed the National Labor Relations Act (Wagner-Connery) in 1935 which, among other things, upheld the right of employees to join labor organizations and to bargain collectively through their representatives. But the act went on to specifically exclude public employees: "The term employer includes any person acting in the interest of an employer, directly or indirectly, but shall not include the United States, or any state of political subdivision thereof." [67] President Roosevelt, certainly a friend of labor, had furthered this principle when he wrote to the National Federation of Federal Employees in August of 1937 stating: "All government employees should realize that the process of collective bargaining as usually understood cannot be transplanted into the public ser-

vice." [68] The issue was further muddled by the fact that some
state courts had deemed the relationship between boards and
teachers to be legislative and not contractural.[69]

Just where this left the teachers was anybody's guess and
the ajudication required to clarify the issue continues even
today. But even with the right of bargaining resolved the question of enforcement by teachers would remain unsettled. Alternatives to the work stoppage were not available to teachers. In
any industrial setting "soldiering," or purposefully slowing
down production, was one possible alternative. But even the
most radical teacher would have considered slowing down the
teaching-learning process as immoral and unthinkable. Direct
appeals to legislatures, boards of education, and the general
public had a long history of being unsuccessful. The work stoppage seemed the only avenue of enforcement left to the
teachers.

The first work stoppage, or strike, of national consequence
came in 1946 in Norwalk, Connecticut, among teachers affiliated with the National Education Association. The local association in Norwalk had tried unsuccessfully to "democratically
persuade" the board of education to accede to their demands.
This failing, the teachers collectively refused to sign contracts.
NEA Executive Secretary Givens defended this action distin-
guishing between the principle of "no contract, no work" and a
strike violating an existing agreement.[70]

The AFT's policy against strikes had remained intact for
thirty years. Now in 1946 the question was to be seriously
raised. The no-strike policy had been formulated in deference
to the public sentiment that opposed work stoppages by public
employees and in realization of the timidity of teachers. But the
situation seemed different in 1946. Organized labor had been
effective and the labor strike had come of age in America.
Many members of the AFT felt that their power as bargaining
units was seriously diluted without the threat of a possible
strike.

The question was officially reopened at the convention in
1946: "By action of the convention, the AFT Executive Council
was instructed to reexamine the non-strike policy of the American Federation of Teachers and to arrange for a full discussion

in the *American Teacher* of the possibilities of a strike technique as a means of arousing the American public to an appreciation of the desperate needs of its children." [71] In the November and December issues of 1946 the problem was aired with arguments both for and against teacher strikes. Those favoring the strike argued along two basic lines: the tradition of the right to strike, and the proven effectiveness of the strike. The argument of tradition was based on the history of American labor and pointed to the common and statutory laws that accepted the strike as a legitimate activity. Effectiveness was easy to demonstrate and innumerable cases could be mustered to show the relationship between work stoppages and gains of workers. Those who argued for the strike thought education to be an especially critical arena since the situation seemed so dire in many communities that, as one writer put it: "the citizens are so apathetic that only drastic action, such as a teacher's strike, will rouse them to take necessary steps to improve their schools." [72]

Those AFT members who favored retention of the no-strike policy argued that the use of the strike was illegal and unethical. The legality issue has already been discussed. The ethical question is equally moot. The argument, simply stated, was that: (a) teachers entered the profession and accepted a position with the full realization that it was a public service function, and work stoppages were more than a retaliation against employers, they were violations of public trust; and (b) a strike was unethical to children since it was counter to the child's recognized right at receiving an education in a democracy.

After a suitable hearing debate was resolved at the AFT convention of 1947 when the assembled delegates voted to retain the no-strike pledge. During the same summer the NEA convention passed the following resolution: "The Association condemns the violations of contracts by teachers, believes the strike is an unsatisfactory method of solving professional problems, deplores the existence of conditions which have caused teachers to strike, and urges those within the profession to assume a large share of responsibility for the removal of those conditions." [73] On the surface it would appear that the two teacher organizations were in accord on the strike issue. This, however, was not the case, and the presence of a growing number of members in the AFT who favored the strike caused the national office to move in ways less pure than the policy.

The confusion relating to teacher strikes and the various teacher organizations was well illustrated in the Buffalo teacher strike of 1947. The teachers in New York state, as elsewhere, were loudly protesting the insufficiency of their salaries. The whole area of school budgets was complicated nationwide by the fact that city school districts were often subsumed under municipal budgets. These budgets were made and modified by political processes. The school officials, with characteristic unwillingness to involve themselves, had to rely on the altruism of the city fathers in doling out the schools' portion. Predictably the share was always too small.

Buffalo, New York, was caught in just such a dilemma. Like other large cities in New York State, it was depending more and more on aid from the state. The teachers in Buffalo were a splintered group with the vast majority belonging to the Buffalo Teachers Federation which was independent of both the AFT and NEA. A smaller number of teachers belonged to the Buffalo Men Teachers Association (AFT), the Buffalo Teachers Union (AFT), and a smaller number still to a Buffalo Teachers Union which was affiliated with the State and Municipal Workers (CIO).

On February 2, 1947, the larger Buffalo Teachers Federation, realizing that their demands before the city's school committee were not going to be met, voted to strike by February 25.[74] The news of a major metropolitan teacher group threatening to strike infuriated various legislators in Albany. One who was particularly rankled was William F. Condon, a Republican representative from upstate, who offered a bill on February 12 that barred strikes by state employees and, in addition to the normal threat of loss of job and tenure, included a penalties section that punished those employees who were retained by reducing their salaries to minimum levels and requiring that they remain there for three years. Said Raymond Ast, president of the Buffalo Teachers Federation, the bill is "a shotgun aimed at our heads."[75]

At the local level the threatened strike took on even more

interesting dimensions when on February 19 the president of the AFT's mens' local announced that his group would not participate in any strike, since it was contrary to the policies of the national.[76] On February 21, the other AFT local likewise denied support.[77] Such refusals to participate were interesting in terms of policy but not in terms of numbers since of the 2,960 teachers in the district, 2,700 of them belonged to the independent federation.

The Buffalo Teachers Federation was asking for a $500 cost-of-living bonus and a minimum salary range of $2,400 to $3,600.[78] As the strike deadline approached, the situation became more tense in Buffalo. On February 21, school superintendent Robert Bapst contacted 2,732 teachers in his district to discover that about 2,000 of them were planning not to show up for work on February 24.[79] The following day the CIO local gave the strike its support, but this was more than counterbalanced by a statement from Dr. Arvis Eldred, executive-secretary of the New York State Teachers Association, who condemned the strike.[80]

The "absention from work" as federation President Ast termed it, began on the morning of February 24 with "observation lines" being established in front of the schools. Seeing the reality of the situation, both AFT locals refused to cross the picket lines and gave support to the strike. Buffalo Mayor Bernard J. Dowd, while expressing some sympathy for the teachers, generally condemned the action as unfortunate and expressed fears that "the strike might create chaotic conditions which would harm the children." [81]

As the teachers manned the picket lines in the zero degree weather of the strike's second day, eighty of the districts' ninety-eight attendance centers were closed. The city's corporation counsel made public statements about the gravity of the situation and threatened dismissal of striking teachers and the bringing in of replacement teachers. The latter threat must have amused the teachers, since the nation was in the throes of a massive teacher shortage and it would have been extremely difficult to have found twenty-five hundred teachers in February.

No word came from State Commissioner Francis Spaulding's office in regard to the work stoppage.[82] The *New York Times* ran an editorial on February 25 condemning the strike and terming it both illegal and immoral.[83]

By the third day the strike was recognized as the worst teacher strike in the history of the country. Coal drivers were delivering just enough coal to the schools to keep the pipes from freezing. By the third day all attendance centers were closed. Governor Thomas Dewey was silent.[84]

Mayor Dowd begged State Commissioner Spaulding to intervene, and a statement was issued by Spaulding on March 1 ordering teachers back to work.[85] At this same time, Governor Dewey's Special Committee on Education rushed out its report which called for an increase in the state's minimum pay for teachers. While an improvement, it was hardly a Magna Charta for teachers, and the expectations that it would immediately resolve the Buffalo situation were short-lived. In fact, the New York City's Teachers Guild (AFT) threatened to strike itself, and the Syracuse Teachers Association (NEA) condemned the Dewey plan and sent two representatives to witness the techniques being employed by the Buffalo work stoppage.[86]

The ultimatum by Dr. Spaulding was to take effect Monday morning, March 3. Late Sunday evening the teachers emerged from a meeting with the mayor who promised raises of from $300 to $625. Reasonably satisfied with the increment and no doubt convinced that further strike action would be imprudent, the teachers returned to their classes.[87]

The Buffalo strike of 1947 was extremely important. It was important because of its magnitude and duration, it was important because it served as a model for subsequent teacher action, but it was certainly most important because it served to generate public interest in the strike issue and served to crystalize the viewpoints of educators, politicians, and teacher groups. During the strike the *New York Times* carried hundreds of column inches of supporting materials that helped to show the impact of the issue. When a *Times* reporter polled the various teacher-training constituencies of New York City about the strike, he uncovered viewpoints which were probably indicative of the opinion of educators nationally. Dean Francis M. Crowley of Fordham's School of Education condemned the strike.

Teachers College John K. Norton, while sympathetic to the needs of teachers, was opposed. Ernest O. Melby, Dean of the School of Education at New York University, stood alone in his public acceptance of the strike as the teachers' last weapon. Twelve educators who were interviewed at City College tended to support the Buffalo teachers but ended their interview with a frank recognition of their own vulnerability by requesting anonymity.[88]

Concurrent with the work stoppage in Buffalo, the American Association of School Administrators met in Atlantic City for its first convention since 1942. One of its opening exercises was an address by W. E. Peik, president of the National Society of College Teachers of Education and dean of the School of Education at the University of Minnesota, on the "Emergency in Education." Dean Peik condemned the strike as "unsocial." Said Peik: "Like war, the strike should be made socially unnecessary through education." Commented Benjamin Fine, the education editor of the *New York Times* and reporter of the AASA meeting: "Great significance was attached to Dr. Peik's position as it is believed to represent the viewpoint of the nation's top educators who are meeting here." [89]

There was also political reaction to the Buffalo strike. The same year New York passed legislation barring strikes of public employees, but not as severely as had the proposed Condon Bill. The states of Ohio, Michigan, and Texas also passed bills that same year modeled after the New York legislation.[90] The interest in the strike issue got beyond education journals into the more popular public magazines. In October of 1947, the *Ladies Home Journal* carried a feature entitled: "Should Teachers Strike?" The issue was handled by looking at two different teachers, Miss Margaret Mobie of Westport, Connecticut, and Mr. Millard Scott of Buffalo. The approach used by the *Journal* was more than informative, it was instructive of the differing positions and situations faced by teachers. Miss Mobie taught elementary school in a wealthy suburban district where parents were interested in their children and placed a high value on education. Miss Mobie, being single, could manage to live within her income even though it was small. She was opposed to strikes thinking that they widened the breach between teachers and community and that they would upset her children. Millard Scott, on the other hand, taught in an urban setting where parental interest and local concern could not always be guaranteed. Scott had a wife and three children and a mortgage on his home. He taught high school during the day and adults at night to make ends meet. His take-home pay in 1947 was less than it had been in 1932 while the cost of living had tripled. Scott favored the strike and had participated in the Buffalo work stoppage.[91]

For the AFT, the strike issue continued to be a problem as several of its locals became involved in work stoppages. In the winter of 1948, the Men's Federation of Minneapolis announced a strike vote over their failure to get a $400 across the board increase despite the fact that the school district's general fund had a $750,000 surplus at the end of its fiscal year.[92] The Womens' Federation soon followed in support. Before the teachers could actually strike, the janitors went out and the teachers simply honored the picket lines. Even after the personal intervention of Governor Luther Youngdahl, who managed to mollify the janitors, the teachers refused to return. When the governor declared the schools to be opened anyway, the custodians turned off all the heat. The teachers finally accepted compromise after pressure from the Central Labor Union.[93]

In the summer of 1949, the teachers of Oglesby, Illinois, began picketing when the board of education refused to tenure one of its members. This was probably the most explosive of all the work stoppages undertaken by an AFT local, since the issue was the right of a board of education to terminate the services of a probationary teacher. The situation deteriorated to the point where a prolabor crowd actually threatened the assembled board of education physically into retaining the teacher. The AFT local was loudly condemned by the local superintendent, the board of education, the state superintendent of public instruction, the Illinois Education Association, and the Illinois School Board Association.[94]

These and other incidents were a real problem for the AFT since it retained its no-strike policy. The posture it adopted was one of aid and comfort but not official sanction. Its position of aid and comfort included the advisory services of Secretary-

Treasurer Kuenzli and the AFT's legal counsel, John Ligtenburg. But typically the national refused to issue appeals for support from other locals (although it did in the Pawtucket, Rhode Island strike of 1951), and refused to make public statements supportive of strike efforts.

In analyzing teacher work stoppages nationally in the period 1940 through 1952, several conclusions seem warranted: 1. Teacher organizations, like the AFT, officially adopted a hands-off policy; 2. The general public was opposed to teacher strikes; 3. "The increase in teachers' strike activity after World War II was closely related to the rapid rise in prices in postwar years." [95]

Of special concern to the American Federation of Teachers was the further analysis of this data by Bernard Yabroff and Lily Mary David in the *Monthly Labor Review* that showed that "strike action in 29 per cent of the teacher stoppages accounted for four-fifths of the days idle, was taken by unions affiliated with the A.F.L. . . . Local professional associations of teachers took part in a fourth of the stoppages, accounting for a tenth of the days idle. CIO and unaffiliated unions participated in approximately 16 per cent respectively, and for smaller proportions of total idleness." [96] Even with a no-strike policy, the AFT had emerged as the leader in teacher work stoppages.

Overview of the Forties

During the period 1941–54, the AFT made significant strides. Their successes in attracting members and in moving financially into the black were very important. Also during this time the national office was increased in size and scope. The consolidation of the jobs of the president and the secretary-treasurer was an appropriate administrative operation. For the first time in its history, the national office was the capstone and not a subsidiary of the organization.

Old efforts were redoubled and new efforts were accomplished. The old efforts included combating the forces of antiunionism, female subservience in education, racial bigotry, and political chicanery. New battles were accomplished in the greater professionalization of the teacher and in the concept of the democratic school organization.

Early in the year 1948, the AFT announced the appointment of Florence R. Greve as research director.[97] The appointment fulfilled a long-standing need. The AFT had operated for thirty-six years without a research director and the consequences were all negative.

The AFT sought new outlets for its political beliefs in the period 1941–54 and were aided by an attitudinal transformation in the parent AFL that moved it from its political docility into activity. The AFT was even more directly aided by the political activities of its own membership who successfully sought high public office and were able, in the long run, to introduce legislation and to support policies long advocated by the federation. Such a case would be that of Michael Mansfield, from the Montana University Teachers Union, who was elected to Congress in 1942.[98] Mansfield eventually joined fellow AFT members Hubert H. Humphrey and Paul H. Douglas in the United States Senate.

The greater political activity on the part of the American Federation of Labor was also important to the union teachers. Early in 1948, the AFL formed a Labor's Educational and Political League undoubtedly as a reaction to the CIO's effective Committee on Politics and Education (COPE). The LEPL formation was a frank recognition of the need to give systematic thought and activity to the political arenas.

The AFT, who long before had shown political interest, continued to be interested in politics in the 1940s. In 1948, they had sent questionnaires to the three presidential candidates—Thomas Dewey, Harry Truman, and Norman Thomas—asking their views on such educational issues as federal aid.[99] This was an important issue since the death of Franklin Roosevelt in 1945 left the office of president wide open and meant the entrance of someone whose feelings about national educational issues would be less known. The AFT had undertaken a similar questionnaire in 1936 when Roosevelt had shown them a much more favorable position on education than had Alfred Landon. All three of the candidates of 1948 sent their replies, and all three took positions acceptable to the AFT.

Chapter 7

Coming of Age
1954–1961

Educational Critics and National Concerns

The fifties in the United States gave witness to an intense national self-assessment. With Normandy long since secured and with the Marshall Plan and the Truman Doctrine well established, the nation's attention was now being turned inwardly. Domestic institutions were to be carefully and critically scrutinized. The schools were to be a major center of this national interest.

The schools faced serious problems. Wartime priorities had sidetracked local building programs, and the growing tax burden necessitated by the war debt and the maintenance of our role as a world leader made citizens hesitant to accept the further burden of bringing school programs up to better levels. The period found the schools suffering from overcrowding, low morale among the teachers, and a growing chorus of vocal critics that would attack the public schools from nearly every angle.

The overcrowding was the most obvious problem. In 1953 the United States Office of Education was reporting 59,652 one-room school buildings still in use.[1] By 1957 the USOE was estimating that the school year had started with a shortage of 247,000 classrooms. This figure did not take into account the nearly 100,000 more estimated as necessary to replace existing classrooms that were unsuitable and unsafe. In 1957 approximately 840,000 pupils were attending schools on a shift or some other part-time basis. And the situation could not be quickly resolved. Nearly twice as many children were born in 1956 as were born in 1936.[2]

Symptomatic of many urban areas was Chicago where Superintendent Benjamin Willis reported that in 1956, 17,000 children were attending Chicago schools on split shifts. Enrollment in that year alone had increased by 14,000. Willis and the teachers faced this growing enrollment with about one-third of the district's schools having being built before 1900. These buildings, while often usable, were extremely costly to maintain and usually lacked gymnasiums, auditoriums, and library facilities. Some of Chicago's schools were over one hundred years old.[3]

These conditions were realized on Capitol Hill but action was not forthcoming. President Eisenhower was sympathetic to the school building program and favored a system of matching state and federal monies for school construction. While the president could sell Congress on this principle to build the millions of miles of highways that characterized the Eisenhower administration, he could not sell Congress on a similar scheme for schools.

The situation in Congress was a stalemate. As bills concerning federal aid for school construction were offered, they were forwarded to the House Committee on Labor and Education chaired by Harlem's flamboyant representative, the Reverend Adam Clayton Powell. Chairman Powell amended every one of these measures so that no federal money would go to districts having racial segregation. This effectively killed every measure since many of Powell's Democratic colleagues, from both the South and the North, would refuse to pass the amended bills while the delighted Republicans, savoring the sight of a severely split majority party, would support Powell's amendments.[4]

Congress never did get together on school construction, and the burden had to be faced by the local and state governments. At first the response of the general public was good. But by the sixties, the goose was rebelling against laying any more golden eggs. By the sixties, a full-scale taxpayers revolt was underway.

The problems of underpaid teachers were the same old song, though now being sung by the teachers in less harmonic fashion. The old enemy inflation was again the factor. The fight against this enemy was being waged best by teachers that had some collective strength and organization. Many benefits such as tenure and retirement plans had been won by the teachers over the years. But working for decent salaries was to be the most difficult thing to achieve. In 1954 the union was recommending a single salary schedule with a range of $4,500 to $8,000 a year at the bachelor's degree level.[5] The AFT would experience growth as it proved that it was the undeniable leader in improving salary benefits for teachers.

The attacks on the schools were scurrilous in the period 1954 to 1961. The right wing, the business and tax-cutting interests, the national defense alarmists, the superpatriots, and the basic education enthusiasts all took turns criticizing the schools.

The activities of the right wing in the period gained their momentum with the McCarthy hearings and progressed almost unchecked until the junior Senator from Wisconsin had been officially censured by the Senate and publicly discredited. The best organized of the right wing extremists was the John Birch Society. Its founder, Robert Welch, wrote to his followers in *The White Book of the John Birch Society*, for 1961, about the schools: "Join your local PTA at the beginning of this school year, get your conservative friends to do likewise, and go to work to take it over. You will run into real battles, against determined leftists who have had everything their own way. But it is time we went on the offensive to make such groups the instruments of conservative purpose, with the same vigor and determination that the "liberals" have used for opposite aims. When you and your friends get your local PTA group straightened out, move up the ladder as soon as you can to exert a wider influence." [6]

The business interests continued to press their demands for economy in school management. The National Association of Manufacturers was largely silent, but the battle was continued by the U.S. Chamber of Commerce and local taxpayer groups. Neal Gross's study of Massachusett's school superintendents and board of education members, published in 1958, showed that the greatest pressure placed on both of these elements was from groups protesting tax increases and bond proposals.[7] The same study showed that taxpayers' associations were conceived by the superintendents as the fourth greatest source of pressure with business or commercial organizations being ranked seventh. This is compared to labor unions which ranked fourteenth out of a list of nineteen individuals or groups who exerted pressure.[8]

The national defense alarmists became prominent after the launching of the Soviet satellite in 1957. The leader was Vice-Admiral Hyman Rickover whose book, *Education and Freedom*, published in 1958, condemned the schools for their failure to conduct education with the academic rigor of the European educational systems. This failure, he claimed, would cause the country to fall helplessly behind the Russians. Rickover's contribution to education was a mixed blessing. In a negative sense it prompted other self-styled experts on the failures of American education to preach and publish their hostile views. In a positive sense, however, it frightened Congress into passing the first massive federal aid measure for public education when in 1958 the National Defense Education Act became law. The Soviet satellite was able to accomplish in less than a year what the teacher groups had reasoned and begged for for over two decades.

Basic education groups were also active in the 1950s. Led by such organizations as the Council for Basic Education, great pressure was brought to bear upon school districts to upgrade instruction in the basic areas of language instruction, science, history, and mathematics while downgrading such curricular offerings as physical education, social problems courses, and others deemed less "basic."

The superpatriots continued to press for loyalty oaths for teachers, the inclusion of programs of Americanism in schools, and randomly attacked school texts that they considered less than exuberantly patriotic. All in all, the period 1954 to 1961 probably witnessed the largest and widest-spread assault on public education in the United States.

Organizational Responses

American public schools continued to boom in the fifties. By 1958, the U.S. Office of Education reported that there were 47,600 school districts in the United States and that total enrollment in all levels of education had reached 42.4 million.[9] One-fourth of the nation was in school. The total number of teachers employed had risen to 1,677,000 and men now represented 34 percent of this number.[10]

Like every other decade, the fifties had critical problems for educators. Juvenile delinquency seemed to be the foremost problem to be faced by all agencies concerned with young people, but there were other items as well. School district consolidation, continued teachers shortages, increased popularity and growth of the junior high school, the dropout rate, and the real development of audio-visual technology all received critical play in the school journals. The AFT, as expected, spent much of its time in discussing and debating these issues.

Congressional investigations of subversive and radical groups took the center stage in the first half of the 1950s. The cold war gave rise to intense fear over questions of internal security and espionage. In characteristic fashion these investigatory agencies often trod heavily upon civil liberties. Most of the energies of these agencies were reserved for political activities, but there was some effort at looking yet once again at the nation's schools. Of interest to the AFT was the use of the Fifth Amendment in these proceedings. As more and more witnesses refused to answer questions on the grounds of possible self-incrimination, the belief that such an invocation was equivalent to guilt began to rise. The AFT's response to this trend came with the following convention resolution: "That while we oppose the employment of Communists in our schools, we decry the dismissal of competent employees solely on the grounds that they avail themselves of their legal and constitutional rights guaranteed in our Bill of Rights."[11] In 1955, three teachers of the Newark local were dismissed for "conduct unbecoming a teacher" when they had invoked the Fifth Amendment privilege before congressional hearings. The AFT's executive council voted them $1500 for aiding them in their legal defense.[12]

Several of the states were passing antisubversive acts especially designed to remove teachers from service. One of the most noteworthy of such laws was the Feinberg Law passed in New York in 1949. The law required the state to establish and maintain a list of subversive organizations. This list was in large part taken from similar lists maintained by the U.S. government. If a teacher was found to be a member of any of these organizations, the membership was to serve as "prima facie evidence of disqualification for appointment to or retention in any office or position in the public schools of the state." [13]

The law was challenged in the early fifties in two different court actions. "Its opponents argued that it was a bill of attainder and an ex post facto law. They also charged that the word "subversive" was vague. But the main contention was that it represented an abridgment of freedom of speech and assembly as guaranteed by the due process clause of the Fourteenth Amendment. And, in addition, it was pointed out that making membership in an organization listed as subversive an automatic ground for dismissal was a denial of procedural due process." [14] The opponents of the law won in the state supreme court but lost in the appellate courts thus setting the stage for a hearing before the U.S. Supreme Court. The Court upheld the law but the dissent of Frankfurter, Douglas, and Black provided the most provocative ideas. Said the dissenting judges:

The law inevitably turns the school system into a spying project. Regular loyalty reports on the teachers must be made out. The principals become detectives; the students, the parents, the community become informers. Ears are cocked for tell-tale signs of disloyalty. The prejudices of the community come into play in searching out the disloyal. This is not the usual type of supervision which checks a teacher's competence; it is a system which searches for hidden meanings in a teacher's utterances . . .

What happens under this law is typical of what happens in a police state. Teachers are under constant surveillance; their pasts are combed for signs of disloyalty; their utterances are watched for clues to dangerous thoughts. A pall is cast over the classroom. There can be no academic freedom in that environment. Where suspicion fills the

air and holds scholars in line for fear of their jobs, there can be no exercise of the free intellect. . . . The teacher is no longer a stimulant to
adventurous thinking; she becomes instead a pipe line for safe and
sound information. A deadening dogma takes the place of free inquiry. Instruction tends to become sterile; pursuit of knowledge is dis-
couraged; discussion often leaves off where it should begin.[15]

Another arena of interest to the AFT was the litigation concerning the issue of segregated schools. The capstone of the
AFT's historical fight for the rights of American Negroes came
with the U.S. Supreme Court decision in 1954 that declared
separate schools to be inherently unequal. The AFT's concern
for the legal battle over segregated schools began in 1950 when
the delegates to the convention had instructed John Ligtenberg, the union's legal counsel, to file *amicus curiae* briefs in
cases then pending in the courts. Similar instructions were
given by the delegates in 1952 and 1953.[16] The attorney was instructed to offer the following contentions:

1. The equalization of the segregated school systems of the nation
is impractical. Since it cannot be done effectively, equal protection can
be achieved only by abolishing segregation.
2. . . . the doctrine of "separate but equal" facilities is falla-
cious . . .
3. Segregation in public schools inevitably results in inferior educational opportunities for Negroes . . .
4. Segregation in public schools deprives the Negro student of an
important element of the education process and he is thereby denied
the equal educational opportunities mandated by the Fourteenth
Amendment.[17]

The victory scored by the National Association for the Advancement of Colored People in the *Brown* v. *Board of Education*
decision was loudly applauded by the American Federation of
Teachers.

Moving in the spirit of this decision the AFT had amended
its constitution in 1953 to provide that "no charter of the
A.F.T. which defines or recognizes jurisdiction on the basis of
race or color, or permits the practice of such jurisdiction, shall
be recognized as valid, and the practice of any such local in
limiting its membership on account of race or color, shall
render its charter void." [18] In 1954, the convention instructed

the executive council to order all AFT locals not racially integrated to submit reports giving cause why they were not so
integrated.[19] By 1955, locals in New Orleans, Mobile, Chattanooga, Atlanta, and Birmingham had submitted such reports.
No reports were received from all white locals in Capitol
County and Fulton County, Georgia.[20]

The 1956 AFT convention was largely devoted to the issue
of racially segregated locals and was predictably stormy. The
convention was characterized by long debates and serious consideration of both the idealistic and realistic aspects of the issue.
But finally a resolution was hammered out that decreed that all
locals not integrated by January 1, 1958, would be compelled to
surrender their charters. Rather then comply, several AFT
locals voluntarily withdrew from the national causing an immediate loss of about 2,000 members. The largest single loss was
Local No. 89, Atlanta. Local No. 89, the first to achieve 100
percent membership, the pride of the AFT for over three decades withdrew its 1,855 members in December of 1956.[21]

The internal organization of the union continued to be
strengthened. In the period 1954 to 1961, the AFT was to have
one president, Carl J. Megel. Megel was keenly aware of the
needs of the national office and worked diligently to build it.
His early successes in centralizing the national and attracting
membership caused him to say in 1956, "this is a new era—for
forty years we have been on the defensive—now, for the first
time, we are on the offensive." [22] As of May 30, 1954, the AFT
had 45,140 members,[23] and Megel was wishing out loud for
twenty-two full-time organizers and a membership of 100,000
by 1960. That goal was not reached, but it was not due to
Megel's lack of effort. In October 1957, the AFL-CIO withdrew
its $13,000 annual subsidy to the teachers' union. The AFT was
now on its own financially.[24] This caused a pinch on the budget
and hurt organizational efforts. From four full-time organizers
the AFT dropped back to two. This placed greater emphasis on
the organizational role of the state organizations. Fortunately
these organizations had come to maturity in the fifties. Prior to
this the state federations were usually just paper organizations
without either a central office or staff. By 1960 the AFT had
ten state federations—Arizona, California, Colorado, Illinois,

Indiana, Michigan, Minnesota, New York, Pennsylvania, and Wisconsin—that had full-time executive secretaries who were active in servicing old locals and in organizing new ones.[25]

The financial picture also improved in the fifties. By 1960 financial stability was reached with the union closing out the year with all bills paid, some investments in securities, and a cash reserve of $30,000 in the bank.[26]

During the fifties, Megel's pet project had been the use of a professional public relations firm, and he happily reported to the 1954 convention delegates that the Caylor Agency had done more for AFT public relations in one year than all previous years combined.[27] Whether this was enough was still questionable though since the AFT public relations budget for 1957 was still only $7,000 while the NEA spent $2 million that same year on its public relations program.[28] Marie Caylor reported to the 1960 convention that that year over 20,000 column inches of newspaper space had been written about the American Federation of Teachers. She reported that the *American Teacher* magazine had a circulation of 63,209.[29] In 1954 Mildred Berleman had resigned after eleven years as editor of the *American Teacher*. In its new push for professionalization, the AFT's executive council passed the editorial chores over to its public relations firm.[30] With this change in editorship came a new format and some new decisions effecting the journal. Beginning the next December the *American Teacher* became a quarterly publication.

It was also during the fifties that a growing element of the membership of the union was giving consideration to moving the national office to Washington, D.C., where there were the natural advantages of proximity to both Congress and the national office of the newly merged AFL-CIO. But by 1961, the national office remained in Chicago.

The New York Situation

One of the more interesting phenomena to happen in the 1950s was the rise to power of the New York Teachers Guild. This was accomplished by planning, political events, and personalities that came together at the right time in the nation's first city.

The guild had been growing in numbers and influence ever since the purge of 1941 but had never been the potent power that it was to eventually become. The teachers of New York City continued to be splintered into several teacher groups and the guild was just one of those groups competing for the numbers. In 1951 Charles Cogen was elected president of the guild, and he must be credited in guiding local five into national prominence. Cogen understood the city well, having been born in Manhattan and schooled in Brooklyn. After graduating from Cornell, he had returned to Brooklyn to teach and to chip away at graduate study picking up a master's degree from Columbia in economics and a law degree from Fordham.[31] In becoming the president of the guild he certainly possessed all the experience and education that the membership could hope for. A second man important to the emergence of the guild was David Selden. Selden was educated and taught in the Michigan area before coming to New York City as a teacher of junior high school social studies. In 1941 his interest in the unionization of teachers got him the job of organizer for the New York local—a job he fulfilled so well that he was later brought into the national AFT office as organizer and as assitant to the president. The third member of the triumvirate was Albert Shanker. After education in the Midwest, he had returned to the city and had become active in union affairs. In 1959 Shanker was hired by the national office as an organizer and proved to be most effective in this capacity. He concentrated his energies in the New York area and worked closely with the guild. In 1962 he resigned his position as national organizer to return to the New York local as secretary and close associate of President Cogen.

The decision was made by the American Federation of Teachers in the late fifties to concentrate on New York City. This was made possible by special organizing funds made available to the AFT by the AFL-CIO's Industrial Union Department. The union's special friend, Walter Reuther, was president of this department.

Such external sources of funds were supplemented by the

AFT. In October of 1960 the national loaned the New York local $20,000 of its $22,000 reserve fund for an organizational drive. A special fund-raising drive conducted among the AFT general membership netted an additional $1,500.[32] In 1960 the New York Guild (Local No. 2) merged with some dissident elements of the Social Studies Teachers Association to form the United Federation of Teachers.[33]

If the AFT was to become a viable force in New York City it would have to prove itself as an organization that could deliver and not just another do nothing organization. The strategy employed by the UFT was to stage a strike and then gain recognition as at least the "unofficial" bargaining agent for teachers. It was a desperate strategy—and it worked.

The first vote for a strike came on October 5, 1960, when the United Federation of Teachers Delegate Assembly approved the motion for a work stoppage. The complaint was that Superintendent John J. Theobald had promised the previous May that the board of education would give consideration to a dues checkoff plan and to a collective bargaining election. Other issues concerned sick pay for substitutes, a fifty-minute lunch period for teachers, and an adjustment in the salary schedule. As of October, the board had not considered any of these issues. The approved motion to strike was finally settled on October 19 when the entire UFT membership was to convene and to vote on the strike proposal.[34]

Anticipating the final vote, the *New York Times* printed an editorial on October 18 opposing the strike, terming it both illegal and unethical. The *Times* was to condemn the strike on three subsequent occasions as well.

The ethics of the matter was debatable. The legality of the matter was clear—strikes by public employees were illegal in New York State. The Condon-Wadlin Law, which forbade them, had been passed on the heels of the Buffalo teachers strike. The penalty for violating the law called for loss of tenure, probationary status for five full years, and a freeze on the salary schedule for three years. On October 19 the UFT met, and 90 percent of the approximately thirty-five hundred teachers present voted to strike on November 7. [35]

The reaction of the superintendent, the board, other

teacher groups, and several leading educators was unanimously opposed. Superintendent Theobald termed the threatened strike "a shameful reach on the part of a few for organizational power and self-aggrandizement." [36] The superintendent threatened to invoke the Condon-Wadlin Law if a stoppage did occur and refused to meet "with anyone while under threat of a strike." [37]

Charles H. Silver, president of the board of education, accused the teachers of acting in bad faith and posited that: "The spectacle of teacher abandoning their pupils is as unthinkable as parents deserting their children, . . . any thing interfering with the orderly education of our children cannot be tolerated by the community." [38] Mayor Wagner, though not totally unsympathetic with the teachers, supported Theobald and Silver throughout the controversy. Five leading parent groups had rejected the unions' position by November 1, and other groups were equally unsupportive.[39] The NEA's affiliates all publicly condemned the threatened action.[40] Even the old teachers union (formerly AFT Local No. 5), jeered at the prospects of a strike. Meeting on November 1, 1960, it claimed that the UFT was overestimating its strength and its strategy.[41] From retirement came the voice of the dean of American progressive educators, William Heard Kilpatrick. Said Kilpatrick in a letter to the editor of the *Times:*

> It is with great regret that I read in the *Times* that certain teachers of the New York City system have decided to strike on November 7. I feel this regret because I thoroughly accept the reasoning of the *Times* editorial upon the subject.
>
> I feel that the teachers should accept an even stronger moral obligation than the policemen to obey the law forbidding striking because any disrespect of the law on the part of teachers cannot fail to have serious effect on their pupils. As one who has given his life to the teaching profession I cannot fail to express my deep regret for any failure to live up to the highest standards of the profession.[42]

Despite such objections and overwhelming condemnations, President Cogen and the United Federation of Teachers continued to plan for the strike on November 7. As the strike day grew nearer, Superintendent Theobald vacillated between firm opposition to the union and conciliation. At first, he showed his tough side by prohibiting the use of the city's schools by teachers who desired to meet to discuss the strike issue.[43] He urged building principals to begin to recruit retired teachers for teaching during a strike. His mood for conciliation shortly followed, however, and on November 2 he rescinded his no-meeting ultimatum and summoned the UFT representatives for meetings.[44] The board did concede to the demand for a collective bargaining election, which it promised would be held before April 1, 1961. But the UFT thought this concession to be too small and the strike-planning continued.[45]

On November 7, 1960, the United Federation of Teachers of the American Federation of Teachers went on strike—the first strike by teachers in the history of New York City public education. President Cogen claimed at days end that it was a victory for the union with 7,500 pickets out and with 15,000 of the city's 39,000 teachers failing to report. Police and board of education estimates were far more conservative claiming that only about 2,000 teachers had picketed 267 of the district's nearly 800 attendance centers, and that only 5,949 teachers failed to report to work with 1,349 of them having legitimate reasons. Theobald, with board approval, charged 4,600 teachers with "conduct unbecoming a teacher," which carried the same penalties as violation of the Condon-Wadlin Law.[46]

The wheels of government and organized labor moved quickly to mediate the strike. AFL-CIO President George Meany appointed Vice-Presidents David Dubinsky and Jacob Potofsky to a board along with Harry Van Arsdale, Jr., president of the City Labor Council. The doors of Gracie Mansion, the mayor's official residence, were open for business.[47]

On Tuesday, November 8, 1960, the American people went to the polls to choose between John F. Kennedy and Richard M. Nixon for president of the United States. On the same day the United Federation of Teachers returned to their classrooms. Earlier promises of Superintendent Theobald were reaffirmed, all charges against striking teachers were dropped.

The union had proven itself, it was strong enough to disrupt the school operation, it was popular enough to command the attention of teachers who were not even members, and it was able to make the superintendent and board listen to its demands. The lessons learned from this brief work stoppage were great enough to change the course of teacher organization in New York City. From this point on, the teachers were more than simply employees occasionally placed in an advisory capacity—they were full partners with the community, the board, and the administration in the educational process.

In the spring of 1961 a collective bargaining election was held. The United Federation of Teachers received 20,045 votes, the Collective Bargaining Organization (NEA) 9,770, and the teachers' union came in last. Seeing the handwriting on the wall, the latter union voted to disband in November of 1963.[48]

The work stoppage in New York City and the subsequent election were more than isolated local events. New York's position as the communication and mass media capital of the United State meant that any event the least bit newsworthy would be enlarged to national proportions. A successful teacher strike in New York City would be talked about in every educational circle. By 1965 students at teachers' colleges in even the most remote locations would be reading about the AFT and discussing the issues of teacher strikes.

In 1960 Myron Lieberman, himself a member of the AFT, wrote a book entitled *The Future of Public Education*. After carefully analyzing the background of teacher organizations in the United States, Lieberman concluded by saying: "The foremost fact about teachers' organizations in the United States is their irrelevance in the national scene. Their futility in protecting the public interest and the legitimate vocational aspirations of teachers is a national tragedy, much more dangerous to our democratic institutions than the excessive power wielded by such familiar bogeys as 'Madison Avenue,' 'labor bosses,' 'captains of industry,' 'military high brass,' and the like. Because their organizations are weak, teachers are without power, power is exercised upon them to weaken and to corrupt public education." [49] The events in New York City of late 1960 and early 1961 successfully challenged Professor Lieberman's dismal description. Teacher power and organizational strength had become a reality.

Chapter 8

Historical Themes
1916 – 1961

General Themes

The birth of the American Federation of Teachers in 1916 and the subsequent trials it experienced helped to shape the philosophy of the organization. Born with the desire to advance the cause of the classroom teacher, it had fostered original hopes of influencing the National Education Association. When it found out that the NEA was not interested in having its teachers so vocal and active and that the NEA was hostile toward the labor union model, it withdrew. These realizations caused the federation to adopt a highly critical opinion of the NEA and its leadership—a view which became the source of many verbal assaults upon the association. Realizing that it would receive no assistance from the NEA, the AFT tied itself closer to organized labor. Such ties led to the increasing use of both the language and methods of the labor union. Such an affiliation proved to be a mixed blessing, however. Tied with organized labor, the AFT could use the state and local trades councils for their advantage in either organizing new locals or in influencing educational legislation or decision-making processes. The spirit of activism and reform, which was often associated with certain labor groups, was now the advantage of the AFT. Where unions were strong, the AFT locals usually prospered and were influencial.

But the close identification with labor was also a disadvantage. Education leaders and most teachers, regardless of their geographic location, were bred in a middle-class attitude that spurned union membership and usually envisioned the labor movement as a low-class phenomenon beneath the dignity of teachers. Labor unions were thought to be power hungry, without ethics, and grossly materialistic. In the smaller cities and many towns of America, there were no strong labor groups to aid AFT locals and influence local thinking. Where this was the case, the organizational efforts of the AFT were usually doomed to failure. This meant that the move to unionize teachers was dependent upon local labor strength and at the mercy of public attitudes toward labor. In attempting to court even a modicum of public acceptance the AFT entered the 1950s with a no-strike policy. Undoubtedly this was a carry-over from the public hostility toward strikes in general and strikes of public employees in particular that was the dominant attitude in the 1920s. The AFT never considered itself strong enough to change the no-strike policy until the fifties.[1]

In terms of educational issues, the association between the AFT and the AFL was usually an agreeable alliance. The AFT found the platform of the AFL easy to live with. Only once, that being the period prior to 1929, was there even small disagreement. The issue was the development of the junior high school. Most educators accepted the notion. Some unnionists saw it as an attempt to provide a terminal education for the lower class, which would have reserved high school only for the elite. Their fears undoubtedly grew out of suspicion that was engendered over the earlier debate on the establishment of separate vocational schools. That argument, despite the practical appeal, amounted to the promotion of a *de facto* class segregation. There is also evidence that many unionists saw intelligence testing as a similar conspiracy.[2] Whenever resolutions were formulated by AFT conventions, great care was given to offer only guarded support for such testing.

It was during the period of 1916–29 that the AFT adopted a social platform that remained consistent through the sixties. The major points the AFT fought for were:

1. Greater pay and better-working conditions for all teachers.

2. Equal pay for teachers regardless of race, creed, or sex.

3. Tenure provisions for teachers.

4. The granting of sabbatical leaves for teachers.

5. Equalizing the pay and benefits between elementary and secondary teachers.

6. The political freedom of teachers to belong to organized parties, participate in political activities, and espouse political candidates outside of their teaching duties.

7. The inclusion of teachers on boards of education.

8. Academic freedom for teachers to discuss national and international issues in the classroom setting.

9. Protection of women teachers from unfair hiring practices, dismissals due to marriage, and the failure of boards of education to provide maternal leaves.

10. Recognition of the special educational plight of the black American and his teacher. Promotion of equal pay and school facilities and recognition of the need to publicize the inequities of Negro education.

11. Gaining a role for the teacher in the process of school administration especially in matters pertaining to the profession or in the instruction of children.

12. The inclusion of laboring-class peoples on boards of education.

13. Condemnation of plans that would separate vocational programs of education from regular school settings.

14. Resistance to those groups who sought to use the schools to indoctrinate children, such as the National Association of Manufacturers, U.S. Chamber of Commerce, American Legion, and others.

15. Opposition to secondary school ROTC and military training courses.

16. Support for the workers' education movement.

17. Federal aid to education.

18. The establishment of a cabinet-level Department of Education

Perhaps all of these points were adequately summarized in Resolution No. 25 passed by the delegates to the AFT's fifteenth annual convention. Called "The Social Policy of the A.F.T.," it contained four statements:

1. That all restrictive regulations by Boards of Education on out-of-school activities of teachers be abolished as dangerous to the aim of public education.

2. That all teachers study the operation of the social forces in the world about them in order that they maintain that position of leadership which makes for an appreciation of their rightful place in the life of society.

3. That all teachers seek with unfailing persistence such levels of wages, such security of tenure, and such protection for old age or disability as is in keeping with the high standing of schools as social institutions.

4. That to achieve these ends teachers unite in professional organizations with the wildest social affiliations and with no subservience to any other organizations or vested interests.[3]

From the period of 1931 to 1935, many of these objectives had to be temporarily set aside. The realities of the depression caused the AFT to have to fight hard in order to simply hold the line against retrenchment. The struggle found the educators beset by powerful financial interests with the additional burden of having professional educators reluctant to take a firm stand. On the personal level, certainly a teacher who was hoping to retain his or her position even at a 10 percent pay cut, would have been dismayed by the failures of local people to support education and by picking up a local newspaper with a letter to the editor such as this one: "There are plenty of nice, fine American girls on the eligible list, over 5000 of them, waiting for the position of school teacher who would be glad to take the position at half the salary the present school teachers get. Why not let some of us graduates who have graduated with honors have a chance?" [4]

By 1929 the AFT had become an institution of crisis. Such a crisis complex is easily diagnosed and understood. Born into an uncaring world, weaned on the controversies of the First World War era, raised in a hostile environment, the AFT developed as a child of the streets into an adult who thrived on crisis. The AFT's whole cause for existence was based on the belief that crisis existed in the school system and that teachers needed to confront it. The AFT had had its best luck in organizing local unions of teachers when such teachers were faced with a dilemma that led them to believe that affiliation with organized labor and the adoption of militant union strategies would help to solve their problem. The small staff of the national and the general poverty of the federation helped this crisis-orientation to grow since it could best respond to specific crises rather than undertake more costly long-range planning and organizational campaigns. This crisis-complex was also the product of a union working hard just to survive. One writer characterized the AFT during the thirties as a "desert tribe, devoting most of its energies to a relentless struggle for existence." [5]

The AFT entered the period of the thirties with an established reputation as the most vocal of teacher groups in matters of teacher welfare and freedom. Said Lawrence Cremin about the NEA and the AFT: "The American Federation of Teachers, founded in 1916, was infinitely more vocal, and indeed more effective, in the defense of academic freedom and the campaign for adequate tenure laws in the several states." [6] In viewing the AFT from 1929 to the present, it becomes useful to see the events from the perspective of this crisis-complex and crisis-orientation.

1929–1941: The Middle Period

The period 1929 through 1941 was in many ways a search for identity for the AFT—a search that was in a large part successful. The federation entered the decade of the 1930s with a platform for education that was clearly delineated but without a program for its implementation. Never in the position to influence national policy, it had to work through locals for realization of different objectives. This was complicated by the fact that most AFT locals were organized by a minority of teachers within the system. Where the AFT locals were able to organize over one-half of a district's teachers, such as in Atlanta and Chicago, the locals were able to translate the national platform into local programs. But equally important was the fact that many locals of small size and percentage of a district's teachers were disproportionately successful in influencing local education. Efforts to realize the AFT's platform were probably aided by a high degree of unanimity of the general membership in regards to the national platform. Thus, identity was no particular problem. Although specific notions varied—the average member of the AFT knew what the organization stood for.

Members of the AFT were convinced that the NEA was unwilling to fight for teachers and education. This belief was based on both the publications and actions of this larger teacher association.

The printed record of the National Education Association was ambiguous. In its convention resolutions the NEA came across as liberal and vital. This is especially true in the resolutions passed by the NEA's Department of Classroom Teachers. In looking at these the author found that they favored a position similar to that of the AFT. Here is a list of some of their resolutions with the date they were offered indicated in parentheses:

1. Tenure for teachers, (1929)
2. A U.S. Department of Education, (1929)
3. Less clerical work for teachers, (1929)
4. Equal salary schedules, (1929)
5. A greater share for teachers in school policy-making, (1929)
6. Retirement programs, (1929)
7. Sabbatical leave for teachers, (1930)
8. A program for world peace, (1930)
9. Cumulative sick leave, (1931)
10. A stronger child labor law, (1931)
11. Establishment of credit unions for teachers, (1931)
12. Keeping teacher loads constant despite depression, (1931)
13. Opposition to teacher loyalty oaths, (1935)
14. Opposition to war propaganda and ROTC, (1935)
15. Support for kindergartens, (1936)

By simply looking at the resolutions of the AFT and the Department of Classroom Teachers one would have to conclude that there was little difference. In fact, one investigator, using this very methodology came to the conclusion that "No significant differences have existed in the basic, broad, education goals of the National Education Association and of the American Federation of Teachers." [7]

But most of the publications of the National Education Association counseled patience or low key activity such as committee study of problems. In calling for "A Program of Action" in 1934–35 the NEA suggested:

1. A vigorous campaign to insure the educational opportunity for every child. This calls for continued federal emergency aid in states and communities unable to maintain schools either because of general economic conditions or by drought.

2. A fearless insistence, backed by action, that teachers are entitled to adequate salaries, secure tenure, retirement allowances, and academic freedom.

3. Comprehensive studies of educational conditions thruout [sic] the country to determine the needs of the public schools.

4. Increased participation of the teaching profession in the solution of the social-economic problems of our day.

5. An aggressive campaign of publicity in newspapers, magazines, and over the air, designed to increase public appreciation of the schools.

6. A legislative service to provide state and local groups with up-to-the minute information regarding school legislation in the various states.

7. A professional JOURNAL for every teacher, second to none in inspiring content and progressive spirit.[8]

It would be difficult to be critical of the intent of such statements. What needs to be examined, however, are the many questions that emerge from such statements that are left unanswered: What is meant by a "vigorous campaign"? How can teachers gain "increased participation"? Who shall undertake or coordinate the "aggressive campaign of publicity"? In short, the most militant statements are left terribly vague and underdeveloped. What does come through clear is the call for "comprehensive studies," "legislative service," and a "journal for every teacher."

Internal Problems

The largest group of problems facing the AFT in its history were internal problems. The budget was always too small. There was simply not enough money to run a large enough national office, throw an impressive convention, publish a highly regarded journal, fill an adequate defense fund, and place organizers in the field. The heart of the matter in the early decades was dues—they were too low. In an early attempt to attract membership, it was decided to keep dues low. This decision proved to be nearly fatal. In 1929 Secretary-Treasurer Hanson reported to the convention that the average contribution to the union's organizational work was fourteen cents per member per year.[9] As late as 1946 the dues schedule shown below indicates the reason for a shallow treasury.[10]

Salary	Monthly Dues	Yearly Dues
Under $1,000	$.10	$1.20
1,000–1,500	.15	1.80
1,500–2,000	.20	2.40
2,000–2,500	.25	3.00
2,500–3,000	.30	3.60
3,000–3,500	.35	4.20
Over 3,500	.40	4.80

Another grave internal problem was the regionalism that continually cropped up. It could be argued that the causes of such feelings had roots other than geography but for the participants geography became a convenient category. The founding of the AFT in 1916 was largely the joint enterprise of New York and Chicago, and by 1970 these were still the power blocs, although each had expanded their spheres of influence. The Chicago bloc had always been more associated with the American Federation of Labor. Their union philosophy was what some labor historians would describe as "Gomperism" or "pure and simplism." That is, they tended to be associated with bread-and-butter issues rather than social concerns. The New York bloc, on the other hand, tended to be more cosmic and ideological in their interests and less interested in the AFL.

As the federation grew in the 1930s each of these two blocs extended its influence. Most of the AFT's locals in the Midwest found themselves in agreement with Chicago more than New York. The larger locals in Detroit, Cleveland, and Gary were often in Chicago's camp. The local in Atlanta provided a special case. During the era of the 1930s, the Atlanta local was important since it had the highest percentage of that school district's teachers in its membership. Atlanta was the first local to achieve 100 percent membership. Since 100 percent membership was quite naturally the goal of every local and since Atlanta was a relatively large city its importance was great. It provided much of the early national leadership in the AFT and became a key element in organizing school districts in the South. But Atlanta was a southern city and as such rather conservative. It often found itself anchoring Chicago in squabbles with New York. The New York bloc gathered as its allies most of the WPA teachers organized in the thirties, many of the Washington, D.C. teachers, and several of the small locals whose nucleus of leadership was ultraliberal. AFT locals organized from 1935 often found themselves more sympathetic with New York. This seems to be due to the fact that all locals organized after 1935 were without question developed during a period of extreme turbulence and confrontation and were attracted to the conspicuous militancy shown by New York.

A much smaller issue that was related to regionalism was an undertone of religious differences. It is difficult to document this satisfactorily since no official papers or minutes would reflect such differences. But within the personal correspondence of Selma Borchardt appears a few brief references to such a controversy. In his 1938 investigation of Chicago, George Counts pointed out that Margaret Haley's organization of Local No. 1 was accomplished through the efforts of a core of Catholic teachers. Counts suggests that it was this Catholic identification that kept Local No. 1 from ever becoming the union for all teachers.[11] In the latter part of the 1930s there was an informal Catholic caucus organized within the AFT. The locus of this effort was in the Boston local under the presidency of Mary Cadigan. The purpose of this caucus was to promote the cause of federal aid to both public and nonpublic education.

A significant percentage of the New York local was always Jewish—at least by ethnic background if not by religious practice. Placing these two facts together, that is, the existence of an identifiable Catholic and Jewish element, one can only speculate on the effect that these had in trying to organize small midwestern and western teachers.

The religious question never blossomed into a floor debate at the convention or made the columns of the *American Teacher*.

Evidence of its existence comes from interviews with the participants. Apparently it was a source of underlying friction. The only public awareness of religion and the AFT came in the 1960s when some militant blacks in New York City, frustrated by the UFT's opposition to decentralization in Oceanhill-Brownsville, charged the UFT with protecting the jobs of Jewish principals and teachers.

Communication

The problems of communication faced the AFT on all levels: national office to local unions; local unions to other local unions; national office to the leadership; AFT officers to other AFT officers; and the AFT to the parent AFL.

Communication from the AFT national office to the local union was especially critical. Locals were often organized by field organizers or regional vice-presidents whose major work was in just such a process. But once they were organized, the locals could at best hope for only infrequent visits from national office representatives. This became an important problem for those locals organized in communities where labor was not especially strong and where the distance was great from the regional vice-president. Let us suppose, hypothetically, that a group of teachers in a southern Florida community might have shown interest in the AFT in the 1930s. The regional vice-president was in Atlanta, Georgia—a goodly distance by train and bus, especially for a regional vice-president who was a full-time classroom teacher. The number of visits such a person might be able to make over the Christmas and Easter vacations would be understandably limited. Or, again hypothetically, a group of teachers were interested in AFT affiliation in Texas. During the latter 1930s this responsibility would have fallen to Vice-President Paul W. Preisler, a full-time professor at the Washington University Medical School in St. Louis. About the only regular communication that a local could hope to receive from the national office was notification of dues assessment. This placed an additional burden on the *American Teacher* since it was expected to aid in this problem by printing notifications from the national office, reporting the convention proceedings and resolutions to those members who did not attend, and, in general, letting the membership know what was going on in Chicago.

Communication from one local federation to another was likewise difficult. The basic organization of the American Federation of Teachers was such that the individual locals were to be the focal point of the structure rather than having the national as a capstone. This being the case, it was up to the individual local to organize its own programs of action based on local conditions. In the stronger locals this was no particular problem and local leadership was continually cultivated and utilized. But in a small struggling local the maintenance of successful local-action programs was often beyond hope. Although better vehicles for communication may not have saved many of such struggling locals, it might have aided all locals in knowing what other locals were facing, what their programs were, and what original ideas were being formulated. This would have assisted locals in anticipating problems, utilizing the successful schemes of others, and sharing in local victories. The only extent that this was done was through the pages of the *American Teacher*. But the allowance given the locals in terms of space was too small. The larger locals, like Chicago, Atlanta, and New York, had enough space. But news from small locals was relegated to the inside front cover or a specific section sometimes entitled: "With the Locals." Here two short paragraphs were allotted to such news items. In reading the issues of the *American Teacher* this writer can testify to the high probability of skipping over such sections with only a cursory glance.

The officers of the AFT were located all over the country. The scheme was to have them closer to various geographic regions, this was important. The result, however, was to have the most important policy-making and policy-executing body cast to the winds. The executive council did get together a few days before the summer convention and again over the Christmas break. This was about as much as could be expected from working teachers. But the summer council meeting was usually absorbed by making last minute convention arrangements and determining the agenda. The Christmas session of the executive council was given to deciding what convention resolutions meant in terms of administrative planning. The continual shortage of money left the executive council to contact each other through the mail—a process which under-standably consumed a great deal of time.

Communications between the national office and the president of the federation was equally irregular. The organization of the AFT made the president the most important figure. The secretary-treasurer was a full-time paid officer but was faced with duties of running the business end of the operation and in no way resembled the executive-secretary of the National Education Association such as J. W. Crabtree or Willard Givens, who had a lot of policy-formulating power and was the chief officer of that association. The president of the AFT was its chief officer. During the 1920s when Charles B. Stillman of Chicago was president, the communication problem was minimized. In the mid-thirties Jerome Davis was able to take up residency in Chicago. But in the early 1930s with the presidency of Henry R. Linville and again in the late 1930s with the presidency of George S. Counts, these men were in New York City while the secretary-treasurer and the national office were in Chicago. Using the mail to coordinate a nationwide operation was as difficult as the prospect suggests. This also helps to account for the limited effectiveness of AFT committees. Committees were organized to look into national educational issues, but the work load was squarely upon the shoulders of a committee chairman. For a breakdown of the 1940 national committees and their chairmen, see the example below.[12]

Committee	Chairman
State Federations	E. Glenn Baxter
National Educational Policies Commission	Lillian Herstein
Pension and Retirement	Florence Rood
Academic Freedom	Alice Hanson
Social and Economic Trends	Frances Comfort
Vocational Education	Samuel Barth
Public Relations and Publicity	Hazel Murray
Insurance and Credit Unions	Maurice Crew
Taxation and School Finance	Samuel Greenfield
Workers Education	Eleanor Coit

These committees, while certainly important, never published reports with national impact.

Communications did improve with the advent of the fifties. This was due to at least three reasons: the centralization of the national office, the growth of state federations, and the general improvement in travel and telephone service. The centralization that took place with the presidency of Carl J. Megel has been described. Its impact was significant.

The growth of state federations was also a critical factor. State federations of the AFT in the 1970s now employ one or more full-time persons and a secretarial staff to service the locals of the state. The state federations make real sense due to increased state involvement in public education. But the real strength is the day-to-day servicing function of periodically visiting the locals, getting to know local officers and problems, and advising the teachers as to solutions for their local problems. With the growth of collective bargaining in education, the role of the state federation officer in serving as a consultant and advisor has been fundamental to a profession that has no training or experience in this area.

The general improvement in telephone and air service has also been fundamental to the improvement of communications.

Crisis Orientation

As previously pointed out, the American Federation of Teachers entered the decade of the 1930s with a crisis orientation. This orientation continues. Being able to respond only to the most pressing problems and attracting a membership through such crisis situations proved to be more problematic than beneficial. In talking with this writer, Paul W. Preisler, a part-time AFT organizer in the mid-thirties and regional vice-president in the late 1930s, characterized his experience in organizing locals as following a general pattern. Usually, he pointed out, a local grievance grew out of the case of one individual teacher—usually very popular with the other teachers—who was being threatened by the board of education with the loss of his job. This leads to several critical questions: What happens if the issue is resolved to the satisfaction of the grieved party? What happens if the grieved person leaves the district? What happens when the particular grievance fades into time? The answer to all of these questions is the same—the local dissolves. This is what often happened and helps to account for the amazingly short-life-span of many locals even up to today. The AFT must share the blame for much of this. For in addition to experiencing difficulties in maintaining locals due to lack of proper communication, the AFT declared and nurtured the idea that it was best equipped to handle emergencies and crisis situations. In so doing they often received the first call for help but found themselves ignored after the dissipation of local emergencies or by teachers in communities who never quite reached the breaking point. This view of the AFT as having plans for fighting wars but no strategies for peace was engendered by the *American Teacher* who quite naturally hammered away on the small victories and stunning defeats felt by the federation in its formative years.

In trying to account for the failure of many locals, Secretary-Treasurer Irvin Kuenzli sent to the locals a questionnaire in the fall of 1939 which asked the respondents to evaluate the reasons for local failures. The return replies indicated the following reasons for failure shown here in descending order of importance.

1. Lack of leadership in locals.
2. Chartering locals which are too small to function effectively.
3. Neglect of locals after they have been chartered.
4. Fear of losing positions—on the part of teachers.
5. Failure of International Union to educate new locals in effective methods of organizing and operating local unions.
6. Opposition of Superintendents of schools and other officials.
7. Organizing locals in communities where there is no labor movement.
8. Lack of state federations of teacher unions.
9. "Red scares" and other propaganda of anti-Labor forces.
10. Failure of locals to concentrate on actual class-room teacher problems.
11. Teachers drop out of the Union when their objectives are accomplished.
12. Locals are destroyed by reactionary or anti-labor political machines which come into power.

13. Organizing locals for some immediate purpose such as passing a tax levy or securing a new salary schedule.

14. Dues are too high in proportion to those of non-union teachers' associations.

15. Lack of cooperation of local labor bodies.

16. Failure of locals immediately to solve all problems "over night."

17. Controversies and political bickering in locals.

18. Too much politics in International Unions.

19. Local union officers "bought-off" by promises of advancement of increases in salary.

20. Rapid turn-over in the teaching profession itself.

21. Admitting to membership persons who are not really teachers.[13]

This crisis orientation continues today. The American Federation of Teachers has become action personified. Its publications scream at the reader to contribute to the militancy fund, wear the militancy button, and to press for greater teacher rights. The picutres of the *American Teacher* magazine were characterized throughout the 1960s and early 1970s with this spirit of militancy. Pictures of President David Selden entering jail and leaving jail for violation of court injunctions were often featured. Similar pictures of the UFT's Albert Shanker were shown. The pages abound with photographic evidence of pickets and protest. The negative consequence of all this is the branding of the AFT as a one issue organization—teacher welfare.

Liberality

The position that the AFT took on the Negro, the woman, and academic freedom did prove to be positions that were important throughout the history of the federation. The AFT cannot be questioned in its sincere espousal of such positions, and it often held them at a time when to do so was unpopular and very likely detrimental to its own development. But the federation held to such views and can now look back with pride. It has lived to see its position on women teachers become the conventional wisdom. Its definition of academic freedom and the support of such a definition was important in seeing such tenets survive for the public-school teacher during the turbulent period of McCarthyism. In 1954 the Supreme Court of the United States ruled in favor of ending school segregation. The victory was given to the National Association for the Advancement of Colored People as it rightly should have been. But those who knew the evolution of the case gave witness to the importance of AFT support in the long struggle.

The Character of the AFT

Critics of the American Federation of Teachers have pointed out that the federation has failed to come to grips with specific school issues. They can show, for example, that the Progressive Education Association was much more influential in the field of curriculum and teaching methodology. The AFT has been relatively silent on these issues, making only general statements about the curriculum reflecting democracy. The many committees of the National Education Association were much more successful than AFT committees in offering advice on a wide range of contemporary school issues, and in publishing such advice in highly palatable forms and in giving such publications wide circulation. Certainly the NEA's Department of Superintendence played a larger role than did the AFT in formulating broad educational policies. Such criticisms of the American Federation of Teachers are basically valid.

Any rebuttal that can be mustered in favor of the AFT must hinge on the question of priorities. The editorial stance and content of the articles of the *American Teacher* make it obvious that the AFT considered that the teacher's welfare and freedom were the most important issues. It saw the teacher as the central point in the massive educational system. Working for the realization of material benefits and freedom, both personal and academic, became its focus. To criticize it for doing little else begs several questions: Could the AFT have existed in trying to compete with the NEA's Department of Superintendence or Educational Policies Commission in becoming the policy voice of education? Did it have the financial means and resources to undertake curricular research and reformation?

Didn't it run the risk of spreading its all-too-meager resources too thin? The AFT believed that the key to reform in education was in creating a teaching profession that was well paid, informed, secure, powerful, and proud. This it saw as the first step. It could be argued that the AFT took no further action simply because step one was absorbing its entire energies and has yet to be completed.

The Significance of the Purges

The most important thing to happen to the AFT in the thirties and forties was the purge of three of its locals on grounds that grew out of communism. This activity was certainly central from 1935 onward and it leads to several legitimate questions: Was communism a real danger? What were the practical reasons, if any, for voting out Locals Nos. 5, 192, and 537? How just were the charges and proceedings against the three locals? What happened to Local No. 5 in New York City after the purge?

Certainly George Counts and the executive council that was elected in 1940 believed that communism was a threat to the teachers' union. At the time, their judgment was based on reports given to the council by John Connors who had attended the New York State Communist party convention and returned with his report that said that the party members were bragging about having already made inroads into the AFT and that they controlled the New York Local No. 5. The executive council was also very much aware of the contemporary affairs. At the actual point of expulsion, the amount of documentary evidence that the AFT's executive council could put its hands on was limited. Subsequent events, however, gave them documentation for its feelings. In the 1953–54 hearings of the House Un-American Activities Committee, several things happened. Testimony by several teachers, former members of both the AFT and the Communist party, indicated a link in the affiliations. The historian Daniel J. Boorstin testified that he was a member of the Communist party from about 1938 to 1939. During that time he was also a member of the Harvard Teachers Union and indicated that there had been talk about the importance of education and the necessity of developing a Communist position.[14] Testimony by Wendall H. Furry, a physicist at Harvard from 1934 onward and member of the Harvard Teachers Union, took the fifth amendment on the question of Communist party membership, which whetted the appetite of the committee.[15] Testimony of Granville Hicks, who admitted Communist party membership from 1934 to 1939 had also been a member of the Harvard Teachers Union.[16] The most complete testimony regarding communism and the teachers' union given at this session was from Robert Gorham Davis, who had been a professor at Harvard from 1933 to 1943.[17] The heart of his testimony is contained in the following examination by the committee's council, beginning with questions concerning his particular activities in the local Communist cell.

Mr. Tavenner.   Will you state how frequently the group met?

Mr. Davis.   During the academic year I think it was once a week. Certainly it was as often as twice a week.

Mr. Tavenner.   Where were these meetings held?

Mr. Davis.   In the apartments of the members.

Mr. Tavenner.   What was the nature of the business that was conducted at the meetings?

Mr. Davis.   It consisted, as I remember it, of three activities: First, discussing the policies of organizations to which we belonged, like the teachers' union, or the front organizations, and determining upon the role that the individual member should play in those organizations; secondly, the question of Marxist education—organizing study groups to which teachers would be invited; and, thirdly, various fund-raising activities for united front organizations or for the party itself.

Mr. Tavenner.   Let us consider each of those functions in the order in which you named them. Now what was the policy of the Communist party with reference to your activities in outside organizations?

Mr. Davis.   We were to assume positions of leadership so that their policies would be as close to the policies desired by the Communist part as possible.

Mr. Tavenner.   How was that information transmitted to you as to what organizations you were to infiltrate?

Mr. Davis.   I think it hardly needed to be transmitted, because our immediate concern was with the teachers' union and with organizations like the (American) League for Peace and Democracy.

Mr. Tavenner.   It may be well at this point for you to give us the names of all the organizations which your cell or group of the Communist part infiltrated or endeavored to infiltrate.

MR. DAVIS. The so-called front organizations change so rapidly that it is hard for me to remember them. But during the period in which I was active we were concerned dominantly with the teachers' union.

MR. TAVENNER. Was that merely a local union at Harvard, or was that a national union?

MR. DAVIS. It was the national union affiliated with the American Federation of Teachers, which belonged to the AFL.

MR. TAVENNER. Do you recall what instructions were given you by the Communist party, or any functionaries of the Communist party, with regard to that organization?

MR. DAVIS. I think we were left pretty much to ourselves as far as the local organization is concerned, because we all read the party press and were aware of what the general line was. We got the various publications of the teachers' union—

MR. KEARNEY. But isn't it also true that from time to time you received instructions from national headquarters on your procedure?

MR. DAVIS. Oh, yes. As I say, persons like Frankfield sat in with us, but that was on the whole to educate us because the party felt we were liberals and progressives and we were not thoroughly grounded enough—not thoroughly disciplined enough—so that, as I recall these conversations, they were of a fairly general nature since the persons who came to visit us were not very well informed about the teachers' union itself. On a national scale the situation was different. There was a Communist party faction which did receive—

MR. KEARNEY. Pardon me. Was Frankfield a member of the teaching profession?

MR. DAVIS. No. So far as I know he had no connection with it.

MR. TAVENNER. You were familiar with the teachings of Lenin on the subject of the activity of teachers and what they should endeavor to do, I assume?

MR. DAVIS. I have seen a passage quoted often since. I don't recall it from those days.

MR. TAVENNER. I have before me volume 23 of Lenin and I find at page 499 this statement: "But today the chief task of those members of the teaching profession who have taken their stand with the International and the Soviet Government is to work for the creation of a wider and, as nearly as possible, an all-embracing teachers' union."

MR. DAVIS. Yes, that is correct.

MR. TAVENNER. And again on page 500 there is this statement: "Your union should now become a broad teachers' trade-union embracing vast numbers of teachers; a union which will resolutely take up its stand on the Soviet platform and the struggle for socialism by means of a dictatorship of the proletariat." You are aware of those purposes and of that thinking of the Communist party?

MR. DAVIS. Yes.

MR. MOULDER. Was that book referring to the teachers in our educational institutions, or just as representatives?

MR. TAVENNER. This has reference to the teachers' trade-unions throughout the world and not any one particular country or any one segment of the country.

MR. DAVIS. Of what date are those passages? Lenin was not speaking of the United States, of course.

MR. VELDE. We hope not.

MR. TAVENNER. What activity did your group engage in which might be said to have carried out the policy as expressed by Lenin of assisting in the organization of teachers' trade-union movements which would be adaptable to the purposes of the Soviet Union?

MR. DAVIS. We worked very hard to build up the teachers' union in Harvard and to build up teachers' unions generally, and we did this with a comparatively clear conscience because our objectives, our immediate objectives, were to improve teaching conditions, raise salaries, and so on; but also obviously we wished teachers to take the same position that we took on public questions.

MR. TAVENNER. Was there a local of that organization at Harvard?

MR. DAVIS. Yes.

MR. TAVENNER. Did it have a name?

MR. DAVIS. It was called the Cambridge Union of University Teachers, as I recall.

MR. TAVENNER. Will you explain the manner in which the Communist members of your group functioned within the teachers' union, your local teachers' union?

MR. DAVIS. We usually discussed before a meeting what policies we would urge at the meeting; and whenever there were elections we would decide in advance what candidates we would propose or support.

MR. TAVENNER. And the purpose of that was to make certain that the plans of your group were carried out because the vast majority of members of your local were non-Communist?

MR. DAVIS. Yes.

MR. TAVENNER. Can you recall any specific instance?

MR. DAVIS. No, I can't, but they would have to do again with the national political situation at the time. The Communists supported the

New Deal, supported the Roosevelt administration until the Russian pact of 1939; and many of the measures which they supported were, I think, good measures—against anti-Semitism; against fascism; for minority rights.

Mr. Tavenner. Did your group of Communist party members endeavor to control the selection of delegates from the local teachers' union to national conventions?

Mr. Davis. Yes.

Mr. Tavenner. Of what district was the local at Harvard a member?

Mr. Davis. The Massachusetts Teachers Union—whatever its title was.

Mr. Clardy. Can I interject here? Were you successful in your efforts to obtain that control in the selection of delegates?

Mr. Davis. During that period, yes.

Mr. Clardy. Was that because you had been a cohesive body, knew where you were going, and worked hard at it?

Mr. Davis. And also, because, as I say, the policies we supported were policies supported by many liberals and progressives at the time.

Mr. Clardy. And you had the support of many other people who would probably have rebelled at communism as a word or party?

Mr. Davis. I am not even sure the last is true, because many were willing to work with Communists in the united front at the time.

Mr. Clardy. Even though they knew they were working with Commies?

Mr. Davis. Yes.

Mr. Doyle. What year was that please?

Mr. Davis. That was between 1937 and 1939.

Mr. Clardy. We are talking now about those in the teaching profession particularly?

Mr. Davis. Yes.

Mr. Clardy. You understand that?

Mr. Davis. They would have said, though, they objected strongly to certain Communist policies, they felt the good ends justified the means of collaboration at that time.

Mr. Schere. I believe you said, Professor, that the group, party, at that time opposed anti-Semitism?

Mr. Davis. Yes. That's why I was particularly interested in the position of Louis Harap.

Mr. Clardy. I don't follow you there.

Mr. Davis. Because, as editor of the magazine, whatever it may be called, *Jewish Affairs*, I believe, he is now defending the Prague trials, contending that they are not anti-Semitic.

Mr. Clardy.   Do you happen to have a copy of that available? I would like to see one.

Mr. Davis.   No, I don't.

Mr. Clardy.   If you could obtain one and send it to me, I would appreciate it. We may have it in the files, but I would like to see a recent issue.

Mr. Tavenner.   Now, will you proceed, please, to describe the method by which you endeavored to control the selection of delegates to the district and national convention of the teachers' union?

Mr. Davis.   One reason why Communists were successful was because in these organizations all service was voluntary. The teachers were very busy; trips were expensive, and very frequently those who offered to go were asked to go because no other persons were available; and if a member of the Communist party offered to go his offer was usually accepted, if he offered to go to a national convention.

Mr. Tavenner.   And were those offers made as a result of a decision by your Communist party group that they should be made?

Mr. Davis.   Yes. Again, if persons were willing to go, even within the Communist group, there was not immediate pressure or orders which had to be carried out. That is, the members of this group still retained a great many of their liberal attitudes and were handled, on the whole, with kid gloves by the officials.

Mr. Tavenner.   Did you attend a district or state or national convention of the teachers' union?

Mr. Davis.   I went to two national conventions.

Mr. Tavenner.   Will you state whether or not Communist party influences were brought to bear on the conventions that you attended?

Mr. Davis.   There was always a Communist party caucus.

Mr. Moulder.   What years—

Mr. Tavenner.   Describe that—

Mr. Moulder.   What years were those?

Mr. Davis.   These were in the academic years 1937–38 and 1938–39. The convention I remember most clearly was at Buffalo, and it occurred just at the time of the pact in late August 1939.

Mr. Clardy.   Witness, are you sufficiently acquainted with the facts as of today to tell us whether or not the same techniques are being followed today?

Mr. Davis.   Oh, I'm sure that can be taken for granted. The Communists always meet and consult together.

Mr. Clardy.   And the things you've been describing as taking place in the thirties, in your judgment, are taking place today?

Mr. Davis.   Yes, except that the situation probably requires much more secrecy. These activities were comparatively open at that time.

Mr. Clardy. You think there is more of an underground now than there was at that time?

Mr. Davis. Yes, and a much smaller one. And I should like to interject at this point the fact at the present time among teachers the influence of Communists is very slight because the times have changed and because the teachers have been so shocked by the events in the Soviet Union in the last eight years.[18]

Another important witness for the government was Bella Dodd, who had served as the legislative representative for the New York local and was considered to be an influential advisor to President Hendley of Local No. 5. Both in testimony before investigatory agencies and in her book, *School of Darkness,* she admitted active Communist party membership and said she was interested, as a Communist, in gaining a foothold in the American Federation of Teachers. Although the complete reliability of Bella Dodd might be questioned, it would seem accurate to say that there were Communist party members in the AFT and that some of them entertained the notion of controlling federation policy. History has seemingly verified the fears of the executive council in 1941.

The practical reasons for ridding the AFT of the three locals were abundantly apparent to the 1940 executive council of the AFT. To begin with the AFL was putting pressure on the AFT. The AFL could not vote out individual locals of the AFT, but it could vote out the entire national union. The steps taken against those unions in the AFL who had worked with the CIO made it increasingly clear that they were ready to tolerate little unconformity. It was also obvious that the AFT needed the AFL. The AFL had made up its mind—Local No. 5 had to go.

A second practical reason concerned organizational efforts. By 1940 the press of the United States was acutely aware of the leftist elements in the AFT. Through the press the unorganized teachers were reading about the charges of communism in the federation. This became ammunition for any competing teacher organization or enemy of the federation. It seemed to many of the AFT leaders that quick, spectacular, and decisive steps were going to have to be taken if the federation could entertain hopes for national growth.

An analysis of the charges offered against Locals Nos. 5, 192, and 537 and an evaluation of the procedure used against these three locals has led this writer to conclude that the public charges against them were not sufficient for expulsion but that the procedures employed were satisfactorily democratic. The actual charges against Locals Nos. 537 and 192 were especially weak and probably could not have stood on their own feet if it were not for the chain of events described in this book. The charges against Local No. 5, while more extensive, seem to this writer to be adequately rebutted in statements made by Local No. 5. The key issue, communism, could only be skirted due to lack of documentary evidence, but it was clear to the voting membership that this was the crux of the matter. The agreement between the general membership and the executive council as to the guilt of the locals was proven in the vote. In terms of procedure, some criticisms could be leveled against the executive council, but very few. The only charges of validity stemmed from the accusation by spokesmen of Local No. 5 that they were not given enough time to construct their case from the time the first charges were issued in December of 1940 until February of 1941.

After being voted out of the American Federation of Teachers, Local No. 5 in New York remained independent for a couple of years. In September of 1943 Michael Quill, president of the Transport Workers Union, welcomed them into the CIO as Local No. 555 of the State, County, and Municipal Workers. Said Quill: "You are coming home when you join the C.I.O." [19] They took a great deal of interest in the CIO and the leadership of No. 555 was active in the National Educator's Committee for the Re-Election of Franklin Roosevelt in 1944 and in the campaign for Henry Wallace in 1948. [20] During the same period of time the Teachers' Guild, which had been formed by Henry R. Linville in 1935, became the New York local of the AFT. In 1960, the guild joined forces with the Secondary School Teachers Association to form the United Federation of Teachers. [21] In November of 1960, the United Federation of Teachers of the AFT had its first strike. This was critical for both the UFT and former Local No. 5, for the success of the strike established the UFT as *the* teachers' union.

The association of the American Federation of Teachers with communism was difficult to erase from the public's mind. During World War II, the AFT formed a Commission on Education and the Post-War World. In 1943 the commission published a book entitled *America, Russia, and the Communist Party*.[22] It took a very firm stand against communism. It warned its readers that Communists possessed

the power of a disciplined, conspiratorial group, operating, on the principle that the end justifies the means and having its objectives and its strategy authoritatively determined by centralized leadership, . . . They are trained in the art of public speaking, in the mastery of the tricks of parliamentary tactics, in the ways of delaying and speeding up action in public meetings, in the methods of wearing down opponents and of confusing issues, in the techniques of creating division, particularly by the introduction of resolutions cunningly devised for the purposes, and generally in an ever developing variety of means by which the procedures of democratic group deliberation and decision can be manipulated by a minority in order to attain predetermined ends.[23]

The AFT's swift action against the locals in Los Angeles, San Francisco, and Seattle is evidence of its determination to wipe out the specter of communism.

Just in case the public needed further reminding, the House Un-American Activities Committee published a pamphlet in 1949 called: "100 Things You Should Know about Communism and Education." In a series of turgid questions and answers the pamphlet unfolded:

1. *What is Communism?*
   A conspiracy to conquer and rule the world by any means, legal or illegal, in peace or in war.
2. *Is it Aimed at Me?*
   Right between your eyes.

. . . .

95. *Are Communists very active in teachers' unions?*
   Yes. For instance, the American Federation of Teachers (A.F.L.) in 1941 expelled three of its New York City teachers' unions [*sic*] with 8,000 members, because the locals were Communist-controlled.[24]

The Impact of the American Federation of Teachers

In analyzing the many problems of the American Federation of Teachers and in trying to assess the relative effectiveness of the organization, it must be pointed out that the total membership has always been small. As one student of the AFT has pointed out, "A.F.T. membership in 1940 represented only 3 percent of the entire teaching profession." [25] This same person, in an article about the AFT in the thirties, finishes by saying: "Nevertheless, if the conclusion reached by Professor H. K. Beale in his book *Are American Teachers Free?* is accurate, that the overwhelming majority of teachers during the 1930's were really unaware of or indifferent to the conditions of their profession, then perhaps the outstanding feature of the A.F.T. during this period is not that it failed to secure the widespread support of the teachers in the U.S. but that it succeeded in activating as many as it did." [26] Measuring the impact of the American Federation of Teachers is admittedly difficult. But the evidence seems to show that:

1. Among teachers the AFT was influential only in those communities where a local federation has been organized and where the labor movement is strong.

2. The influence of the AFT among professors of education is small. There has been union activity in other colleges and universities but generally not among the members of the education departments. During the period, however, the small number of professors of education who were interested in the AFT made many contributions in terms of service and publication.

3. The singular strength of the AFT in influencing state or national legislatures has been small, but in a collective sense effective, since the AFT could usually speak in the name of organized labor on education issues.

4. The AFT has been regarded as an ally of most organizations of liberal persuasion, and its support in matters concerning national education is often sought.

Chapter 9

Epilogue: The AFT
1961 – Present

Growth of Teacher Militancy

The ecstasies of the successful collective bargaining elections in New York City were short-lived. The fact that teacher groups could be victorious in pressing their demands was encouraging but also sobering. The more reflective and somber sort took pause to realize that a whole new era of teacher-board and teacher-community relations had arrived. Power, if it was to be used wisely, must be used to support well-planned and worthy ideals. Teachers, not used to such power, had to develop future-mindedness as well as present-mindedness if their new role was to be effective.

The concept of power was probably less important to the ordinary classroom teacher than the daily reality that was a consequence of power. The opportunity to teach in better-equipped rooms, the chance to exercise one's professional judgment in matters of curriculum and instruction, and the new incentives that resulted from the realization that salaries would be improving gave new vitality to the teaching profession. This vitality fastened a new spirit of optimism among teachers and gave renewed life to the idea of the school as a fundamental agency in the process of social change.

But this new possession of power and vitality by those few teachers who had gained it through the process of collective bargaining in the sixties also served as a grim reminder to the

bulk of American teachers who continued to labor for inadequate pay in unprofessional environments that they must take
action. This sense of desperation drove a significant number of
teachers to militantness.

The sixties might be known in the future as the militant decade. It began with black militancy and ended with the beginnings of environmental and consumer militancy. Sandwiched
somewhere in between was teacher militancy. The causes and
consequences of teacher activism are difficult to assess. Some
say the increased percentage of men into the profession was a
major causal factor. Others point to the model of civil disobedi-
ence advocated and carried out by Dr. Martin Luther King, Jr.,
and his associates as being influential in convincing teachers
that social policy could be altered in public protest. Still others
point to the National Defense Education Act of 1958 as serving
just to whet the appetite of educators and igniting within them
new hope for financial support to cause needed change in education. Whatever the causes, unrest and activism among
teachers spread from urban centers to small towns.

This new spirit of activism was to be divisive for the National Education Association. A growing discontent among
classroom teachers within the NEA surfaced. The result was internal feuding, political manipulation, and general confusion.
What was clear to the NEA was its need to reappraise its longtime opposition to collective bargaining, teacher power, political participation, and work stoppages.

This new spirit of activism was ready-made for the American Federation of Teachers. The time was ripe for new organizational efforts. The times had final finally caught up with the
philosophy of the teachers' union. By 1972 the AFT had nearly
250,000 teachers as members. This represented about 12 percent of the 2,063,000 teachers in America, and the membership
was growing.[1]

The Crumbling Détente with Organized Labor

As the AFT moves into the decade of the seventies, its relationship with organized labor needs to be once again reex-
amined. By the 1960s the AFL-CIO had grown stodgy. Its

slowness in championing the cause of racial equality, its refusal to speak out against the war in Vietnam, and its growing cooperation with the "establishment" caused suspicion among the ranks of the liberals.

The union movement has been successful. Despite local inequities, the American blue-collar worker is enjoying unrivaled prosperity. High wages, reasonable working conditions, and increasing welfare benefits have made the ordinary worker feel rather contented. The war to establish the power of the workers has been won. With this new prosperity, the blue-collar worker has cast his lot with the established order of things. The militant spirit of the thirties that caused the worker to think about social issues as well as material benefits is dead. Early in the presidential campaign of 1968, pollster Louis Harris reported that 24 percent of the members of American unions supported George Wallace. Even though the political arm of the AFL-CIO fought this trend and was able by election time to lower it to 12 percent, it was only a short run reversal. By December of 1968, Harris was reporting that 70 percent of the people classified themselves as either conservative or middle of the road.[2]

Late in the 1960s, a reaction to this new state of being emerged. The conflict between President Meany and Vice-President Walter Reuther reached the breaking point with Reuther withdrawing with his United Auto Workers from the AFL-CIO. This was significant to the AFT since the UAW had been instrumental in aiding organizational efforts among New York City teachers by providing funds. The loss of the UAW also meant the loss of Walter Reuther, perhaps the greatest friend the teachers ever had. Reuther's ties to the AFT were close. He was a frequent speaker at AFT functions and his wife May, a schoolteacher, was a member of the Detroit Federation of Teachers, Local No. 231.[3] His departure was a blow to teacher unionism.

The relations between the AFT and the parent AFL-CIO were strained on several fronts. The war was one issue. The AFT gave consideration to the war and even had a national referendum on the war in 1971. Although the results of this referendum were too inconclusive to publish, it was obvious that a significant portion of the AFT membership was opposed to the war, despite the position of George Meany.

Another issue was politics. The AFL had strongly supported Democrats John F. Kennedy in 1960, Lyndon B. Johnson in 1964, and Hubert H. Humphrey in 1968 for president of the United States. Suddenly in 1972 the AFL executive council, hammered into line by a determined Meany, refused to support any national candidate and instructed the national unions to do likewise. This advice was stoutly rejected by the American Federation of Teachers when at its convention of 1972 it strongly supported its former member, George McGovern, for president.

More important than the growing rift between the AFT and the AFL-CIO is the broader question of blue-collar support for public schools. The ability of local school districts at passing either bond issues or tax referenda has diminished to the point where over three-quarters of them fail. Of concern to the teachers, who depend upon the passage of such measures to maintain conditions and salaries, is the realization that they have lost the support of local labor. A national public opinion poll showed that in 1971 52 percent of those questioned were against new taxes while only 40 percent said they would approve if a need could be shown. A more-refined analysis showed that those favorable did not include the working class.[4]

The strike experience of certain AFT locals has been equally disappointing. Several have reported reticence on the part of local labor councils to support teacher work stoppages. Even those local labor councils who reluctantly approved support would follow with demands for quick settlement and actually apply pressure upon the local teachers for acceptance of board of education offers. More than one local has honored the picket lines of custodians or cooks only to have these people violate theirs. Increasingly teachers are finding themselves at cross purposes with organized labor, and the AFT is caught in the middle of such a struggle.

The Possibilities of Merger

Growing teacher militancy and a mutual concern for school issues brought the National Education Association and the

American Federation of Teachers closer together in the sixties than they had ever been before. In 1968 NEA President Elizabeth D. Koontz made informal overtures toward AFT President David Selden concerning the prospects of merger talks. Selden's response was one of interest. But before anything further could be developed, the rug was pulled out from the negotiation possibilities by the NEA's hierarchy. In 1970 the NEA officially banned national merger talks. But despite such an official ban, merger continued to be the hottest topic among the delegates to the NEA conventions.

At the NEA convention in the summer of 1972, its board of directors responded to the issue of merger by presenting the delegates with a paradox. "On the one hand, the board rescinded its 1970 position against NEA-AFT merger talks at the national level, and endorsed the concept of a confederation of public-employee unions, including the AFT. On the other hand, the board introduced a resolution barring any future merger agreements by NEA or its affiliates requiring affiliation by the AFL-CIO." [5] This simultaneous willingness to seek merger and spurn organized labor has become the official line of the National Education Association. The NEA's incoming president in 1972, Catharine Barrett, echoed this sentiment when she said: "I would not enter into talks with the AFT unless they agreed to the precondition of disaffiliation with the AFL-CIO." [6]

This national policy means that merger will probably proceed from the bottom up rather than from the top down, since the leadership of the AFT is more inclined to defend the AFL-CIO's affiliation then the rank and file. In 1972 the New York State NEA affiliate merged with the AFT's United Federation of Teachers, and the example caused new hope and serious discussion for even further consolidation efforts. The potential of a united teaching profession staggers the imagination.

The Prospects for the AFT

The future prospects of the American Federation of Teachers looks promising if not unconditionally bright. The growth rate will probably continue to increase. Of the 2,063,000 elementary and secondary schoolteachers in the

United States, there are still nearly 900,000 that belong to neither the NEA nor the AFT. As the percentage of those who join teacher organizations grows, so, undoubtedly, will the membership of the AFT.

One area of special interest are those teachers involved in higher education. The college and university faculties continue to be difficult to organize, but there are high hopes for the junior college faculties. During the sixties the AFT found special success in organizing such junior colleges. In 1961 the junior colleges enrolled 517,925 students.[7] By 1972 the number had grown to 1,679,127.[8] The junior college faculties have usually faced the dilemma of attempting to apply college and university ideals of instruction and scholarship, which their degrees and training reflect, in settings controlled by public-school administrative types who endeavor to enforce traditional ideas of administrative efficiency and control. The result has often been rebellion on the part of the faculties and a growing militancy that has led many of these faculties into the arms of the American Federation of Teachers.

Numbers are important to the AFT since education continues to be dominated by political processes and politicians that respect numbers above all else. For this reason the AFT's voice in national educational policy-making will probably continue to be small. But its chance for influencing state legislatures look promising. This promise grows as individual states move to pass collective bargaining laws for public employees. This should prove to be advantageous to the union since it should find them better prepared to advise and counsel teachers than their competitors.

And yet despite these hopes for the future, the AFT will be caught in several dilemmas. Merger with the much larger NEA could well mean that the AFT would be swallowed up. The delegate strength and structure of the new permanent bureaucracy could prove to be the death knell for the fighting liberalism of the teacher-union movement. Without merger, the problem would be to continue to attract new membership. The AFT has been characterized by brashness and boldness. The question is whether such characteristics will ever have mass appeal among teachers as a class. If the AFT is to become a truly

national spokesman for American public education, it will
probably have to assume a more responsible role and will have
to soften its image. This will very likely lead to the loss of support of the activists in education and to the possibility of even
more splintering among teachers. The paradox seems inescapable.

And finally, it could be argued that predictions based on the
contemporary scene are largely irrelevant since we seem to be
on the verge of an institutional revolution of sorts that could
change the basic fabric of our system of schooling. In any case,
the past, present, and future of teacher unionism in the United
States needs to be recognized as a vital element in the evolution
of American education.

References
Notes
Index

References

Books

Arnold, Thurman W. *The Folklore of Capitalism* New Haven: Yale University Press, 1937.

Bagley, William C. *Classroom Management.* New York: Macmillan Co., 1919.

Barrett, Edward L. *The Tenney Committee.* Ithaca: Cornell University Press, 1951.

Beale, Howard K. *Are American Teachers Free?* Part 12: "Report of the Commission on the Social Studies." Washington, D.C.: American Historical Association, 1936.

Bonnett, Charles E. *History of Employers' Associations in the United States.* New York: Vantage Press, 1957.

Bowers, C. A. *The Progressive Educator and the Depression: The Radical Years.* New York: Random House, 1969.

Bunting, David E. *Liberty and Learning: The Activities of the American Civil Liberties Union in Behalf of Freedom of Education.* Washington, D.C.: American Council on Public Affairs, 1942.

Callahan, Raymond E. *Education and the Cult of Efficiency.* Chicago: University of Chicago Press, 1962.

Chamberlain, Lawrence. *Loyalty and Legislative Action.* Ithaca, New York: Cornell University Press, 1951.

Commission on Educational Reconstruction. *Organizing the Teaching Profession: The Story of the American Federation of Teachers.* Glencoe, Ill.: Free Press, 1955.

Commons, John R., et. al. *History of Labor in the United States.* 4 vols. New York: Macmillan Co., 1935–61.

Counts, George S. *The Social Composition of Boards of Education: A Study in the Social Control of Public Education.* Chicago: University of Chicago Press, 1927.

———. *School and Society in Chicago*. New York: Harcourt, Brace, and Co., 1928.

———. *Dare the Schools Build a New Social Order?* New York: John Day Co., 1932.

Cremin, Lawrence A. *The Transformation of the School: Progressivism in American Education, 1876–1957*. New York: Vintage, 1961.

———, ed. *The Republic and the School: Horace Mann on the Education of Free Men*. New York: Teachers College, Bureau of Printing, 1957.

Curoe, P. R. V. *Educational Attitudes and Policies of Organized Labor in the United States*. New York: Teachers College, 1926.

Danish, Max. *The World of David Dubinsky*, Cleveland: World Publishing Co., 1957.

Dies, Martin. *The Trojan Horse in America*. New York: Dodd, Mead, and Co., 1940.

Dilling, Elizabeth. *The Red Network*. Chicago: Published Privately, 1934.

Dodd, Bella. *School of Darkness*. New York: Kennedy, 1954.

Edwards, G. Franklin. *The Negro Professional Class*. Glencoe, Ill.: Free Press, 1959.

Eells, Walter Crosby. *Teachers Salaries and the Cost of Living*. Stanford: University Press, 1933.

Elsbree, Willard S. *Teachers' Salaries*. New York: Teachers College Bureau of Publications, 1931.

Foster, Charles Richard Jr. *Editorial Treatment of Education in the American Press, 1930–35*. Cambridge: Harvard Bulletin in Education 21, 1938.

Foster, William Z. *Toward a Soviet America*. New York: Coward-McCann, 1932.

———. *History of the Communist Party in the United States*. New York: International Publishers, 1952.

Gellermann, William. *The American Legion as Educator*. New York: Teachers College Bureau of Publications, 1938.

———. *Martin Dies*. New York: John Day Co., 1944.

Gellhorn, Walter. *The States and Subversion*. Ithaca, New York: Cornell University Press, 1952.

Gitlow, Benjamin. *I Confess*. New York: E. P. Dutton and Co., 1940.

Graham, Patricia A. *Progressive Education: From Arcady to Academe*. New York: Teachers College, Bureau of Publications, 1967.

Green, Marguerite. *National Civic Federation and the American Labor Movement, 1900–1925*. Washington: Catholic University Press, 1956.

Haggerty, M. E. *Children of the Depression.* Minneapolis: University of Minnesota, 1933.

Hapgood, Norman, ed. *Professional Patriots.* New York: Albert and Charles Boni, 1927.

Harper, Manley H. *Social Beliefs and Attitudes of American Educators.* New York: Teachers College, Bureau of Publication, 1927.

Hentoff, Nat. *Peace Agitator: The Story of A. J. Muste.* New York: Macmillan Co., 1963.

Hicks, Granville. *Where We Came Out.* New York: Viking, 1954.

Iverson, Robert W. *The Communists and the Schools.* New York: Harcourt, Brace, and Co., 1959.

Jones, Richard Selye. *A History of the American Legion.* New York: Bobbs-Merrill, 1946.

Kandel, I. L. *The Impact of the War upon American Education.* Chapel Hill: University of North Carolina Press, 1948.

Kazin, Alfred. *Starting Out in the Thirties.* Boston: Little, Brown, and Co., 1962.

Kilpatrick, William Heard. *Education and the Social Crisis.* New York: Liveright Inc., 1932.

——— et. al. *The Educational Frontier.* New York: D. Appleton-Century-Crofts, 1933.

Krug, Edward A. *Salient Dates in American Education.* New York: Harper & Row, 1966.

Labor Research Association. *Labor Fact Book.* Volume 4. New York: International Publishers, 1938.

Langford, Howard. *Education and the Social Conflict.* New York: Macmillan Co., 1936.

Lorwin, Lewis L. *The American Federation of Labor: History, Policies, and Prospects.* Washington: The Brookings Institute, 1933.

Lynd, Robert S. and Lynd, Helen M. *Middletown.* New York: Harcourt, Brace, and Co., 1929.

McManis, John J. *Ella Flagg Young and a Half Century in the Chicago Public Schools.* Chicago: McClurg, 1916.

Mitchell, Broadus. *Depression Decade: From the New Era through the New Deal, 1929–1941.* New York: Harpers, 1947.

Morris, James O. *Conflict within the AFL.* Ithaca, New York: Cornell University, 1958.

Morris, Richard B., ed. *Encyclopedia of American History.* New York: Harper & Row, 1953.

Mort, Paul R., and Reusser, Walter C. *Public School Finance.* New York: McGraw-Hill, 1941.

Myrdal, Gunnar. *An American Dilemma.* New York: Harper and Bros., 1944.

Newell, Barbara Warne. *Chicago and the Labor Movement: Metropolitan Unionism in the 1930's.* Urbana: University of Illinois Press, 1961.

Pitkin, Royce S. *Public School Support in the United States during Periods of Economic Depression.* Battleboro, Vt.: Stephen Daye Press, 1933.

Rippa, S. Alexander. *Education in A Free Society.* New York: David McKay Co., 1967.

Robinson, Aileen W. *Critical Evaluation of the American Federation of Teachers.* Chicago: American Federation of Teachers, 1934.

Saposs, David J. *Communism in American Unions.* New York: McGraw-Hill, 1959.

Shannon, David A., ed. *The Great Depression.* Englewood Cliffs, N.J.: Prentice-Hall, 1960.

Sinclair, Upton. *The Goslings.* Pasadena: Published Privately, 1924.

Slesinger, Zalmen. *Education and the Class Struggle.* New York: Covici-Friede, 1937.

Spero, Sterling D. *Government as Employer.* New York: Remsen Press, 1948.

Statistical Abstract for 1931. Washington, D.C.: U.S. Government Printing Office, 1932.

Townsend, Mary.; Shannon, David.; and Cremin., Lawrence. *A History of Teachers College.* New York: Teachers College, Bureau of Publications, 1954.

Watson, Carter G. "Teachers and Their Peers." In *The Negro Professional Man and the Community.* New York: Negro Universities Press, 1934.

Wattenberg, William W. *On the Educational Front.* New York: Columbia University Press, 1936.

Welter, Rush. *Popular Education and Democratic Thought in America.* New York: Columbia University Press, 1962.

Wesley, Edgar B. *N.E.A.: First 100 Years.* New York: Harpers, 1957.

Wilkerson, Doxey A. *The Negro People and the Communists.* New York: Workers Library, 1944.

Zeller, Belle. *Pressure Politics in New York.* 1937. Reprint. New York: Russell & Russell, 1967.

Zitron, Celia Lewis. *The New York City Teachers Union, 1916–1964.* New York: Humanities Press, 1969.

Periodicals

American Teacher.

"AFT Reverses Itself." *America,* September 6, 1947, p. 623.

"Is America Safe?" *National Republic,* October 1936, p. 2.

"Attitudes of a German Schoolboy." *Social Frontier,* February 1939, p. 159.

Boardman, Norman. "O Promise Me." *Social Frontier,* February 1936, p. 158.

Brameld, Theodore. "Karl Marx and the American Teacher." *Social Frontier,* November 1935, p. 53–56.

Bunche, Ralph J. "The Programs of Organization Devoted to the Improvement of the Status of the American Negro." *Journal of Negro Education,* July 1939, p. 547.

Butler, Wayne C. "The Oglesby Incident." *Nations Schools,* November 1949, pp. 26, 29–30.

Callis, H. A. "The Negro Teacher and the A.F.T." *Journal of Negro Education,* January 1937, pp. 188–90.

Carlson, Avis D. "Deflating the Schools." *Harpers,* November 1933, pp. 705–14.

"Counts and Communism." *National Republic,* May 1936, p. 26.

Counts, George S. "Business and Education." *Teachers College Record,* April 1938, p. 553–60.

———. "Whose Twilight?" *Social Frontier,* February 1939, pp. 135–40.

"Crisis in the Teachers Union." *Nation,* October 9, 1935, pp. 410–12.

"Current Trends and Events of National Importance in Negro Education: National and State Activities." *Journal of Negro Education,* January 1937, pp. 661–72.

Daniel, Walter G., and Wright, Marion T. "The Role of Education Agencies in Maintaining Morale among Negroes." *Journal of Negro Education,* Summer 1943, pp. 490–501.

Davis, George. "Rule or Ruin." *Social Frontier,* October 1935, p. 25.

Davis, Jerome. "Unionization in the College." *Social Frontier,* November 1936, pp. 46–48.

Dewey, John. "Labor Politics and Labor Education." *New Republic,* January 9, 1929, pp. 211–14.

———. "Why I'm Not a Communist." *Modern Monthly,* April 1934, pp. 135–37.

———. "Education, Democracy, and Socialized Economy." *Social Frontier,* December 1936, pp. 71–72.

——. "Education and Social Change." *Social Frontier,* May 1937, pp. 235–38.

"Educating the Negro." *Newsweek,* August 8, 1938, p. 19.

"Education and Politics." *Social Frontier,* April 1936, p. 205.

"Educators Face the Labor Problem." *Social Frontier,* April 1935, pp. 16–19.

Fordyce, Wellington G. "The Historical Background of American Teacher Unions." *American School Board Journal,* May 1946, pp. 43–44.

Gallant, Joseph. "Militancy Versus Stagnation." *Social Frontier,* October 1935, p. 25.

Gass, Charles E. "Before the A.F.T.: The Texas Experience." *Changing Education,* Summer 1966, pp. 6–9.

Goodsell, Willystine. "Opportunities of American Women in Education and the Professions." *Frontiers of Democracy,* April 15, 1940, pp. 214–16.

Grant, Elliott, M. "In Reply." *Social Frontier,* January 1937, pp. 112–13.

Harper, Manly H. "Social Attitudes of Educators." *Social Frontier,* February 1937, pp. 145–47.

Hullfish, H. Gordon. "Why I'm Resigning from the Teachers Union." *Social Frontier,* January 1937, pp. 110–12.

"Inquisition in the U.S.A." *Social Frontier,* October 1936, pp. 26–27.

Johnson, Orvel, Lt. Col. "Red Mist over Philadelphia." *National Republic,* October 1936, pp. 1–2.

Journal of Negro Education July 1938, p. 582.

Kandel, I. L. "Education and Social Disorder." *Teachers College Record,* February 1933, pp. 359–67.

Lane, Layle. "Report of the Committee on Cultural Minorities of the American Federation of Teachers," *Journal of Negro Education,* Winter 1945, pp. 109–12.

Leipold, L. E. "Teacher Unrest on the Salary Front." *American School Board Journal,* December 1950, pp. 27–28.

——. "A Summary of the Minneapolis School Strike." *American School Board Journal,* April 1951, pp. 31–32.

Linville, Henry R. "Destructive Factionalism." *Social Frontier,* October 1935, pp. 24–25.

——. "How Communists Injure Teachers Unions." *Social Frontier,* March 1939, pp. 173–76.

"The Matthew Woll Incident." *Social Frontier,* February 1935, p. 33.

Mesirow, David. "The AFT's Role in the Thirties." *Changing Education,* Summer 1966, pp. 28–33, 51.

New York Times. February 13, 1947–March 3, 1947.

Newlon, Jesse. "The A.F.T. Moves Forward." *Frontiers of Democracy,* October 15, 1940, p. 6.

Northwestern Associates. "The Work of the Educational Policies Commission." *Frontiers of Democracy,* January 15, 1941 pp. 115–23.

"On the Battle Line." *Social Frontier,* November 1935, p. 58.

"Our Association at Work." *NEA Journal,* October 1934, p. 179.

"Professional Security." *Social Frontier,* October 1934, pp. 9–10.

"Revolt against the High Cost of Government." *Literary Digest,* August 6, 1932, p. 6.

Ricker, David Swing. "The School-Teacher Unionized." *Educational Review,* November 1905, p. 357.

Rinehart, Blance. "Mr. Gompers and the Teachers." *Changing Education,* Summer 1966, p. 16.

Rippa, S. Alexander. "Retrenchment in a Period of Defensive Opposition to the New Deal: The Business Community and the Public Schools, 1932–34." *History of Education Quarterly,* June 1962, pp. 76–82.

———. "The Business Community and the Public Schools on the Eve of the Great Depression." *History of Education Quarterly,* March 1964, pp. 39–40.

Rogge, O. John., and Green, Harold. "Do Teachers Have the Legal Right to Strike?" *American School Board Journal,* May 1947, pp. 27–28, 84.

Rugg, Harold. "Immediate Proposals." *Social Frontier,* October 1936, pp. 12–15.

Russell, William F. "Education and Divergent Philosophies." *Teachers College Record,* December 1937, pp. 183–96.

———. "Are Business and Education Pulling Apart? *Teachers College Record,* April 1938, pp. 545–52.

———. "How to Tell a Communist and How to Beat Him." *Teachers College Record,* November 1938, pp. 89–98.

Schiff, Albert. "Teachers' Strikes in the United States." *Phi Delta Kappan,* January 1953, pp. 33–35.

"The School Executive Looks at the Teachers Federation." *Nation's Schools,* March 1929, pp. 43–46.

"Should Teachers Strike?" *Ladies Home Journal,* October 1947, pp. 225–30.

Social Frontier, December 1935, pp. 70–71.

Social Frontier, February, 1936, p. 136.

"Spasmodic Diary of a Chicago School Teacher." *Atlantic Monthly,* November 1933, pp. 513–26.

"Split in the A.C.L.U." *Nation,* May 18, 1940, p. 610.

Starr, Mark. "Teachers Clear Desks for Action." *New Leader,* September 7, 1940.

Strayer, George Drayton. "Educational Leadership in a Troubled World." *Teachers College Record,* March 1935, pp. 478–89.

"The Taxpayer's New Champions." *Literary Digest,* December 10, 1932, p. 6.

"Teachers and the Class Struggle." *Social Frontier,* November 1935, pp. 39–40.

"The Teachers' Union Controversy." *Social Frontier,* October 1935, pp. 24–25.

Wechsler, James. "Twilight at Teachers College." *Nation,* December 1938, pp. 661–63.

"Who Are the Friends of Human Rights?" *Social Frontier,* October 1934, p. 23.

"Why Chicago's Teachers Unionized." *Harper's Magazine,* June 19, 1915, pp. 598–600.

Yabroff, Bernard., and David, Lily. "Collective Bargaining and Work Stoppages Involving Teachers." *Monthly Labor Review,* May 1953, p. 476.

Pamphlets, Government Documents, Bulletins, and Theses

AFT Commission on Education and the Postwar World. *America, Russia, and the Communist Party in the Postwar World.* Edited by George S. Counts and John Childs. New York: John Day, Co., 1943.

American Federation of Teachers, Local No. 5, College Section. *The College Teacher and the Trade Union.* New York: Local No. 5, 1935.

American Federation of Teachers. *Policies of the American Federation of Teachers,* Chicago: AFT, 1954.

American Federation of Teachers Collection, Wayne State University Labor Archives.

American Federation of Teachers Convention Proceedings. Chicago: AFT, 1928, 1929, 1931.

Arthur Elder Collection, Wayne State University Labor Archives.

Baum, Eugene. "History of the Commission on Relation of School and College of the P.E.A., 1930–1942." Ph.D. dissertation, Washington University, 1969.

Clarke, James Earl. "The American Federation of Teachers: Origins and History from 1870–1952." Ph.D. dissertation, Cornell University, 1966.

College Committee on Academic Freedom. *The Jerome Davis Case*. Chicago: AFT, 1936.

Committee of 100 on the Problem of Tenure. *Teacher Tenure in the United States*. Washington, D.C.: NEA, 1927.

Committee on Academic Freedom. *The Gag on Teaching*. New York: American Civil Liberties Union, 1931.

Committee on Social and Economic Problems, Progressive Education Association. *A Call to the Teachers of the Nation*. New York: John Day, Co., 1933.

Corneliuson, Signe. "Content of State Education Journals during the School Years, 1929–30 and 1930–31." Master's thesis, University of Chicago, n.d.

Counts, George S. *Education and Democracy*. Chicago: AFT, 1939.

Current Conditions in the Nation's Schools, NEA Research Bulletin No. 4. Washington, D.C.: NEA, 1933.

Dewing, Rolland L. "Teacher Organization and Desegregation, 1954–1964." Ph.D. dissertation, Ball State University, 1967.

Educational Policies Commission. *The C.C.C., the N.Y.A., and the Public Schools*. Washington, D.C.: NEA, 1941.

Fordyce, Wellington G. "The Origin and Development of Teachers' Unions in the United States." Ph.D. dissertation, Ohio State University, 1944.

Gaumnitz, W. H. *Salaries and Salary Trends in Rural Schools*. U.S. Bureau of Education. Washington, D.C.: U.S. Government Printing Office, 1929.

Kuenzli, Irvin R. *The Union in 1939*. Chicago: AFT, 1939.

———. *The Union in 1940*. Chicago: AFT, 1940.

———. *The Union in 1941*. Chicago: AFT, 1941.

Lester, Jeanette Ann. "The AFT in Higher Education: A History of Union Organization of Faculty Members in Colleges and Universities, 1916–1966." Ph.D. dissertation, University of Toledo, 1968.

Levitt, Emma. "The Activities of Local Teacher Organizations in Chicago since 1929." Master's thesis, University of Chicago, 1936.

Linville, Henry R. *Oaths of Loyalty for Teachers.* Chicago: AFT, 1935.

National Education Association Convention Proceedings. Washington, D.C.: The National Education Association, 1929, 1930, 1931, 1932, 1933, 1934, 1935, 1936, 1937, 1938, 1939, 1940, 1941.

National Education Association. "Constitution of the Department of Classroom Teachers." *Fourth Yearbook.* New York: NEA, 1929.

New York Academic Freedom Committee, American Civil Liberties Union. *What Freedom in the New York Schools?* New York: 1934.

Nottenburg, Robert A. "The Relationship of Organized Labor to Public School Legislation in Illinois, 1880–1948." Ph.D. dissertation, University of Chicago, 1950.

Opinion in Education Literature, Research Bulletin no. 1, 1932. Washington, D.C.: NEA, 1932.

Personal Conversation with George S. Counts, Spring 1970.

Personal Interview with George Axtelle, March 1, 1972.

Personal Interview with Paul W. Preisler, January 27, 1971.

Peterson, Richard Earl. "An Analysis of the Goals of the National Education Association and of the American Federation of Teachers." Ph.D. dissertation, St. Johns University, 1967.

Pottishman, Nancy. "Jane Addams and Education." Master's thesis, Columbia University, 1960.

Pritchett, Henry S. "The Deflation of Public Education," *27th Annual Report: Carnegie Foundation for the Advancement of Teaching,* pp. 45–49. New York: Carnegie Foundation, 1932.

Reid, Robert Louis. "The Professionalization of Public School Teachers: The Chicago Experience, 1895–1920." Ph.D. dissertation, Northwestern University, 1968.

Schmid, Ralph D. "A Study of the Organizational Structure of the N.E.A., 1884–1921." Ph.D. dissertation, Washington University, 1963.

Tostberg, Robert E. "Educational Ferment in Chicago, 1883–1904." Ph. D. dissertation, University of Wisconsin, 1960.

U.S. Bureau of Census. *Statistical Abstract of the United States, 1931.* U.S. Government Printing Office, 1932.

U.S. Bureau of Education. "Statistics of State School Systems." *Biennial Survey of Education in the United States, 1946–48.*

U.S. Bureau of Education. "Statistical Summary of Education, 1947–48." *Biennial Survey of Education in the United States.*

U.S. Congress. *The House Un-American Activities Committee Hearings.* 83d Cong. 1st Sess., February 25–27, 1953.

U.S. Department of Interior, Commissioner of Education Reports for 1914. *The Tangible Rewards of Teaching,* Bulletin No. 16.

U.S. Department of Interior, Commissioner of Education Reports for 1931. *Biennial Survey of Education, 1928–1939,* Bulletin No. 20.

U.S. House Un-American Activities Commission. *100 Things You Should Know about Communism and Education, 1949.*

Notes

Chapter 1. Education and Unionization

1. Welter, *Popular Education and Democratic Thought,* p. 183.
2. Curoe, *Attitudes and Policies of Organized Labor,* pp. 81–88.
3. Ibid.   4. Ibid., p. 90.
5. Commission on Education Reconstruction, *Teaching Profession,* p. 21.
6. Reid, "Public School Teachers," p. 44.
7. Counts, *School and Society in Chicago,* p. 92.
8. Reid, "Public School Teachers," pp. 45–49.
9. Ricker, "School-Teacher Unionized," p. 357.
10. Reid, "Public School Teachers," p. 53.
11. Ibid., p. 55.   12. Ibid., p. 57.
13. Ibid., p. 59.   14. Ibid., p. 66.
15. Ibid., pp. 78–79.
16. Ricker, "School-Teacher Unionized," pp. 356–57.
17. Clarke, "American Federation of Teachers," p. 84.
18. Reid, "Public School Teachers," pp. 89–94.
19. "Why Chicago Teachers Unionized," p. 598.
20. Ibid.
21. Reid, "Public School Teachers," p. 95.
22. "Why Chicago Teachers Unionized," p. 600.
23. Reid, "Public School Teachers," p. 101.
24. Ibid., p. 102.
25. McManis, *Ella Flagg Young.*
26. The relation of teachers with the superintendents who followed Mrs. Young is described in Counts's *School and Society in Chicago.*
27. Commission on Educational Reconstruction, *Teaching Profession,* p. 21.
28. "The Chicago Decision," *American Teacher,* May 1917, pp. 72, 77.
29. Fordyce, "American Teacher Unions," pp. 43–44.
30. Gass, "Before the A.F.T.," pp. 6–9.
31. Reid, "Public School Teachers," p. 208.
32. *Ibid.,* pp. 209–10.
33. Schmid, "Structure of the N.E.A.," p. 125.
34. Ibid., p. 128.   35. Ibid., p. 125.   36. Ibid., p. 199.

37. McManis, *Ella Flagg Young,* p. 157.

38. "The American Teacher and Democracy," *American Teacher,* January 1912, p. 5.

39. "Credimus," *American Teacher,* December 1912, p. 140.

40. "A Call to Organize," *American Teacher,* February 1913, p. 27.

41. The Chicago Federation of Teachers, *Federation Bulletin,* May 4, 1914, p. 1.

42. Commission on Education Reconstruction, *Organizing the Teaching Profession,* p. 26.

43. Clarke, "American Federation of Teachers," p. 120.

44. Commission on Educational Reconstruction, *Teaching Profession,* p. 27.

45. Hugh Frayne, "Public School Teachers in Affiliation with the American Federation of Labor," *American Teacher,* February 1916, pp. 18–19.

46. Rinehart, "Mr. Gompers and the Teachers," p. 16.

Chapter 2. The Formative Years

1. Ricker, "School Teacher Unionized," p. 348.

2. Schmid, "Structure of the N.E.A.," p. 125.

3. Spero, *Government as Employer,* p. 316.

4. Clarke, "American Federation of Teachers," p. 154.

5. Stecker, "How the A.F.T. Began," pp. 13–14.

6. Ibid., p. 14.   7. Ibid.   8. Ibid.   9. Ibid.

10. Clarke, "American Federation of Teachers," pp. 158–59.

11. Ibid., p. 92.   12. Ibid., p. 170.

13. *American Teacher,* April 1920, pp. 88, 99.

14. Clarke, "American Federation of Teachers," p. 170.

15. Ibid., p. 182.   16. Ibid., p. 121.

17. Reid., "Public School Teachers," p. 252.

18. "Report on the American Teacher," (n.d.), AFT Collection.

19. Cremin, *Republic and the School,* p. 15.

20. "Democracy and the Teacher," *American Teacher,* March 1912, p. 21.

21. Louise Hall, "The Boston School Committee and Political Activity by Teachers," *American Teacher,* April 1913, pp. 55–56.

22. "Tweedledum," *American Teacher,* November 1913, p. 138.

23. "Professional Security," pp. 9–10.

24. Spero, *Government as Employer,* p. 299.

25. "O Promise Me," *Social Frontier* 2 (February 1936): 158.

26. Bagley, *Classroom Management,* p. 262.

27. Harper, *Social Beliefs.*

28. Harper, "Social Attitudes of Educators," p. 145.

29. *American Teacher,* February 1912, p. 24.

30. Sinclair, *The Goslings,* p. 103.

31. Ibid., p. 80.   32. Ibid., p. 76.   33. Ibid., p. 78.

34. Dewey, "Professional Organization of Teachers," pp. 99, 101.

35. Committee on Academic Freedom, *The Gag on Teaching,* p. 1.

36. Hapgood, *Professional Patriots,* p. 22.

37. Ibid., p. 23.

38. Chamberlain, *Loyalty and Legislative Action,* p. 12.

39. Ibid., p. 16. 40. Ibid., pp. 40–41.

41. "Statement of Principles Presented by the American Federation of Teachers and Endorsed by the American Federation of Labor in National Convention, Baltimore, November 24, 1916," *American Teacher,* December 1916, p. 168.

42. Callahan, *Education and the Cult of Efficiency.*

43. Sinclair, *The Goslings,* pp. 401–2.

44. Lester, "The AFT in Higher Education," p. 54.

45. Ibid., p. 60. 46. Ibid., p. 75.

47. Ibid., p. 93. 48. Ibid., p. 56.

49. The three that continued were: No. 79—Milwaukee Normal founded in 1919; No. 194—Commonwealth College in Mena, Arkansas founded in 1922; and No. 204—Yale University founded in 1928.

50. Arnold Shukutoff, "Progress in Cooperation," *American Teacher,* May–June 1936, p. 18.

51. "The School Executive Looks at the Teachers' Federation," p. 43.

52. Ibid., pp. 43–46.

53. Ricker, "School-Teacher Unionized," p. 349.

54. Ibid., p. 373.

55. Benjamin Morrison, "The Cleveland School Board and the Teacher," *Nation's Schools,* May–June 1936, p. 18.

56. Zitron, *New York City Teachers Union,* p. 19.

57. Personal interview with Paul W. Preisler, January 27, 1971.

58. William F. Russell, "Are Business and Education Pulling Apart?" *Teachers College Record,* April 1938, pp. 542–45.

59. *American Teacher,* February 1919, pp. 42–43.

60. *American Teacher,* January 1928, pp. 3–6.

61. Ibid., pp. 5–7.

62. "Between 1920 and 1929 the membership of the American Federation of Labor fell from 4,093,000 to 2,769,700. Practically all unions except those in building construction, public service, and entertainment lost membership." Mitchell, *Depression Decade,* p. 268.

63. Kuenzli, *The Union in 1939,* table 2.

64. Letter from Mary Barker, August 26, 1927. Quoted in Robinson, *A Critical Evaluation of the A.F.T.,* pp. 12–13.

65. Clarke, "American Federation of Teachers," pp. 171–74.

66. *American Teacher,* September 1918, p. 150.

67. Clarke, "American Federation of Teachers," p. 189.

Chapter 3. The Depression Years

1. Lynd, *Middletown,* pp. 218–19.

2. Arnold, *Folklore of Capitalism,* p. 107.

3. Ibid., pp. 108–9.

4. Elsbree, *Teachers' Salaries*, pp. 217–19.

5. Eells, *Cost of Living*, pp. 66–67.

6. *Statistical Abstract.*

7. Eells, *Cost of Living*, p. 68.

8. Ibid., p. 69.   9. Ibid., p. 60.

10. Ibid., p. 73. "In 1911 there were but two states that required any professional training for certification; in 1925 there were 30."

11. Ibid., p. 81.

12. Elsbree, *Teachers' Salaries*, p. 116.

13. Educational Policies Commission, *The C.C.C., the N.Y.A.*, p. 9.

14. Shannon, *The Great Depression*, pp. 104–7. Thirteen thousand men and three thousand women worked for all of their expenses in college. One-half of all men and one-fourth of all women earned some money.

15. Ibid., p. 91.   16. Ibid., p. 92.   17. Ibid.

18. Ibid., p. 92.   19. Ibid., p. 51.   20. Ibid., p. 52.

21. Ibid.   22. Ibid., pp. 53–54.   23. Ibid., p. 94.

24. *Current Conditions in the Nation's Schools*, p. 98.

25. Sumner Slichter, Harvard Professor of Business, testified before the Senate Subcommittee on Manufactures in 1933 that delinquency rates on property taxes were 20–30 percent. Shannon, *The Great Depression*, p. 37.

26. Eells, *Cost of Living*, pp. 86–87.

27. Ibid.   28. Ibid.

29. Carlson, "Deflating the Schools," pp. 705–13.

30. Corneliuson, "Content of State Education Journals," pp. 20, 47.

31. Pritchett, "The Deflation of Public Education," pp. 45–46.

32. Ibid., p. 47.   33. Ibid.

34. Shannon, *The Great Depression*, p. 95.

35. Ibid., p. 97.

36. Wattenberg, *On the Educational Front*, p. 35.

37. Ibid.

38. "On the Battle Line," p. 58.

39. Eells, *Cost of Living*, p. 85.

40. Pitkin, *Public School Support.*

41. Mort and Reusser, *Public School Finance*, p. 80.

42. Rippa, "Retrenchment," pp. 76–82.

43. "Revolt against the High Cost of Government," p. 6.

44. "The Taxpayer's New Champions," p. 6.

45. "Revolt against the High Cost of Government," p. 6.

46. E. E. Schwarztrauber, "The Tax Reduction Hysteria," *American Teacher*, April 1933, pp. 12–15.

47. Rippa, "Retrenchment," p. 77.

48. Ibid., p. 79.

49. Harry L. Tate, "Education Breakdown," *American Teacher*, October 1932, pp. 8–9.

50. Graham, *Progressive Education*, pp. 90–93.

51. Baum, "History of the Commission."

52. *N.E.A. Proceedings: 1934* (Washington, D.C.: NEA, 1931).

53. Northwestern Associates, "Educational Policies Commission," pp. 115–23.

54. Ibid.

55. *N.E.A. Proceedings: 1931* (Washington, D.C.: NEA, 1931).

56. Joseph Rosier, "How Professional Organizations Help in Solving the Present Emergency," *N.E.A. Proceedings: 1932*, p. 77.

57. *Social Frontier*, December 1935, pp. 70–71.

58. Ibid.

59. *AFT Convention Proceedings* (1931).

60. Ibid., p. 11.

61. Harold J. Laski, "The Teachers Union in a New Social Order," *American Teacher*, February 1933, p. 4.

62. Charles J. Hendley, "The Dictatorships of the Bankers," *American Teacher*, February 1933, p. 4.

63. John Dewey, "The Crisis in Education," *American Teacher*, April 1933, pp. 5–9.

64. Levitt, "Teacher Organizations in Chicago," p. 7.

65. "Spasmodic Diary," p. 515.

66. Levitt, "Teacher Organizations in Chicago," p. 7.

67. Ibid., p. 8.

68. Counts, *School and Society in Chicago*, pp. 85–88.

69. Levitt, "Teacher Organizations in Chicago," p. 49.

70. Ibid., pp. 12–13.   71. Ibid.

72. "Spasmodic Diary," p. 517.

73. Ibid., p. 523.

74. "The Chicago Riots," *American Teacher*, June 1933, pp. 18–19.

75. "Spasmodic Diary," p. 525.

76. Ibid., p. 515.

77. Spero, *Government as Employer*, pp. 323–24.

78. Ibid.

79. "Spasmodic Diary," p. 525.

80. Clarke, "American Federation of Teachers," pp. 255–56.

81. "Who Are Your Friends? Two Programs—Choose," *American Teachers*, April 1933, p. 16.

82. *Social Frontier* 2:136.

83. By the 1950s this system had evolved so that fifteen vice-presidents served the following fifteen areas: 1. Mich.; 2. Ohio, W.Va.; 3. D.C., Md., Va., N.C.; 4. N.H.; 5. R.I., Conn.; 6. Chicago, La., Neb.; 7. Wis., Minn., N.D., S.D.; 8. La., Miss., Tex.; 9. Ind., Tenn.; 10. Mont., Wyo., Ind., Col.; 11. Wash., Ore., Ala., Hawaii; 12. Calif., Nev., N.M., Ariz.; 13. N.Y., Pa., Del., N.J.; 14. Ill., Okla., Ark., Kans., Mo.; 15. Ill., Ky.

84. Ester Peterson (organizer for New England), "Breaking Ground," *American Teacher*, March–April 1937, p. 10.

85. Personal interview with Paul Preisler. Preisler reported to the author that a letter from the United Mine Workers or the Progressive Miner's Union was often necessary in organizing work in the coal regions of southern Illinois. The trick was to present the right letter in the right town.

86. Hugh DeLacey, "Help from Trade Unionists," *American Teacher*, May–June 1937, p. 14.

87. This theme of importance of a strong local is picked up in several places—e.g., Mary Herrick, "Following Contacts," *American Teacher*, May–June 1937, p. 14.

88. Jerome Davis, "Unionization in the College," p. 46.

89. Ibid., p. 47.

90. Arnold Shutokoff, "Progress in Cooperation," *American Teacher*, May–June 1936, p. 19.

91. Jerome Davis, "Unionization in the College," p. 4.

92. "The College Teacher and the Trade Union," p. 27, AFT Collection.

93. Cremin, *Republic and the School*, p. 181.

Chapter 4. Social and Philosophical Concerns

1. Watson, *The Negro Professional* (p. 43) offers this indication of the number of Negro teachers in the United States by year: 1890, 15,100; 1900, 21,267; 1910, 29,432; 1920, 35,422; 1930, 54,439.

2. "The War and the Colored Schools," *American Teacher*, November 1918, p. 186.

3. Julian S. Hughson, "The Negro and Educational Reconstruction in the South," *American Teacher*, April 1919, pp. 82–85.

4. Callis, "The Negro Teacher and the A.F.T.," pp. 188–90.

5. *AFT Convention Proceedings* (1928), Resolution No. 2.

6. Zitron, *New York City Teachers Union*, p. 94.

7. Ibid., p. 91.

8. Daniel and Wright, "Role of Educational Agencies," pp. 490–501.

9. "Educating the Negro," p. 19.

10. Ibid.

11. "Current Trends" pp. 661–72.

12. Bunche, "Programs of Organizations," p. 547.

13. Dewing, "Teacher Organizations and Desegregation," pp. 61–62.

14. Ibid.

15. Myrdal, *An American Dilemma*, p. 319.

16. Ibid.

17. Charles H. Thompson, "Needed—An Educational New Deal for the Negro," *American Teacher*, March–April 1937, pp. 24–27.

18. Ibid., p. 24.   19. Ibid.   20. Ibid.   21. Ibid.

22. Ibid., p. 25.   23. Ibid.   24. Ibid.   25. Ibid.

26. Ibid., p. 27.

27. Letter from Allie Mann, March 31, 1934. Wayne State University Labor Archives, Selma Borchardt Collection.

28. "Proceedings of the Executive Council of the A.F.T.," August 15–19, 1938, AFT Collection.

29. *Journal of Negro Education* 7 (1938):582.

30. Dewing, "Teacher Organizations and Desegregation," p. 63.

31. Personal interview with Paul W. Preisler.

32. Unpublished letter from Irvin Kuenzli to George S. Counts, dated May 21, 1941 (AFT Collection, Wayne State University Labor Archives).

33. Layle Lane, "Negro Teachers Win Fight for Equal Pay," *American Teacher,* February 1941, pp. 5–6.

34. Ibid.   35. Ibid.

36. In 1910 women held 78.9 percent of all teaching positions. In 1920 they held 85.9 percent and in 1928 83.4 percent. *Statistical Abstract of the United States,* p. 109.

37. Schmid, "Structure of the N.E.A.," p. 53.

38. Ibid., p. 93.   39. Ibid., pp. 98–99.

40. *Opinion in Educational Literature,* pp. 15–20.

41. Ibid.

42. Goodsell, "Opportunities of American Women," p. 216.

43. Cremin, *Transformation of the School,* p. 181.

44. Ibid., p. 220.   45. Ibid., p. 228.   46. Ibid.

47. John L. Tildsley, "Why I Object to Some Proposals of the Frontier Thinkers," *Social Frontier,* July 1938, pp. 319–20.

48. Cremin, *Transformation of the School,* pp. 261–62. Also on the committee were Sidney Hook, Merle Curti, John S. Gambs, Willard Beatty, Charles L. S. Easton, and Frederick Redefer.

49. Ibid.

50. Counts, *Dare the Schools,* pp. 6–7.

51. Ibid., p. 28.

52. Rugg, "Immediate Proposals," pp. 12–15.

53. Kandel, "Education and Social Disorder," pp. 364–66.

54. Russell, "Education and Divergent Philosophies," pp. 183–96.

55. Wechsler, "Twilight at Teachers College," p. 661.

56. Slesinger, *Education and the Class Struggle.*

57. Wechsler, "Twilight at Teachers College," p. 663.

58. Townsend, Shannon, and Cremin, *A History of Teachers College,* p. 168.

Chapter 5. The Critical Period

1. Letter dated October 14 from Lila Hunter to Irvin Kuenzli, AFT Collection. An argument introduced in Philadelphia was that the WPA teachers couldn't afford membership in any other union.

2. Letters from Harold J. Gibbons dated 1936 and 1937, AFT Collection.

3. Conversation with Harold J. Gibbons, February 15, 1971.

4. Letter from Mary Herrick, AFT vice-president, to Irvin Kuenzli, dated February 6, 1939, AFT Collection. "I have tried to lean over backwards in being fair to the W. P. A. locals, although I do not believe that our major effort should concern itself in organizing them."

5. John L. Lewis, "The Teacher's Relation to Labor," *American Teacher,* March–April 1937, p. 8.

6. Harold J. Gibbons, ed., "Special Bulletin," WPA Section, May 15, 1937, p. 1. AFT Collection.

7. "Shall We Affiliate with the CIO," *American Teacher*, September–October 1937, p. 2.

8. Emil Mortel and Irving F. Friedman, "For the Affirmative," *American Teacher*, May–June, 1938, p. 24.

9. Celia Lewis, "For the Affirmative," *American Teacher*, September–October 1937, pp. 13–14.

10. Selden C. Menefee, "For the Affirmative," *American Teacher*, March–April 1938, p. 26.

11. Doxey Wilkerson, "For the Affirmative," *American Teacher*, March–April 1938, p. 26.

12. Daryl Belat, "For the Negative," *American Teacher*, March–April 1938, p. 27.

13. Lillian Herstein, "For the Negative," *American Teacher*, May–June 1938, p. 25.

14. *American Teacher*, January–February 1938, p. 4.

15. Ibid., p. 7.   16. Ibid., p. 17.

17. Wilkerson, *Negro People and the Communists*, p. 2.

18. Saposs, *Communism in American Unions*, p. 9.

19. Ibid., p. 10.   20. Ibid., p. 15.

21. Gitlow, *I Confess.*

22. Ibid., pp. 211–12.   23. Ibid., pp. 294–95.

24. Gitlow, *I Confess*, p. 404.

25. Hicks, *Where We Came Out*, p. 35.

26. "Teachers and the Class Struggle," pp. 39–40.

27. Ibid.

28. Brameld, "Karl Marx," pp. 53–56.

29. Ibid.   30. Ibid.

31. Langford, *Education and Social Conflict*, p. 179.

32. Richard Frank, "The Schools and the People's Front," *Communist*, May 1937, quote inserted into volume 1 of the hearings of the House Un-American Activities Committee.

33. "Attitudes of a German Schoolboy," p. 159.

34. Dewey, "Why I'm Not a Communist," pp. 135–37.

35. Zeller, *Pressure Politics in New York*, p. 5.

36. Ibid., p. 158.

37. Iverson, *Communists and the Schools*, p. 21.

38. Ibid., p. 22.   39. Ibid., pp. 26–27.

40. Dodd, *School of Darkness*, p. 72.

41. Iverson, *Communists and the Schools*, p. 32.

42. Zitron, *New York City Teachers Union*, p. 24.

43. Iverson, *Communists and the Schools*, p. 35.

44. Ibid., p. 36.   45. Ibid., pp. 37–38.

46. Ibid., pp. 38–43.   47. Ibid., p. 44.   48. Ibid., p. 41.

49. "The Matthew Woll Incident," p. 33.

50. Ibid.

51. Rippa, *Education in a Free Society*, pp. 266–74.

52. Gellermann, *The American Legion as Educator*, pp. 18–22.

53. Ibid., p. 200.   54. Ibid., pp. 219–20.

55. Jones, *A History of the American Legion*, p. 274.

56. Gellermann, *American Legion as Educator*, p. 24.

57. Ibid., p. 26.   58. Ibid., p. 128.

59. Linville, *Oaths of Loyalty for Teachers*, p. 5.

60. Ibid., p. 3.

61. Bunting, *Liberty and Learning*, pp. 130–31.

62. Hapgood, *Professional Patriots*, pp. 52–54.

63. *National Republic*, July 1936, pp. 27–28.

64. Johnson, "Red Mist over Philadelphia," pp. 1–2.

65. "Counts and Communism," p. 26.

66. John E. Wright, "The A.B.C.'s of the Fifth Column," Wayne State University, AFT Collection.

67. Dilling, *The Red Network*, p. 124. Characterization of the AFT is generally true except for Garland Fund. This investigator found no record of contributions from the Garland Fund to the national.

68. Ibid., She also included Robert Maynard Hutchins, A.O. Lovejoy, Harold Rugg, Carleton Washburne, and several other noted educators.

69. Bunting, *Liberty and Learning*, pp. 1–3.

70. Ibid., pp. 22–30.   71. Ibid., pp. 109–10.

72. Ibid., pp. 117–21.

73. John Dewey, "Education, Democracy, and Socialized Economy," pp. 71–72.

74. Fordyce, "American Teacher Unions," p. 25.

75. Ibid.

76. Hullfish, "Why I Am Resigning," p. 111.

77. Counts, "Whose Twilight?" p. 137.

78. "Woll, Matthew," *The American Labor Who's Who*, ed. Solon DeLeon (New York; Hanford Press, 1925), pp. 253–55.

79. Green, *National Civic Federation*, p. 475.

80. Hentoff, *Peace Agitator*, pp. 25–39.

81. James O. Morris, *Conflict within the AFofL*, pp. 94–95 ff.

82. Ibid., p. 97.   83. Ibid., p. 113.

84. When President Green was asked to speak at the AFT convention of 1930 he refused saying he was already speaking before the NEA's convention. His refusal to re-arrange his schedule was related to the Brookwood disagreement. Clarke, "American Federation of Teachers," p. 207.

85. Fordyce, "American Teacher Unions," p. 25.

86. Ibid.

87. Commission on Educational Reconstruction, *Organizing the Teaching Profession*, p. 235.

88. Ibid., pp. 236–37.

89. *New York Post*, September 6, 1935, AFT Collection.

90. Ibid.

91. "Crisis in the Teachers' Union," pp. 410–12.

92. Teachers' Union Controversy," pp. 24–25.

93. Ibid.

94. George Davis, "The Washington Hearing," *American Teacher*, May–June 1936, p. 4.

95. Letter from George Davis to Selma Borchardt, dated May 19, 1936. Wayne State University Borchardt Collection.

96. "To the Local Unions of the AFT," a copy of an unsigned petition. AFT Collection.

97. Ibid.

98. Stanton Smith, "A Communication to Local Unions of the A.F.T.," *American Teacher*, March–April 1936, pp. 10–12.

99. Ibid., p. 11.

100. Smith, "Communication," p. 11.

101. Ibid., p. 10.

102. Zitron, "New York City Teachers Union," p. 28.

103. Ibid.   104. Ibid., p. 30.   105. Ibid., p. 29.

106. All of these characterizations are made on the basis of the minutes of the executive board, correspondence, and other AFT documents. Both Paul Preisler and Harold J. Gibbons were invited to contribute to or contest these characterizations.

107. College Committee on Academic Freedom, *Jerome Davis Case*, p. 5.

108. Arnold Shutokoff, "Lessons of the Jerome Davis Case," rough draft of what appears to have been a 1937 bulletin, AFT Collection.

109. Ibid.

110. Iverson, *Communists and the Schools*, p. 113.

111. Ibid., p. 115.

112. Personal conversation with George S. Counts, spring of 1970.

113. Danish, *The World of David Dubinsky*, pp. 94–95.

114. Ibid., p. 330.

115. Iverson, *Communists and the Schools*, p. 115.

116. Counts, *Education and Democracy*, p. 2.

117. Letter from Counts to Green dated April 2, 1940. AFT Collection.

118. "Split in the A.C.L.U.," p. 610.

119. "A Statement of Principles and a List of Candidates," Joint Progressive Caucus, AFT Collection.

120. Ibid.

121. Starr, "Teachers Clear Desks for Action."

122. Ibid.

123. Ralph Bunche, the slate candidate for vice-president at large, was disqualified from running since he had forgotten to pay his local union dues. He had been on sabbatical leave from Howard University that year. Layle Lane, a candidate favorable to the slate, ran in his place and defeated Doxey Wilkerson.

124. "Report of the Council Acting as a Committee of the Whole on the Investigation of Local Five," *American Teacher*, January 1941, p. 4.

125. Ibid.   126. Ibid.   127. Ibid.

128. "Official Statement of the Executive Council." Wayne State University, AFT Collection.

129. "Answer of Local 5 to Charges Made against It by the Executive Council," *American Teacher*, February 1941, pp. 9–11.

130. "The Familiar William Green Stiletto," *Daily Worker*, March 11, 1941, AFT Collection.

131. "The Executive Council's Proposal to Save the AFT," *American Teacher*, April 1941, p. 2.

132. Ibid.   133. Ibid., p. 4.   134. Ibid., pp. 4–7.

135. Ibid., p. 8.   136. Ibid., p. 9.   137. Ibid.

138. Ibid.   139. Ibid., p. 11.

140. Ibid., pp. 12–13.

141. Local No. 453 was "suspended" by the executive council on February 16, for non-payment of national dues. "For a United and Effective AFT," *American Teacher*, April 1941, p. 3.

142. Ibid., pp. 12–13.

143. "The Executive Council's Proposal to Save the A.F.T.," p. 15.

144. "For a United and Effective AFT," p. 3.

145. "Regulations for Conduct of the Referenda," *American Teacher*, April 1941.

146. Letter from Mark Starr to Irvin Kuenzli, AFT Collection.

147. Iverson, *Communists and the Schools*, p. 208.

Chapter 6. The Hot and Cold War Era

1. *American Teacher*, November 1943, p. 6.

2. Ibid., p. 29.

3. Personal interview with George Axtelle, March 1, 1972.

4. Walter Johnson, "Paul H. Douglas of the U.S. Marines: A Teacher in Action," *American Teacher*, February 1944, p. 14.

5. Kandel, *Impact of the War*, p. 18.   6. Ibid., p. 22.

7. Ibid., p. 24.

8. *American Teacher*, October 1942, p. 28.

9. Willard W. Beatty, "Democracy at the Crossroads," *American Teacher*, November 1942, p. 8.

10. *American Teacher*, October 1943, p. 20.

11. George S. Counts, "A Challenge to AFT Members," *American Teacher*, December 1942, p. 30.

12. "AFT Passes 1000 Mark in Five Cities," *American Teacher*, October 1942, p. 10.

13. "Secretary-Treasurer's Report," *American Teacher*, October 1943, p. 10.

14. *American Teacher*, October 1944, p. 10.

15. *American Teacher*, October 1947, p. 2.

16. "Status of Locals Chartered by AFT Since December 21, 1944," AFT Collection.

17. Letter from Marie L. Caylor, November 17, 1952, AFT Collection.

18. Wayne State University Labor Archives, Arthur Elder Collection.

19. "Statement of Your President Concerning the Kuenzli Matter," March 11, 1954, AFT Collection.

20. Ibid.

21. "Minority Opposing Majority Reasons for the Dismissal of Irvin R. Kuenzli," AFT Collection.

22. Ibid.

23. *American Teacher,* February 1949, p. 5.

24. Ibid.   25. Ibid., pp. 6–8.   26. Ibid.

27. Ibid., p. 8.   28. Ibid., p. 9.   29. Ibid.

30. *American Teacher,* May 1949, p. 5.

31. *American Teacher,* October 1949, p. 3.

32. Barrett, *The Tenney Committee,* pp. 1–10.

33. Ibid., pp. 121, 167.   34. Ibid., p. 158.   35. Ibid., p. 166.

36. *American Teacher,* November 1944, p. 2.

37. "Minutes of the Meeting of the Commission on Educational Reconstruction," December 10, 1944, p. 2, AFT Collection.

38. Ibid., p. 13.

39. Letter from Irvin R. Kuenzli, June 26, 1945, AFT Collection.

40. "Resume of Proceedings—Commission on Educational Reconstruction," November, 13, 1949, AFT Collection.

41. Letter from Kuenzli, June 26, 1945.

42. *American Teacher,* January 1944, p. 10.

43. Ibid., p. 12.

44. *American Teacher,* March 1944, p. 11.

45. Ibid., p. 17.

46. *American Teacher,* December 1944, p. 15.

47. *American Teacher,* October 1946, p. 39.

48. "AFT Council Takes Action on British Loan, UNESCO, and Cultural Relations Bill," *American Teacher,* May 1946, p. 3.

49. "Comprehensive Education Program Adopted by AFL Convention," *American Teacher,* January 1945, p. 4.

50. "Bayonne Teacher Makes Study of Economic Status of Bayonne Teachers," *American Teacher,* February 1945, p. 20.

51. *American Teacher,* January 1944, p. 14.

52. "AFT Reverses Itself," *America,* p. 263.

53. *American Teacher,* April 1947, p. 5.

54. U.S. Bureau of Education, "Statistics of State School System," pp. 4–5.

55. Ibid.

56. U.S. Bureau of Education, "Statistical Summary of Education, 1947–48."

57. Kandel, *Impact of the War,* p. 65.

58. *American Teacher,* October 1945, p. 7.

59. AFT, *Policies of the American Federation of Teachers.*

60. "Teachers Union and Board of Education Sign Collective Bargaining Agreement," *American Teacher,* November 1944, p. 6.

61. Ibid.   62. Ibid.

63. *American Teacher,* November 1946, p. 18.

64. Yabroff and David, "Collective Bargaining," p. 476.

65. Ibid.   66. Ibid.

67. Rogge and Green, "Legal Right to Strike?" pp. 27–28.

68. Ibid.   69. Ibid.

70. Yabroff and David, "Collective Bargaining," p. 479.

71. "Should Teachers Strike?" *American Teacher,* October 1946, p. 38.

72. "Should Teachers Strike?" *American Teacher,* November 1946, p. 8.

73. Leipold, "Teacher Unrest," pp. 27–28.

74. *New York Times,* February 13, 1941, p. 1.

75. Ibid., p. 26.

76. *New York Times,* February 20, 1947, p. 6.

77. *New York Times,* February 22, 1947, p. 1.

78. *New York Times,* February 20, 1947, p. 6.

79. *New York Times,* February 22, 1947.

80. *New York Times,* February 23, 1947.

81. *New York Times,* February 24, 1947.

82. *New York Times,* February 25, 1947, p. 1.

83. Ibid., p. 24.

84. *New York Times,* February 26, 1947.

85. *New York Times,* March 1, 1947, p. 1.

86. *New York Times,* March 2, 1947, p. 1, 39.

87. *New York Times,* March 3, 1947, p. 1.

88. *New York Times,* February 27, 1947, p. 16.

89. *New York Times,* March 1, 1947, p. 2.

90. Schiff, "Teachers' Strikes in the United States," pp. 133–35.

91. "Should Teachers Strike?" pp. 225–30.

92. Leipold, "Minneapolis School Strike," pp. 31–32.

93. Ibid.

94. Butler, "The Oglesby Incident," pp. 26, 29–30.

95. Yabroff and David, "Collective Bargaining," p. 478.

96. Ibid.

97. *American Teacher,* February 1948, p. 7.

98. *American Teacher,* March 1949, p. 5.

99. *American Teacher,* November 1948, p. 16.

Chapter 7. Coming of Age

1. "Reporting the Progress of Public Education," *School Life,* October 1953, p. 3.

2. Elaine Exton, "About the School Construction Stalemate," *American School Board Journal,* January 1957, pp. 62–63.

3. *AFT Convention Proceedings* (1931), pp. 115–16.

4. Exton, "School Construction."

5. *AFT Convention Proceedings* (1954), p. 151.

6. Quoted in Roald Campbell, Luvern Cunningham, and Roderick McPhee's *The Organization and Control of American Schools* (Columbus, Ohio: Charles E. Merrill Publishing Co., 1965), p. 347.

7. Neal Gross, *Who Runs Our Schools?* (New York: John Wiley, 1958), pp. 45–60.

8. Ibid.

9. "Statistical Survey of Education, 1957–58," *Biennial Survey of Education in the United States* (1956–58), pp. 2–4.

10. Ibid., p. 7.

11. John Ligtenberg, "AFT Policy with Respect to Communist Teachers and the Fifth Amendment," *American Teacher*, February 1954, pp. 4–5.

12. *AFT Convention Proceedings* (1955), p. 109.

13. Isidore Starr, "Recent Supreme Court Decisions: The State, the Teacher and Subversive Activity," *Social Education*, November 1952, pp. 309–10.

14. Ibid.   15. Ibid., p. 311.

16. *AFT Convention Proceedings* (1954), p. 143.

17. "AFT Files Amicus Curiae Brief in Segregated Schools Case," *American Teacher*, February 1954, p. 14.

18. *AFT Convention Proceedings* (1954), p. 145.

19. "AFT Convention Sets Policy on Vital Issues in Education," *American Teacher*, October 1954, p. 4.

20. *AFT Convention Proceedings* (1955), p. 129.

21. "Address by President Carl J. Megel to the 41st Annual Convention," *AFT Convention Proceedings* (1957), p. 10.

22. *AFT Convention Proceedings* (1956), p. 15.

23. *AFT Convention Proceedings* (1954), p. 5.

24. "Presidential Address," *AFT Convention Proceedings* (1957), p. 16.

25. AFT Convention Proceedings (1960), p. 21.

26. Ibid.

27. *AFT Convention Proceedings* (1954), p. 6.

28. "Address by President Carl J. Megel to the 41st Annual Convention," *AFT Convention Proceedings* (1957), p. 12.

29. *AFT Convention Proceedings* (1960), p. 45.

30. "We Bow Out," *American Teacher*, October 1954, p. 14.

31. Robert H. Prall, "Militant Man of the Classroom," *New York World Telegram*, May 3, 1963.

32. *AFT Convention Proceedings* (1962), p. 34.

33. Ibid., pp. 41–42.

34. *New York Times*, October 17, 1960, p. 31.

35. *New York Times*, October 20, 1960, p. 37.

36. *New York Times*, October 25, 1960, p. 21.

37. *New York Times*, October 24, 1960, p. 31.

38. *New York Times*, October 22, 1960, p. 25.

39. *New York Times*, November 1, 1960, p. 38.

40. *New York Times*, October 30, 1960, p. 76.

41. *New York Times*, November 2, 1960, p. 41.

42. Ibid., p. 38.

43. Ibid., p. 41.

44. *New York Times*, November 3, 1960, p. 41.

45. *New York Times*, November 5, 1960, p. 25.

46. *New York Times*, November 8, 1960, p. 1.

47. *New York Times*, November 9, 1960, p. 1.

48. Zitron, *New York City Teachers Union*, pp. 47–52.

49. Myron Lieberman, *The Future of Public Education* (Chicago: University of Chicago Press, 1960), p. 179.

Chapter 8. Historical Themes

1. "On the Strike Issues," *American Teacher*, March–April 1935), p. 31. In 1935 the Delegate Assembly of Local No. 5 rejected the no-strike clause.

2. Letter from Mary Barker, January 1, 1925, AFT Collection.

3. *AFT Convention Proceedings* (1931), pp. 115–16.

4. "A Lesson," *American Teacher*, December 1932, p. 13. Appeared originally as a letter to the *Brooklyn Daily Eagle*, July 27, 1933.

5. Mesirow, "The AFT's Role in the Thirties," p. 28.

6. Cremin, *Transformation of the School*, p. 272.

7. Petersen, "An Analysis of the Goals."

8. "Our Association at Work," *NEA Journal*, October 1934, p. 179.

9. *AFT Convention Proceedings* (1929), p. 30.

10. Fordyce, "American Teacher Unions," p. 23.

11. Counts, *School and Society in Chicago*.

12. *American Teacher*, October 1940.

13. Copy of questionnaire with tabulations in the AFT Collection.

14. U.S. Congress, *House Un-American Activities Committee Hearings*, vol. 1, 83d Cong., 1st Sess., 1953, p. 48.

15. Ibid., pp. 62–66.

16. Ibid., pp. 95–105.   17. Ibid., pp. 1–28.

18. Ibid., pp. 9–11.

19. Zitron, *New York City Teachers Union*, p. 38.

20. Ibid., pp. 38–40.   21. Ibid., p. 46.

22. AFT Commission, *America, Russia, and the Postwar World*.

23. Ibid., pp. 67–69.

24. U.S. House Un-American Activities Committee, *100 Things*, pp. 1–17.

25. Mesirow, "The AFT's Role in the Thirties," p. 51.

26. Ibid.

Chapter 9. Epilogue

1. Betty Jo Foster, *Statistics of Public Elementary and Secondary Day Schools*, U.S. Office of Education (Fall 1971).

2. Gus Tyler, "The Future of the Liberal Coalition," *American Federationist*, January 1969, pp. 1–2.

3. "Walter Reuther: Unflagging Defender of Teacher Rights," *American Teacher*, June 1970, p. 13.

4. "The Third Annual Survey of the Public's Attitudes Toward The Public Schools, 1971," *Phi Delta Kappan*, September 1971, p. 37.

5. Laura Tracy, "NEA Convention Debates Merger," *American Teacher*, September 1972, p. 21.

6. Ibid.

7. *Standard Education Almanac* (Orange, N.J.: Academic Media, 1972), p. 111.

8. Garland Parker, "The Growth of the Junior College," *Intellect*, April 1973, p. 457.

Index